A Manual of Staff Management in the Hotel and Catering Industry

A Manual of Staff Management in the Hotel and Catering Industry

J. PHILIP MAGURN

Senior Training Adviser
Hotel and Catering Industry
Training Board

HEINEMANN : LONDON

William Heinemann Ltd
10 Upper Grosvenor Street, London W1X 9PA

LONDON MELBOURNE TORONTO
JOHANNESBURG AUCKLAND

First published 1977
Revised reprint 1980

434 91198 4

Filmset by Willmer Brothers Limited, Birkenhead, Merseyside
Printed in Great Britain by
Redwood Burn Limited
Trowbridge & Esher

To my devoted wife Betty,
who endured it all

Foreword

Whatever else managers may do, they manage people. Some of them are better at it than others but, if they are only frank with themselves, most would admit that they have something to learn about it.

Recent studies by the industry trade association, the British Hotels, Restaurants and Caterers Association, the Economic Development Committee for Hotels and Catering, the Hotel and Catering Industry Training Board, the professional body for the industry, the Hotel Catering and Institutional Management Association, and several others have highlighted the manpower problems of the industry, as well as the key role of management in their solution. It is increasingly recognized that the future prosperity of the industry depends as much on the management of people in its hotels, restaurants and other establishments, as it does on investment and on the marketing of its services.

Few other industries have such close relations between the staff and customers, and between the managers and the managed. Few other industries offer so much scope for giving satisfaction to others, and for getting satisfaction from work. Managers hold the key to creating both.

The author of this manual has performed a service to managers in the hotel and catering industry by showing them how to become better at recruiting, selecting and retaining their staff. He has done so in a most readable and practical way. He has had many years of experience in hotels, as well as running training courses in staff management and supervision for this industry while on the staff of the Hotel and Catering Industry Training Board. What he says, therefore, has been tested first.

For the personnel specialist this manual will serve as a refresher and a reference book. For the owner or manager who so often has to be his own accountant, buyer, marketeer, as well as personnel officer, the manual will provide what he needs to know and do if he wants to be an effective and respected boss and employer. For the assistant manager and departmental head, who often have responsibilities for staffing in their units, it will be a guide and mentor. Last but not least, it should help the student of hotel and catering management translate what he is learning about personnel management in the classroom into practice.

If a few thousand managers in this industry read, inwardly digest, and follow this manual's rules and suggestions, the manpower problem in the industry may disappear overnight.

Professor S. Medlik, M.A., B. Com., F.H.C.I.M.A.,
Department of Hotel, Catering and Tourism Management,
University of Surrey

Preface

It is, at first sight, rather surprising that an industry ranking fourth in the United Kingdom in terms of numbers employed, in turn employs so few professional personnel managers. Since the hotel and catering industry is composed largely of small units, the responsibility of staff management falls either on the manager himself and becomes just one more of his managerial duties, or in large hotels often becomes the delegated responsibility of a relatively junior assistant manager. Our industry has frequently been criticized in study reports for treating man management as the Cinderella of general management and for devoting so little of its resources to developing the skills of those entrusted with responsibility for staff. Doubtless much of this criticism is valid; after all in a service industry the people-resource must be seen as a prime determinant in the success and profitability of even the smallest unit.

However, of one thing I am sure: the failure of our industry to lead the way in sound personnel practice is not attributable to the apathy of many managers who find themselves specifically responsible for the staff. On the contrary, my experience spanning several years in the training of managers in various aspects of personnel management is that such managers and students are consumed with an avidity for learning not matched on other courses. No one can be long in catering of any sort without realizing how much the success of an enterprise depends upon sound staff recruitment and, through the practice of enlightened staff management, the retention of a highly motivated workforce.

Unfortunately very little has been written on the subject specifically for the hotel and catering industry. While many excellent books abound in the general subject area of personnel management, and many guides have been produced to cover the welter of current employment legislation—to which I owe a great deal in preparing this manual—many managers in our industry seem to find it difficult to find time to translate such works for practical application in their businesses. This manual is designed to fill the gap. It is intended as a practical guide to many of the most important subject areas of staff management; before and above all else it is designed as a working document, not a textbook. It aims continuously to provide practical answers to the basic questions of what to do, why and how.

This manual, therefore is meant primarily for the busy line manager, but it is hoped that students preparing to enter the industry by following appropriate Higher National Diploma and Degree courses will also find here the practical application and examples to accompany the theory contained in their business studies and legal textbooks. One frequently voiced criticism of such graduates on entering employment is that 'they think they know everything'. In all honesty they probably do have much to offer their employers from their years of study, but lack the practical experience and application of their theoretical knowledge—a gap that may be reduced by relating what they learn to the practices described throughout this manual.

No attempt has been made to cover every acre of the personnel management field; instead, this manual sets out to give advice on a selected number of major topics likely to support a student's examination answers, and to assist the busy line manager to implement sound staff-management practices. For those readers who wish to pursue any subject in greater detail they may find help in the Bibliographies attached to each part of the manual. There are five such main parts, each containing chapters dealing with subjects that my friends in the industry have indicated are likely to be of special interest to readers. As far as possible the subjects are described factually and without personal theorizing, and each contains a number of 'Practical Tips' derived from personal experience and that of many excellent staff managers in this and other industries. At the close of each chapter there is a checklist, which may serve the dual purpose of determining in advance for the reader whether or not he is likely to benefit from reading that particular chapter, and having done so, providing a ready reminder of action he may wish to take to remedy any weakness in his management approach. A series of appendixes attached to each Part provide the reader with examples of practical documents that can be modified to suit the particular establishment and its needs.

So many people have helped with their advice in preparing this manual that it would be invidious to name selected individuals. However, my gratitude is no less real for all that, and this blanket expression of thanks is meant to be personal to each.

J. P. M.

Contents

PART I

RECRUITING YOUR STAFF

CHAPTER ONE

Attracting the Right Staff

1.1 DESCRIBING THE JOB TO BE DONE

Do you *know what job you want your staff to do*? Whenever a system can be devised to help you in the exercise of your management skills, you would surely be unwise not to install one, even if it took a bit of effort to prepare it initially. Fortunately the recruitment of staff is one area in which a 'system' can be installed. In part this necessitates

1 Preparing job descriptions for each category of staff employed.
2 Drawing up a descriptive account of the ideal person for each job category.

What would you think of a shopper who could describe only in the vaguest manner what he wished to buy from a store? When you recruit staff, you are like the shopper, and the first essential to consider is do you know what you want a new recruit to do? A vague answer to this question usually implies a vague hope that the person you do recruit is suitable for the job. Many proprietors and owner/managers believe they know all about the jobs their staff do. If you are one of these, stop right here and ask yourself, 'Really?' Take the plunge and follow these guidelines and you may well surprise yourself.

To answer the question in such a way as to give us the best chance of getting the most suitable person, let us discipline ourselves to describing briefly on paper what the job is. This is a *job description*.

What must a job description contain? There is no one answer to this question because of the variety of jobs, but we can divide them into two main types: ones that describe a craft or operative sort of job, and ones that describe a supervisory/management type of job. In either case here is a list of broad headings which will help you make a useful start:

Job title, department and location
Job function

Job superior
Job subordinates
Relationships with other people
Main duties
Occasional duties
Limits of authority

Examples of both types of job description may be found in Appendix 1 (p. 55).

The best way to gather information for a job description is by questioning and observing. You can watch the present job holder at work and also interview him about his job, or even have him complete a questionnaire. Likewise you should interview the job holder's supervisor and take the occasion to discuss with him the performance of the successful and unsuccessful job holder, which will give you an insight into the skills of the job. If you have a trainee in the job, discovering his difficulties may also help you draw an accurate description of that job. It may also be a help to discuss the job with anyone else who is affected by the way the job is carried out.

Practical Tips

1 Set out to be brief but accurate.
2 Opposite the heading 'Job function' attempt to describe the reason the job exists in one sentence.
3 When completing the detail under 'Job superior' and 'Job subordinates', write in the titles or appointments rather than the names of the people in these categories. It also helps if you quantify the numbers of subordinates for whom the job holder is responsible.
4 List the 'Main duties' of a person without listing detail. You will find it helpful to start each item with a verb or action word, such as 'Assist', 'Clear', 'Check', 'Inspect'.
5 When the job necessarily brings in other job holders, describe those essential relationships by referring to the appointment rather than the individual names of the other job holders, under the heading 'Relationships with other people'.
6 Under 'Limits of authority' describe anything that limits the job holder's right to act, such as the amount of money he can spend without reference to higher authority, or in disciplining staff.
7 When you have completed your job description, ask the present holder to look at it and check that it faithfully portrays a picture of his or her job. Once completed, make sure you date the job description, for obvious reasons.

When you have completed your job descriptions for all types of job in your business, you have taken the first step in setting up a sound system of recruitment—you have a pen picture of each job for which you may wish to recruit staff. You can now say: 'Yes, I do know what I want a new recruit to do.'

1.2 DESCRIBING THE IDEAL JOB HOLDER

Major errors in selecting staff derive from not knowing what sort of person to look for. The second question to be answered in setting up a sound recruitment system is this: What sort of person will best carry out this job? Already the importance of having an accurate picture of the job first is apparent: it will dictate the background, the education, the training and possibly the personality of the man or woman best suited for that sort of job.

In considering the answer to our question we are now in the personnel management business of attempting to draw up what is known as a 'Man Specification' or a 'Personnel Specification', or, perhaps better, a 'Staff Specification'.

As with the job description you cannot do better than to commit this description to paper—briefly, but accurately. Bear in mind this most important point: you are now setting out to describe a person who may not exist! Does that sound ridiculous? Maybe, but a staff specification's purpose is to give you an opportunity to define the traits and background you would ideally like to see the future job holder possess, because you believe that that is what the job requires. However, with your feet on the ground, you quickly realize that no newcomer will possess all you are describing when he is recruited; he will have at least the essential requirements and the other factors may be added through such things as training and development.

For our purposes you can describe a person under the following headings:

1 *Physical Make-up*

Sex
Age
Appearance
Build
Health
Speech
Eyesight

N.B. With legislation outlawing sex discrimination at work you must think hard before specifying a particular sex. See Chapter 3, which outlines the legislation on sex discrimination.

2 *Education and Training*

School certificates
Further educational attainments
Recognized skills training
Recognized management training
Professional qualifications

3 *Work Experience*. What previous experience of work does the job demand, if any? Examples of what might be specified here are as follows:

Experience in this industry
Experience in this part of the industry
Experience of managing staff
Experience in a similar type of business
No previous work experience

4 *Personality*. You may find most difficulty in this area in describing the type of person the job needs. However, a determined effort to select the qualifications demanded by the job is likely to benefit your selection process enormously. Consider the following factors as examples:

Affability
Honesty
Stability
Concern for others
Qualities of leadership

5 *Personal Circumstances*. What demands does the job make on the holder that might be influenced by his/her personal circumstances, or how might the job affect his personal circumstances? The answers will help to specify the type of person required. Here are some factors that may be considered:

Requirement to work late
Requirement to work shifts
Requirement to live in/live out
Need to be financially bonded

Preparing the Staff Specification

You are now ready to write a portrait in words of the sort of person best suited to do the job you have described earlier. Prepare your paper in three columns, as shown. Under 'Description' list all the factors you believe the job requires of a person under each of the above five headings. For instance, under 'Physical Make-up' you may list Age, Health and Appearance. Opposite each of these you may wish to enter the detail as 'Essential' or as 'Desirable'. Continue to fill in the detail under each column as appropriate until you have completed the staff specification.

Description	*Essential*	*Desirable*
Age	18	25–35

Practical Tips

1 In the first column enter only those items the job dictates.

2 Since this is a working document, avoid entering items, especially under the heading of 'Personality', which you will be unable to check or assess from the application form/letter, or at the interview, or through references.

3 Think carefully about anything you list in the 'Essential' column; it really must be essential, since the purpose is to enable you to rule out of consideration completely anyone who fails to meet even one of your 'essential' requirements!

4 This will be a good opportunity for you to ask yourself how essential it is that a candidate have certain qualifications; how essential is it in the job that he has previous work experience—or particular work experience. Be ruthlessly honest with yourself; it can only be to your advantage in selecting from a wider group of suitable applicants.

Examples of staff specifications are given in Appendix 2 (p. 57).

1.3 ATTRACTING A WIDE SELECTION OF SUITABLE APPLICANTS

With your job description and staff specification before you, you are now ready to implement the third part of the recruitment system—how to throw as wide a net as you can to bring in the largest number of suitable persons from whom you can select.

Application Forms

To be prepared you really should have available forms that would-be applicants can be asked to complete. They can be a bore to draw up initially, but the benefits you reap from them can be significant: they will help you short-list applicants, they will provide a framework of information useful at the interview, they can form the basis of a personnel record system, and they can even be a good P.R. advertisement for your business.

Perhaps you will require to prepare more than one type of form to cover the variety of posts you may wish to fill. Compare what you might require to know in advance about an applicant for a management post with information about an applicant for a still room assistant's post. Here are some guidelines:

1 *Personal Details*. Ask for all the factual information you may need about the person, such as his name, date and place of birth, address and marital status.
2 *Education and Training*. Can any of the requirements you outlined in the staff specification be covered here? You may wish to leave space for him to tell you what examinations he has sat, and their results, what certificates he holds, what his interests and hobbies are, and so on.
3 *Work Experience*. Ask him to tell you here about his previous employment, with names and addresses of employers, length of stay with each, variety of jobs held, and his wage or salary. You might like to add space for him to tell you in his own words what he least likes about his present job, or what he reckons was his greatest success. Apart from the obvious benefit it can also tell you something about the man's ability to express himself in writing (if that is important in your job) and also about his mental outlook.
4 *Personal Circumstances*. Your application form should also allow for the person to tell you about matters that may be important to you in deciding whether or not to entertain his application further. You may wish to include requests for information about work permits, driving licence, mobility or any other personal set of circumstances that could have a bearing on his job. (N.B. Chapter 3 contains a summary of the provisions of the Rehabilitation of Offenders Act 1974, which covers disclosure of criminal records.)

You will have recognized that the categories to be covered in an application form are allied to the headings you used in the staff specification. This is deliberate, since both are working documents and will help you to separate the sheep from the goats when you reach the stage of sifting through applicants. You will also have noticed that it has omitted specific mention of 'personality' at all. This is simply because it is difficult to allow an applicant opportunity to disclose his personality/temperament through an application form, although you may get some indication from what is already suggested for coverage. However, you will need to rely for much of this information on the interview itself.

Now, of course, not every applicant for every post needs to supply all the information exemplified above. That is why it is better to supply yourself with some simpler and some more sophisticated types of application forms for differing applications. Alternatively, you may be able to design an applications form from which you can delete certain sections in certain cases.

Practical Tips

1 Make sure you use wording that is clear and precise enough for the applicant to understand what is required of him.
2 Arrange the layout of the form in such a way that it can be completed quickly and accurately.
3 Leave enough space for replies—more than you think the average person needs.
4 Whenever possible, give printed alternatives that only require ticking or deleting—for instance, 'Male/Female', 'Married/Single/Divorced/Separated'.
5 See if you can arrange the form so that it can also act, at least initially, as a personnel record form.
6 Test any newly designed form on an employee, to see if all your 'straight-forward' questions really are so. If he finds any of them ambiguous, redesign them.

Specimen application forms can be seen at Appendix 3 (p. 59).

Much of the donkey work is now complete. You have word pictures of both the job and the ideal job holder, and you also have suitable application forms for the many applicants you hope to attract.

Sources of Staff Recruitment

How are you going to let people know that you have a job to be filled? There are many ways in which you can notify your vacancies.

Here is a list of the more usual methods, from which you can make your choice, depending on the type of vacancy:

	Internal Methods	*Comments*
1	Transfer or promotion of existing staff	Can be economical, helps to develop staff, can be used for all levels of staff.
2	Present staff may introduce friends and acquaintances.	Saves advertising costs. Staff may be rewarded.
3	Record of previous applications	Free service, suitable for all jobs.

	External Methods	*Comments*
1	Newspaper advertising:	
	National	Wide coverage, high costs, generally applicable to important posts only. Regional editions less costly.
	Local, evening, daily or weekly	Wide local coverage, useful for all jobs, relatively inexpensive.
2	Trade journal advertising	Specialized coverage, costs vary and can be expensive. Be watchful for publishing frequency and copy dates.
3	Local radio	Wide local coverage, costs vary.
4	Employment services division (especially those with hotel and catering sections—HOTCAT offices)	Free service, wide coverage, all posts (if you use the professional and executive recruitment for senior/management posts, there is a fee).
5	Notices and posters—for example, in shop windows	Wide coverage, economical. Care should be exercised in site selection and reducing message to a minimum for easy reading.
6	Direct mail shots—for example, to all householders in a nearby housing estate	Local, relatively cheap
7	Youth Employment Service	Applicable to those under 18, wide coverage, free.
8	University and College Appointments Service	Wide coverage, free service
9	School careers masters	Wide coverage, free service
10	Private employment agencies or management consultants	Specific coverage, you usually pay for results only.
11	Trade unions	Specific coverage, economical
12	'Open House'—inviting people to look around	Free. Good for P.R.

You must decide what medium you think is best in the circumstances, and which will attract the most applicants likely to be suitable for the post to be filled. Clearly this will necessitate weighing the likely costs in each case, not forgetting also the cost of dealing with large numbers of applicants and the time taken in selecting the most suitable. The basic costing of recruitment will be referred to at a later stage in the manual (see p. 80).

Advertising

Perhaps the most usual method of attracting applicants is the use of an advertisement. But a lot of money is spent in bad advertising. Here you should seriously consider the value of professional agencies and copy-writers to help, especially when you are starting. However, if you want to prepare advertisements yourself,

Let Aunt AIDA come to your assistance.

AIDA is a well-known memory aid for salesmen and it stands for

Attention
Interest
Desire
Action

This, in a nutshell, is what your advertisement should aim to do:

1 Attract the Attention of the right sort of person.
2 Create Interest in the mind of that person.
3 Instil Desire to take action
4 Give information on how to take Action so as to be considered for the post.

Your aim must be to produce an advertisement that is 'read most' not 'seen most'. In this case and because advertising is increasingly expensive, everything you say in the advertisement must add something to its pulling power.

Ideally, any advertisement should result in self-selection, but to do so it must reflect accurately, if briefly, the requirements you have already drawn up in the job description and staff specification. Bearing this in mind, let us see how AIDA can be made to work for us.

Attention. Usually the title of the job is what catches a would-be applicant's eye, so make sure it is included as the eye-catcher. Where the vacancy would suit someone who is not necessarily holding a similar post, then attract the attention of the sort of person you would like—for example, 'Young Smart Person'. In this way you are likely to draw the attention of those people who will probably be interested enough to read further.

Interest. Having gained the attention of people, the advertisement must now stimulate a live interest. How? Well, possible applicants will certainly want to know what company or business is advertising the vacant post, what the nature of the work will be, what qualifications and experience are needed (this is where your advertisement should be worded in such a way that the non-suitable type of person will now lose interest), the job location, salary, the prospects. All these things create and sustain interest in the reader.

Desire to do something about it. Here is your opportunity to answer the 'What's in it for me?' question. Fringe benefits qualify for consideration under this heading. Once this stage is reached you must not ignore the final requirement, which is to answer the unspoken question of the reader: 'Good. Now what do I have to do to express my interest?' Your advertisement must therefore indicate a line of action.

Action. Give a telephone number for him to ring, or state whether you expect a letter, whether you would like him to use an application form, or whether he just needs to come and see you.

One last point about your advertisement: before you send it off to the paper or journal, test it out—ask a few people similar in status to those you are aiming at to look at it and tell you what they think of it. Remember that your advertisement may well cost your business more than your salary for a week, so time spent in testing it is not wasted, especially when checking it out first may well increase its effectiveness many times over.

When you are advertising vacancies in the press, you have the option of doing so in one of three basic ways:

1 Display advertisements
2 Semi-display advertisements
3 Classified advertisements.

Examples of each are shown in Appendix 4 (p. 65).

Apart from their layout, these three usually exemplify a descending order of size or prominence and cost. Current rates for each of these will be quoted by the medium you choose to use. Experience shows that bigger and glossier advertisements provide no guarantee of attracting a greater or more suitable number of applicants. Much depends on whom you are trying to attract, their availability and the market situation.

Remember also that, since you are paying for the insertion, you can ask for its placement in a certain position in the paper. Pick up a paper and note that your eyes are first attracted towards the top and to the right-hand columns. It also pays to know the best days for the type of advertisement you intend to use; different papers have their days when that sort of advertisement is known to be included, so that would-be applicants are more likely to buy the paper on that day. Newspapers and magazines may not be able to guarantee specific dates of insertion or positioning on the page, however, so do not be too disappointed if your requests are not wholly met with.

Finally remember that if you want to know the likely coverage your advertisement will have, you can find the normal circulation of the medium you choose by consulting a copy of *B.R.A.D. (British Rate and Data)* at your local library—and the information is free.

Attracting the Right Staff—Summary

	1 Make a list of all categories of jobs you may have the responsibility of filling by recruitment.
Job Description	2 Talk to the present job holders and their superiors so as to get a picture of each job 3 Write a brief accurate description of each type of job. 4 Check your written portrait of the job with the present person in post. 5 Prepare a list of the main things you think each job demands of a successful performer, in the five categories discussed.
Staff Specification	6 Decide which of these items should be marked out as essential, and, where appropriate, write in qualities you would consider desirable and advantageous in the job holder. 7 Prepare application forms to suit the types of person you are likely to recruit, designing them so that they reflect in outline a staff specification.
Attracting Applicants	8 Decide what medium to use in announcing a vacancy. 9 Write out your advertisements, using AIDA. 10 Test your advertisement and then decide the sort of display it calls for.

CHECKLIST

1 Does the job description give the following information:

(a) Job title.

(b) Function of the job.
(c) To whom the job holder is responsible.
(d) The dimensions of the job—numbers controlled, annual operating expenses (budget), limits of authority.
(e) The main duties of the job.
(f) The additional duties required only occasionally.
(g) The working relationships that must be sustained.

2 Have you checked with others that the job description describes the job accurately?
3 Have you made provisions to review and update from time to time?
4 Does the staff specification cover the physical make-up, the educational and work experience, background, domestic circumstances and the personality of the ideal job holder?
5 Are you sure that the items you have listed as essential are really that?
6 Does each item listed justify its place because of the nature of the job?
7 What evidence would you seek from interviewees to establish the presence or otherwise of the items you have listed?
8 Have you considered all the media available to you for notifying the vacancy and compared the costs?
9 If you choose to advertise in the press, ask yourself the following questions:

(a) Is it clear what type of job is being advertised?
(b) Does it describe the main duties in a factual fashion?
(c) Are the company name and location mentioned?
(d) Is the wording appropriate to the type of applicant expected?
(e) Is the advertisement being placed in the right area?
(f) Have you chosen the display, semi-display or classified advertisement approach best suited to your vacant post?

CHAPTER TWO

Making the Right Selection

2.1 BE PREPARED

You have now done the donkey work in drawing up a description of the job to be filled and specifying the person you would like to find to do it. Since you have also prepared an appropriate application form and announced your vacancy, you should also be in the happy position of having a number of people interested in applying for the job. However, before you set about the selection process, you have a little more preparation to do—work that is vitally important if your final decision to employ or reject an applicant is to be the right one.

If the number of applicants is high, or your time schedule is such that you cannot arrange for interviews within a week or so of receiving the applications, then acknowledge the applications briefly and let the applicant know he is being considered. Clearly you should keep this delay to an absolute minimum—after all, you are not the only one in the market place.

Now you must sort the sheep from the goats. With the job description and staff specification before you (make sure they are up to date!) go through each application. You can adopt one of two methods for this: (1) skim through each application and sort them into categories—the *clearly unsuitable* who lack essential qualifications, the *possible* who have most of the requirements but lack detail about others, and the *probable* who seem at first sight to have all the basic requirements; or (2) prepare a sheet of paper with columns for each item of comparison you wish to highlight. It might look like the table below.

Applicant	*Age*	*Qualifications*	*Hotel exp.*	*Jobs in 5 years*	*Present job*
Brady	27	C & G 147	None	2	Cook
Callaghan	41	C & G 147/151	8 yrs.	10	Asst. Catering Manager
Digby	26	C & G 147/151	6 yrs.	3	Chef

The first method may appear quicker, but are you sure you can resist going through each again, and again, to make sure you have the order right? The more detailed second method is likely to be more objective and consistent. You can single out the applicants' weak points, and you can put a line through each applicant as you reject him, thus leaving you with a summary of the main points about each applicant who needs to be considered further.

Do not be put off this initial screening of people; it is never a waste of time. Indeed, most poor selection is caused by the failure to carry out this necessary preparation.

The Short-List

Now that you have decided who is to be asked to attend for interview you have two further basic preparations to make. First, you have to arrange the administrative details: let the applicants on your short-list know where and when to attend for interview, and arrange for an interview room (preferably without a telephone) and someone to meet them on arrival. Secondly, you have your own homework to do in preparing to make your part of the interview process a success. This means quite simply deciding what information of value you want about each applicant that is not already covered by his application form. Here are some general guidelines.

1 *Education and Training*

(a) Difficulty experienced in passing examinations—first attempt or after failures, subject failed, etc.
(b) What difficulties were met with in education and how he coped.
(c) What training courses he has attended.
(d) What his reaction to courses has been.
(e) Likes and dislikes in regard to subjects.
(f) Which subjects were found to be easy or difficult.
(g) What relevance the education and training has for the job.

2 *Work Experience*

(a) Nature of previous jobs—duties, amount of responsibility, etc.
(b) What he liked most and least about the jobs.
(c) What difficulties he met with and how they were tackled.
(d) Why he left jobs.
(e) Is there a career pattern?
(f) What progress he made in each job.

(g) How relevant is this experience to the new job?

3 *Personal Interests*. Since an interview gives little time in which to get to know the person of the applicant, you should think about what you may ask to reveal the real applicant. Be prepared to find out the following:

(a) What interests he has outside of work.
(b) Whether these are deep, time-consuming or merely passing whims.
(c) Have they a relevance to the new job?
(d) Do they indicate a preference for individual or team-type pursuits?

4 *Domestic Circumstances*
(a) Family background.
(b) Attitude of spouse to work and change of job.
(c) Any circumstances that might affect the job.

5 *Health and Stability*
(a) Has any illness or incapacity a likely bearing on the job?
(b) Absence record.
(c) Attitude to punctuality.
(d) Loyalty.

Obviously this sort of preparation should not consist of building up a complete questionnaire to be used during the interview. Think around the guidelines listed and from this prepare a few main questions, which you will ask at the appropriate time. You must trust yourself to build upon these and the answers you get in each case, with all sorts of supplementary questions. Be prepared to take occasional notes during the interview—your memory cannot be relied upon for all relevant details.

Finally, in this section of your preparation, think very carefully about the first two or three minutes of the interview. This is when the applicant is likely to be least at ease and therefore least his true self, and when you, as the interviewer, are most likely to get off on the wrong foot.

2.2 THE INTERVIEW

An interview is a *conversation*, with a purpose. Specifically an employment interview is designed to give you the chance to find out as much as you can about the applicant to see if he is likely to fill the vacant job successfully. But remember, a conversation is a two-way event: the applicant is also using the occasion to find out whether or not he wants to continue with his application. Being properly prepared and conducting the interview skilfully builds up good public relations for you and your business.

Ask yourself, What are the weaknesses of interviewing as a tool to sound selection? You will probably agree that they are basically threefold:

1 The situation is unnatural.
2 Time is limited for all matters to be fully explored.
3 It is mostly a subjective means of judging ability and to that extent unreliable.

When you recognize what hurdles face you, it helps. Now that you have agreed the weaknesses of interviewing as a selection tool, you can take some positive steps to counter them.

Create the Best Atmosphere

Help yourself and the applicant to act naturally by using a quiet room or a corner where interruptions of all sorts can be avoided. See that a comfortable seat is provided on the same level as yourself, preferably without a desk between you (this can be a psychological as well as a physical barrier). Make sure the applicant is not looking into the light or has other distractions to worry about.

Here are some other things you can do to get the interview off to a flying start:

1 Make sure the applicant is not kept waiting more than five to ten minutes before you call him.
2 Introduce yourself immediately and naturally.
3 Adopt a relaxed and friendly attitude.
4 Start with easy general questions.
5 Be polite and ask his permission to make occasional notes as needed.

Ask Questions

Asking questions sounds easy, but it is the most difficult part of the skill of interviewing. This is the area in which you can quickly discriminate between the good interviewer and the amateur.

Another test of a successful interview is to compare how much talking is done by the interviewer and how much by the applicant; a guideline for success here is that the interviewer should not take up more than 30 per cent of the talking time. That can only be achieved if you get the applicant to talk, and that can only be done by asking questions.

First of all avoid all questions that can be answered by a 'Yes' or 'No' or in one word. Such answers reveal nothing about the person being interviewed. Instead ask what might be called 'invitation questions', such as 'Tell me about your greatest success in your present job'. Of course, even the best of interviewers slip up now and then and put a question that receives the answer 'Yes' or 'No'. If you find that has happened, be prepared immediately to come back with the question 'Why?'

Even when you use invitation questions, you may get the reluctant applicant who provides the barest of replies. If so, move in with what you may call 'probing questions', such as 'So you believe introducing a new rota system was your greatest success? Tell me how it worked and what its benefits were'.

You will recall that in planning the interview it was suggested that a few key questions be prepared in advance. Now that the interview is under way these questions may well result in the applicant expressing his views and opinions. This is ideal, since he is now revealing himself as a person. But beware! It is possible for him to express opinions he believes will please you without really holding them very firmly himself. So again, be prepared to probe further: 'And on what do you base that view, Mr X?' or 'How does your experience lend itself to your forming that opinion?'

Appendix 5 gives a number of examples of typical interview questions. (p. 66).

Your Personal Conduct during an Interview

If the mechanics of questioning are important and the need to cover all relevant material is significant, then the way you behave during the interview is even more vital. You can ask good questions covering all the items mentioned, and yet the interview can result in dismal failure. How? By the way you behave towards the applicant. At one extreme you can be brusque, even rude, and at the other extreme you can appear over-friendly, even intimate. In neither case will you be able to encourage the applicant to react and talk naturally and honestly.

So how does a good interviewer behave? Here are some sure-fire pointers:

1 He is relaxed and natural.
2 He is a good listener, attentive to every reply.

3 He gives the impression that no one is more important than the candidate during the interview.
4 He never expresses his own views or opinions on what a candidate says.
5 He shows no special like or dislike of the candidate.

Closing the Interview

Normally interviews are arranged to last for a predetermined period, depending on the type of vacancy. Your skill demands that you use this time fruitfully to obtain enough information on which to base a decision about the applicant. Throughout the interview you should be in control, moving smoothly from subject to subject, ready to interrupt when the applicant's reply is no longer relevant or useful, and using opportunities to summarize from time to time what has been said. To finish the interview is also part of your responsibility for control. Naturally it should not be abrupt or unexpected but as far as you can a natural conclusion. Usually you will end the interview by inviting the applicant to ask you questions about the job or the business. This completed, you can then bring matters to a close by thanking the applicant for attending and giving him an indication of when he may expect to hear of your decision.

Once the interview is over, you must allow yourself time to collect your thoughts, and your notes, before you see the next applicant. Indeed this is another terribly important step that will make or mar your final decision. You must have a factual record, in written form, of all that you have discovered so that your comparison of applicants later can be as objective and accurate as possible. Without such a record facts about each candidate will be blurred and perhaps even wrongly attributed. This information can probably be recorded on the interview rating form referred to below.

2.3 CHECKING REFERENCES AND SELECTING STAFF

You now have all the information about each applicant that your interviewing skill has uncovered, together, of course, with the basic information provided by the application forms. The moment of decision has arrived, subject to you receiving satisfactory references.

Ideally the selection of the successful applicant should be based on an objective assessment of how closely he has measured up to the staff specification you have prepared for that job. Being realistic, however, you will recognize that it is almost impossible to reach such objectivity, and an element of subjective judgement (hunch?) has to be allowed for.

Since no mention has been made here of the use of selection testing, a subject that can be pursued through the references in the Bibliography (p.54), you can devise your own method of being objective in your choice. One way in which you can tackle it is by using an interview rating form.

Look at the example at Appendix 6 (p. 67). You will see that it consists of a list of seven main headings, which you can modify or enlarge upon to suit your own needs. Besides this list appears a self-explanatory five-point scale on which the candidate can be rated. Finally, at the bottom, there is room for 'Notes'. Use this to record any other useful impressions gained from the interview, and specifically two important pieces of information:

1 Unless you have a photograph of the person to attach, give a brief description so as to help you identify him in your memory later on.
2 When you decide to discard an applicant, record the reasons for the decision so as to provide you with prima facie evidence should you be challenged later on the grounds of discrimination (see Chapter 3).

Now that you have completed a rating for each candidate, you have a sounder basis for making your final decision. Of course you still have to make some judgements without any objective evidence: here you might consider, as an example, your judgement about the applicant's attitude to further education, or industrial relations, and so on. Do not shy away from it. You are being paid as a manager, and one of the penalties of management is that you have to make judgements and take the risk that goes with them. If you have followed what at times might have appeared to be tiresome guidelines, you will have given yourself the best chance of success.

Just a final thought or two before you make the decision that the whole recruitment process has been leading up to:

1 Your staff specification described the *ideal* person for the job. No doubt you have now found out the truth of the suggestion that he does not exist.
2 Do not be tempted to select a person that happens to be the best of a bad bunch. Despite appearances, you will be far better off in every way by doing without a job holder for a little longer.
3 Do not judge candidates by how closely they resemble a

previously successful job holder, nor automatically discard candidates who seem to be carbon copies of the previous poor job holder.

4 Equally, avoid the flattering temptation of picking a person whose qualifications and qualities far exceed the job requirements. If you do recruit such a person, you are sure to end up with a frustrated employee, and sooner rather than later another addition to your statistics on staff turnover.

5 Since you will not find the ideal person, try to select the person who will best fit into your business and its way of working rather than fill a rigidly defined job. In the end the best person is the one who makes the job a living part of your business, integrating his own particular skills, strengths and weaknesses into the unit he is assigned to.

6 Do not forget to notify those who have failed. However, if you are fortunate enough to have two or more whom you would accept, do not notify these until your first choice has accepted.

Checking References

The selection is made, but before telling the successful applicant, most employers take out a final 'insurance' that their decision will not be faulted by something vital that they have failed to find out. In other words, they will take up references. Whether references should be asked for before or after interviews is a matter of preference. Where time allows for it, it is probably best in everyone's interest to seek references only for the successful applicant.

Now everyone knows that, to a large extent, checking references gives no guarantee of worthiness; they only have a limited value. Least useful of all, of course, are character references from people chosen personally by the applicant—for obvious reasons they are rarely worth while.

Most references come from educational establishments or past employers. On the whole you should seek confirmation of specific facts rather than personal views about the applicant. You can do this in several ways: by telephoning, by writing, or by visiting. Remember the importance of what you are doing. The job, a person's reputation and perhaps—depending upon the level of job—the possible success or otherwise of your business are all at stake.

Probably the most popular method of obtaining references is by telephone; it is quick and informal, and can be used to obtain immediate comments. Of course its danger is that off-the-cuff and hasty judgements may be made. Again, it is worth repeating: confine your questions to confirming facts—the nature of the job, the dates, salary, health and actual work behaviour, with examples. This information is likely to be much more helpful to you than opinions about such things as honesty, leadership and so on.

Why are references, however obtained, usually so guarded and requiring such care in their interpretation? Frankly, because of what they do not say rather than because of what they do. Referees are conscious of the danger of being cited for defamation of character. Perhaps it is as well to state the legal position: a reference is a privileged document provided it is given in good faith and what is said is believed by the referee to be true.

The subject of a reference may prosecute a referee for damages if he can prove malice on the part of the referee and that the comments were defamatory. This is one of the reasons why references should not be looked at except as an insurance against disaster.

As far as school and college references go, they have their value in so far as they present information concerning achievement or lack of achievement. But again, remember that star pupils do not necessarily make star workers, and college failures can often succeed when they find suitable jobs.

Conclusion

Swallowing all that has been suggested as important in the recruitment process, in one gulp, can sometimes appear to be a prescription for mental indigestion. But once you have undertaken the basic and often boring work of preparing job descriptions, staff specifications and so on, this will provide you with a relatively standard basis to be used time and time again when recruiting your staff, especially if you make sure you keep things updated. As you become more practised, your preparation for interviewing and carrying out the interview itself will become less of a chore and more of a challenge. Perhaps above all considerations think of this. If you recruit staff who are wrongly fitted for the job, or who do not fit into the pattern of your particular business, you will be faced as an employer with two distinctly distasteful, not to mention costly possibilities:

1 Staff will come and go, and your staff turnover figures will continue to be as high as ever.
2 Some very unsuitable staff will hold on to the jobs you have

given them, and to be rid of them may become increasingly difficult and expensive.

Recruitment is one of the most serious tasks you have as a manager. Take it seriously.

Practical Tips

1 Put in hand the administrative procedures for the interview—letters to short-listed applicants, time, a room, and a receptionist.
2 Draw up an analysis sheet covering the main factors obtainable from an application form to help you draw up a short-list of applicants.
3 Practise the use of good interviewing skills by trying them out with staff on a day-to-day basis.
4 Prepare a few basic questions to ask during the interview.
5 Draw up an assessment sheet using a five-point scale, to help you compare all applicants interviewed.
6 Prepare a standard form listing specific factual points to be checked with referees about successful candidates.

CHECKLIST

1 Have you arranged for the acknowledgement of all applications?
2 Have you prepared a format to assist you draw up a short-list of persons for interview?
3 What routine procedures have you established for notifying applicants of the date/time of interview, their reception and the claiming of expenses?
4 What arrangements have you made to carry out interviews in privacy and peace?
5 Are you sure the job description and staff specification are up to date?
6 Have you arranged for time to study the job description, staff specification and application forms and from these to prepare a broad outline of what information you want to get from the interview?
7 Have you thoroughly prepared the first few minutes of the interview, and prepared a few basic questions to cover in the interview?
8 Have you decided how best to make notes during the interview?

9 Have you checked that the physical conditions of the interview room or area are conducive to providing a relaxed atmosphere?

10 Have you made a mental check of the sort of questions you intend to ask to make sure they are 'inviting' types?

11 Have you a prepared guideline to make sure you cover all essential matters during the interview?

12 Are you still conscious of what is required of you in terms of behaviour to make for a successful interview?

13 How much time have you allowed between interviews to record your observations and impressions?

14 Have you a means of recording comparisons between applicants?

15 How are you going to follow up references—by telephone, letter; or personal visit?

16 Have you considered preparing a standard form listing specific factual points you will seek confirmation of from referees?

CHAPTER THREE

Right—in the Eyes of the Law

It cannot be news to anyone reading this manual that the moment you employ a person you immediately become subject to a host of different laws dealing with employment. Look at this list of legislation:

1 Employment of Women, Young Persons & Children Act 1920
2 Young Persons (Employment) Acts 1938 and 1964
3 The Disabled Persons (Employment) Acts 1944 and 1958
4 Payment of Wages Act 1960
5 Factories Act 1961
6 Offices, Shops and Railway Premises Act 1963
7 Race Relations Act 1976
8 Employers Liability (Compulsory Insurance) Act 1969
9 Equal Pay Act 1970
10 Attachment of Earnings Act 1971
11 Trade Union and Labour Relations Act 1974
12 Health and Safety at Work etc. Act 1974
13 Rehabilitation of Offenders Act 1974
14 Sex Discrimination Act 1975
15 Employment Protection Act 1975
16 Employment Protection (Consolidation) Act 1978

And this list is not intended to be comprehensive! However, you will not find in this manual any attempt to cover the provisions of all this legislation, nor even to give a potted version of each Act. This would defeat the principal objective of the Manual which is to be practical and simple but sufficient for the busy staff manager. Clearly then, this chapter must be selective and deal mainly with those aspects of the law that affect the recruitment of staff. It must not be looked upon as anything but a layman's guide to help you establish sound employment practices within the law. If you find that you need more than this in deciding on particular cases, you might well be advised to seek professional advice.

3.1 THE CONTRACT OF EMPLOYMENT

The individual contract of employment is still the keystone of the employer-employee relation in English law. Today, with ever-increasing employment legislation and cases coming before industrial tribunals and courts, the existence and/or the contents of the employment contract have been the central issues. Its importance can be gauged from the following examples illustrating its uses and values:

1 It gives the staff the right to ask for and if necessary, sue for their correct wages.
2 It settles what jobs you can ask staff to do and where you can send staff to do them.
3 No claim for redundancy or unfair dismissal compensation can be made without the claimant being contracted as an employee.
4 It settles both parties' rights if you want to lay workers off.
5 It helps in redundancy situations to check whether staff are being offered new terms and conditions, and in totting up what has been the normal working week.
6 It is the basis of your disciplinary powers.
7 It is the basis for fining staff or otherwise imposing penalties, short of dismissal.

It is surely obvious then that the existence and the content of the contract are vitally important in every situation.

The moment that the person you have selected accepts the job for wages offered, the contract is complete. He can accept the job in writing or by word of mouth, or even simply by turning up on the agreed date to start the job. Naturally if there is nothing in writing, then both parties in a later dispute may find it difficult to prove the terms of the contract.

Mainly because of this difficulty, the Contracts of Employment Act was first passed in 1963 and was subsequently amended until now when its provisions are covered by Ss. 1–7 of the Employment Protection (Consolidation) Act 1978. One of its principal requirements is that each person in employment must be given a *written statement* containing certain terms and conditions of his employment. Here is a list of the items the statement *must* cover:

1 Names of employer and employee.
2 Title of the job for which employed.
3 Date employment began.
4 Whether any previous employment counts as part of the continuous period of employment and, if so, the date on which it began.
5 Scale or rate of pay, including overtime rates.
6 Intervals at which payment is made.
7 Total normal hours of work.
8 Entitlement to holidays, including public holidays, and holiday pay.
9 Provisions dealing with sickness or injury and whether sick pay is payable.
10 Whether pensionable or not, and if so, under what conditions.
11 Grievance procedure.
12 Any disciplinary rules that are applicable.
13 The person to whom an appeal against a disciplinary decision may be taken.
14 Notice to terminate employment.
15 Whether a contracting-out certificate is in force for that employment.

Most of these items are self-explanatory, but you might like to look at a few in more detail:

Date Employment Begins. This can be a very important term since it determines, for example, whether a redundancy payment is earned (after two years' service) or whether a person is entitled to claim 'unfair dismissal' (after twelve months' employment).

Wages/Salary. This item covers more than what you give the staff in their wage packets, which may include a proportion of the service charge. It should also cover fringe benefits such as a company car, free hairdressing, free accommodation and so on.

Hours of Work. You should make it clear whether or not your staff are eligible for payment of hours worked overtime; if they are, the overtime rate should be stated. Do not forget also to cover meal breaks.

Holidays. Whatever you include here, your staff must be able to calculate accurately what is their entitlement to holidays and holiday pay, including entitlement to accrued holiday pay if they leave your employment.

Grievance. What you must be sure of here is that your staff know to whom they can take any grievance and how they can apply for their grievance to be heard. Moreover you must also tell them what the steps are once they have made an application to have a grievance dealt with.

Giving/Receiving Notice. The Employment Protection (Consolidation) Act lays down minimum periods of notice as follows:

After 4 weeks and less than 2 years' employment	1 week
After 2 years' employment	2 weeks
After 3 years' employment	3 weeks
and so on to a maximum of	
12 years' employment	12 weeks

In the case of the employee giving notice to you, unless you make provisions in his contract to the contrary, he is required to give you only 1 week's notice after 4 weeks' employment with you, no matter how long he has been employed by you.

The Contracts of Employment Act applied originally to all staff who were normally expected to work for you for 21 hours a week or more. However, the Employment Protection (Consolidation) Act has now reduced the hours to 16 a week, and even to 8 hours a week once staff have worked for 5 years on a minimum of 8 hours each week.

Remember that the written statement discussed so far is not the contract of employment, but it is good evidence of the terms of the contract and should be kept up to date. In fact you are required under the Act to complete the updating within 4 weeks of any variation. A final few words about the statement itself:

1 It need not contain the full detail about each of the items mentioned. The staff may be referred to other documents that contain the detail, such as the Wages Regulation Orders, booklets about the sick-pay or pension scheme, company handbooks, and so on. There is one proviso, however: if you do refer staff elsewhere for detail, then the documents referred to must be readily available to them in the course of their employment. In practice this will usually mean that you as the staff manager must have the documents, so that your staff can see them whenever they wish.

2 The written statement need not in law be signed by either party.

3 Most of the larger companies issue a standard proforma type of statement to be completed for staff. If you have to draw up and

write your own statement, make it simple and readable; do not try to use legal jargon, it is quite unnecessary.

4 The written statement must be issued within 13 weeks of staff starting work.

You have now looked at what things you *must* include in the written statement you give the staff covering their main terms and conditions of employment. Even so, there are other legal restraints that affect even these essential items—for instance, hours and type of work undertaken by women and young people, minimum wages for all who work under the Wages Council Act 1959, and the influence of the Truck Acts and the Payment of Wages Act 1960, which insist that staff be paid in cash (and not in kind) unless they request in writing to be paid by cheque or bank deposit.

The question now is, What else *might* it be in your interest, as well as that of your staff, to add to this statement, which is first-class evidence of the contract with each party? You are free to fix whatever other terms you wish; the rules simply require that staff accept the terms and are ready, able and willing to work in return for the agreed wage. So what might you consider worth while as additional terms in the contract?

1 *The Code of Practice* (issued at the time of the Industrial Relations Act 1971) suggests that you provide staff with further information on items like job content, training provided, promotion/career prospects and disciplinary offences and procedures.

2 *The Need for Mobility of Staff* (if this applies). If, for instance, you wish staff to work anywhere within an area, or in the case of public house managers, say, that you wish to be free to move them from one house to another, then this degree of mobility should be spelled out as part of a person's contract. Suppose you want to transfer staff, say, because of lack of work, from one canteen to another in the next town and they refuse; if their contract has no mobility clause, then, once dismissed for refusing to move, they could claim to have been made redundant. On the other hand, if their statement covers mobility, then this refusal can be seen as disobeying a lawful order and no redundancy claim would arise.

3 *Power to Search*. There is no right to search members of staff unless this is contained in the contract; even then force may not be used nor may staff be detained without justification,

otherwise you can be sued for damages. Of course, if your staff refuse to submit to a search contrary to contract, they can be disciplined or even dismissed.

4 *Power to Suspend.* Unless the contract provides for this or such a term can be implied from custom, you may not suspend staff without pay.

5 *Restrictive Covenants.* This legalistic term is used to describe terms in a contract that seek to restrain staff from taking certain kinds of employment when they leave you. It probably will not apply much in our industry, but it could in some cases as, for instance, where an employee has influence over your clients. Such a restriction may be valid so long as it does not try to impose longer or wider limits than is necessary for your protection. If you put in clauses that try to prevent ordinary competition when staff leave, they are unlikely to be enforced. In general, courts will only enforce those clauses if they are reasonable between employee and employer and not contrary to public policy.

An example of a 'Contract of Employment Statement' can be seen in Appendix 7 (p. 68).

The Common Law

We have so far considered what terms and conditions must and might be included in the contracts of staff. Now let us look briefly at what other conditions are implied by common law.

First of all, as the employer, you have the following obligations:

1 To provide safe working conditions. This obligation is now of course reinforced by the Health and Safety at Work, etc. Act.

2 Not to impose unreasonable restraints on your staff's rights to take up similar employment after leaving you.

The staff's common law duties include:

1 Being ready and willing to work and to obey lawful and reasonable orders. A 'Go-slow' is therefore technically unlawful.

2 Taking reasonable care in their work.

3 Working honestly and not disclosing confidential information to others. This is a very wide provision and would cover the fact that employees' inventions connected with their employment belong to the employer.

4 Being faithful. This duty is very wide and covers such things as forbidding the taking of bribes or making secret profits from their employment; and, perhaps most commonly of all, restricting an employee's spare-time activities when they are harmful to his employer. This does not mean that staff cannot take on a second job (an express clause in the contract is needed for this); but if the second job affects the staff, for instance, through their being over-tired and thus reduces their ability to do their work, then this could be a breach of contract. However, the common law duty of fidelity in this sense means that a person who actually harms his employer in his spare time is in breach of duty. So staff who work for a competitor in their spare time, and who therefore break the employer's monopoly, may be in breach of contract under common law.

Changing the Contract

Once statements have been drawn up and issued to staff, you need to be conscious that the law's influence does not end there. All eventualities cannot be foreseen, and no doubt you have made provision for those that are by such flexibility in terms as to allow you to cover items like reorganization without redundancies and unfair dismissals.

Suppose, however, that you want to introduce new shift systems or an innovation that means changes in work for the staff, or perhaps you are forced to make changes because of events outside your control, as in the fuel crisis of 1973. Can you change the contract, and, if so, how? The basic guidelines to follow are these:

1 You can make any changes you like by giving staff the same amount of notice about the change as they would be entitled to were you dismissing them. In this way you are really offering them re-engagement on the new terms, and if they continue to work under the new terms, then well and good.

2 If, however, staff reject the changes, then they could claim unfair dismissal.

3 If the change affects any of the items on the written statement required by the Employment Protection (Consolidation) Act, then, no more than one month after the change, you must issue a further written statement notifying the staff of the change.

4 Above all else, try to obtain mutual agreement to the change. If you can do this, there is no need to give any notice, and you are in no danger of a claim against you by the staff.

Since the introduction of 'unfair dismissal' by the Industrial Relations Act 1971, now strengthened in its current form under the Employment Protection (Consolidation) Act, 1978, you will run the risk of being cited for unfair dismissal if you sack staff for refusing to accept changes in their contract. You run the same risk if they resign rather than accept the changes before you actually get round to firing them for refusing to change.

This brings in the whole set of provisions covering unfair dismissal. Suffice it to say at this stage that if staff refuse to accept changes in their contract or are dismissed or resign, then the industrial tribunals will test the case on two counts:

1 Whether refusal to accept the changed terms is a potential reason for dismissal under the Employment Protection (Consolidation) Act, 1978.
2 If that is accepted as a fair reason, go on to test your reasonableness in using it to dismiss.

Practical Tips

1 As far as you can, provide for changes in location and scope and other terms of employment in the contract itself, with due notice to all staff.
2 If other changes are necessary, specify them carefully, consult the staff affected, give them plenty of time to consider the changes, and urge them to use any agreed procedures, if you have them, and to co-operate under both common law and the Code of Practice.
3 If sacking becomes inevitable, warn the staff concerned, hear their side of things, and allow them to appeal.

3.2 OTHER LEGISLATION AFFECTING RECRUITMENT OF STAFF

To complete a look at how recruitment of staff is affected by law it is now necessary to pick out some specific pieces of legislation which you must take into account when starting new staff.

The Rehabilitation of Offenders Act 1974

This Act came into effect on 1 July 1975. One of its main objectives is to help some past offenders to get a job and keep it; an applicant for a job will not generally have to reveal or admit to having a criminal record after a certain period of time. The important parts of this law as far as recruitment is concerned are these:

1 If a person is questioned (in an interview or on an application form, for example) about his criminal record, he can refrain from mentioning 'spent convictions' or their circumstances. He is not liable in law if he fails to acknowledge or disclose such spent convictions.
2 The main sanction for breaking this law is an action for defamation of character. So if a character referee referred to an applicant's spent conviction, it could be defamatory in law.

A conviction becomes 'spent' when a rehabilitation period has passed; in other words, the law will treat a criminal conviction as if it had never happened once a certain time has elapsed. This time varies according to the length of sentence. The main periods are as follows:

	Rehabilitation period
Sentence of 6 months–2½ years	10 years
Less than 6 months' sentence	7 years
A fine or community service order	5 years
An absolute discharge	6 months

Service offences are also subject to this law, as follows:

Cashiering, discharge with ignominy or dismissal with disgrace	10 years
Simple dismissal from the service	7 years
Detention	5 years

Any sentence that exceeds 2½ years' imprisonment can never be 'spent'. In every case it is the sentence given by the court that counts, even if it is a suspended sentence, and not the actual time served in prison.

For persons under the age of 17 at the time of their conviction all the above rehabilitation periods are halved. On the other hand, there are also fixed periods of rehabilitation for sentences that can be imposed on young persons, up to age 21 years, as follows:

	Rehabilitation period
A sentence of Borstal training	7 years
A sentence of detention of 6–30 months for grave crimes under section 53 of the Children and Young Persons Act 1933	5 years
Sentence of detention as above for less than 6 months	3 years
An order of detention in a detention centre under the Criminal Justice Act 1961	3 years

Practical Tips

1 Check the wording relating to police records and convictions on your present application forms. If it is essential that applicants are upright in the eyes of the law, you could ask such questions as 'Have you ever been sentenced to prison for longer than 2½ years?' However, you might prefer something less dramatic and ask, 'Have you received any criminal sentences in the last 5 years (2½ years for those under 20 years of age)?' On the other hand, provided you remember that no spent convictions need ever be declared, you can continue to ask, 'Have you ever had a criminal conviction?'

2 You must expect referees to be even more careful in telling you about the law-abiding habits or otherwise of would-be applicants for employment with you. Remember they must not disclose spent convictions under penalty of defamation. Once again the use of the telephone to check references can be valuable when no written record is made of what a referee might be willing to tell you about the honesty and character of an applicant.

In the end, the whole process of recruitment is one of discrimination. Earlier, you will recall, we talked about 'sorting the sheep from the goats'. Well, of course, this is what it is all about, but more and more laws are being enacted to define what grounds may not be used for discrimination. For example, it can now be unlawful to refuse to employ a chef because he belongs to an independent trade union, because he is coloured, because 'he' is really a 'she', and so on. All this can affect our recruitment effort, from advertising to selecting staff, so let us now review the main legal restrictions you must keep in mind.

Race Relations Act 1976

This Act makes it an offence to discriminate against anyone seeking employment on the grounds of their colour, race, or ethnic or national origin. Of course you can discriminate on grounds of skill, knowledge and other qualifications, and this can mean in our industry that only people of certain nationalities are likely to have these qualifications. What you must be able to do, if challenged, is to show that you selected Bruin rather than Brown because of his knowledge of French or skill in preparing certain dishes, and that your selection had nothing to do with the fact that Bruin was French, or yellow, or Jewish or whatever.

The methods of discrimination you ought to look at under this heading are the following:

1 Are qualified coloured people turned down for jobs in supervisory or management positions in favour of equally qualified white applicants?
2 Are coloured employees confined to the less attractive jobs in terms of pay, hours and working conditions?
3 If you use selection criteria that are not all job-related, do they operate unfairly to the disadvantage of immigrants?
4 Is there any evidence that coloured people receive inadequate notice of your job vacancies?
5 Do you look for higher qualifications from coloured workers than from others?
6 Have you any evidence that minority groups fail to apply for jobs with you because they expect (rightly or wrongly) to meet with discrimination?
7 Have you considered establishing any sort of programme to eliminate immigrant disadvantages? These should not be designed to give any special advantages but merely to reduce the disabilities of immigrants. You might consider under this heading the provision of some sort of staff training in the 'language of work'.

Equal Pay Act 1970 and Sex Discrimination Act 1975

The provisions of both these pieces of legislation can be looked at together since, in a sense, they are complementary.

As far as recruitment is concerned you should note that in deciding the rate of pay for the job, the sex of the person should of itself have no place in your thoughts. Separate rates of pay for women as such are no longer permitted; as from 29 December 1975 the pay of women had to be equal to that of men for the 'same or broadly similar work'. If you have not already taken a long hard look at the implications of all this, and amended wages and the associated written statements issued to the female staff affected, then this must be an immediate priority.

But what is the point of establishing a system of equal pay for women if the doors to the best paid jobs or promotion within your unit are closed to women just because they are women? It is precisely because of this otherwise fruitless exercise that the Sex Discrimination Act has become law. Its effect on recruitment of staff may be much more significant.

You should note immediately that this Act deals with sex indiscriminately—in other words, in addition to seeking to improve the position of women, it equally outlaws discrimination against men. Sex discrimination in employment is illegal in the following instances:

1 A woman is treated less fairly than a man in similar circumstances.
2 A condition applied to both sexes equally is such that it is likely that fewer women could fulfil the condition than men, and it is unjustified to apply it regardless of sex.

In the first case this would be *direct* discrimination, whereas in the second place it would be *indirect* discrimination. This is to prevent unscrupulous employers from continuing to discriminate against women by, for instance, advertising for waiting staff with a minimum height of 5 ft 10 in., when clearly most women could not qualify.

What you must be able to show, if challenged, is that the conditions you apply to any job are requisite because of the job itself. It helps, of course, if you can show that your conditions applied before the Act was passed. For instance, suppose you are advertising for a hall porter and stipulate that membership of the Clefs d'Or is necessary: generally this would exclude all women. If challenged, your best defence would be to show that the job made this qualification necessary and that you had always sought this qualification from applicants.

The Act also makes it illegal in matters relating to employment on grounds of marital status where

1 Any married person is treated less fairly than an unmarried person in the same circumstances.
2 A condition applied equally to married and unmarried persons is such that the number of married people who can comply with the condition is much less than the number of unmarried persons and where it is unjustified to apply it to anyone regardless of their marital status.

One of the practical effects of this part of the Act might well be that you need to be very careful in drawing up your staff specification and marking it *essential* that the applicant be married/unmarried. Notice that the Act refers to 'marital status' and not 'family status'. This presumably means that you can continue to discriminate between those who have dependants and those who do not.

The Act does allow for certain exceptions to the general rule that you must not discriminate against applicants on grounds of sex alone. Broadly speaking, you will not be too concerned with this in the hotel and catering industry unless being a man or a woman is a 'genuine occupational qualification' for a job. Other than cases of married couples holding joint jobs—where the terms of employment can differ, as in public houses—you will be required to prove one of the following:

1 That the job itself demands authentic male/female characteristics.
2 That the normal rules of decency and privacy demand one sex rather than another.
3 That it would be impracticable because the person is required to live in and the accommodation you can offer is designed for one sex only.

Until industrial tribunals have dealt with a number of cases it will be difficult for you to do other than guess how all these might affect you in practice.

Advertising
Perhaps this is the part of the recruitment system you would do best to look at carefully without delay. Unlike other legislation recently the burden of proving that you discriminated on grounds of sex rests on the complainant. You might well believe that if a woman is not offered the job she would have difficulty in proving that the reason you did not short-list or select her was that she was a woman. On the other hand, if you advertise for someone and the title of the job indicates one sex specifically, or the content of the advertisement seems to favour one sex rather than another, then it may give grounds for believing that you intend to discriminate on grounds of sex.

So think carefully about some of the job titles you have used up to now—waiter, waitress, chambermaid, still-room maid, barmaid, and so on—which have a one sex connotation. Likewise, if you overcome this by indicating the job title as favouring neither sex, or specify particularly 'male or female', you must also take care that the rest of the advertisement is equally indiscriminatory in regard to sex. For instance, if you add to the advertisement for a 'Bars Assistant—Male or Female' that the applicant must be 'sober in his habits', this might indicate a preference for a man. Even accompanying your advertisement with a picture showing a man or woman in the role could be open to a charge of discrimination.

If, by now, you are thinking up new job titles that favour neither sex, you must recognize that it may be difficult to get general acceptance for them. Perhaps, at least for the time being, it might be as well to continue with established job titles, and indicate that the position is open to either sex with the appropriate qualifications for the job.

The Shops Act 1960

The Shops Act does affect the hotel and catering industry. For instance, it is illegal to employ waitresses under the age of 18 after 10 o'clock at night, whereas a young waiter of the same age can be employed until midnight, provided he does not have to be on duty before 11 a.m. the following morning. So here is a case where your advertisement for such a job must specify one sex rather than another. However, this is more an apparent exception than a real one, because, you will recall, it will still be legal to advertise for and employ a person of one sex rather than another because the job requires that sex. In this case the Shops Act says so!

The hotel and catering industry employs a tremendous number of women and, as in many other industries, the women have tended in the past to be employed in less rewarding occupations than the men. To be ruthlessly honest, the reason for this was financial. Both the Acts we have been examining seek to remedy the situation by making it more costly for an employer to discriminate than not to discriminate. So, if you employ at least five staff, you will be affected by the Sex Discrimination Act.

But look at it again in another light. Our industry suffers from chronic labour shortages. A famous lady has said: 'The country needs all the wits it can get. It so happens that half the wits are in female heads.' You might like to let that thought simmer, and hopefully learn the lesson it teaches.

Practical Tips

1 Look at all the jobs in your unit and list those that are usually open to and filled by one sex only.
2 Decide which of those jobs can now be justified as 'one sex only' under the Sex Discrimination Act.
3 Ask your colleagues to help you in this decision.
4 Make sure that all your papers dealing with recruitment, such

as staff specifications and advertisements, are aimed at being applicable to either sex.

5 Avoid questions during interviews that could give rise to complaints of discrimination, such as 'Are you planning to get married soon?' or 'When do you intend to start a family?'

6 Select your staff on merit alone.

CHECKLIST

1 Have you issued written statements of terms and conditions of employment to all your staff who are normally employed for more than 16 hours per week within 13 weeks of their starting work?

2 Have you made provision to issue these statements to all those who work even 8 hours a week if they have been in your employment for 5 years?

3 Have you reviewed the content of the written statements to ensure they cover at least what the Employment Protection (Consolidation) Act, 1978 demands? (No need to issue deletions of the earlier requirements under the Industrial Relations Act 1971 to mention rights to belong or not to belong to a trade union.)

4 Have you considered what other terms you might specify on this statement which are not required by law but could be beneficial to both you and the staff?

5 What administrative systems have you got for ensuring that changes required in the statements are issued within 4 weeks of that change applying?

6 What procedure have you agreed with the staff to allow you to agree to changes being incorporated in staff contracts as required?

7 Have you reviewed any recruitment documentation that refers to police records, in the light of the Rehabilitation of Offenders Act?

8 Have you looked at your recruitment process to make sure that it does not discriminate against people on grounds of race or nationality?

9 What action have you taken to effect the changes required by the Equal Pay Act and the amendment afterwards of the written statements to female employees?

10 Have you checked your staff specifications to make sure they

do not discriminate against either sex in the qualities you demand in a job holder?

11 Have you checked that any standard advertisements you may have do not discriminate against either sex without good reason?

CHAPTER FOUR

Right from the Start

4.1 STAFF TURNOVER

Having reached this part of the manual, you may be tempted to think that, if you have implemented all that has been suggested so far, your recruitment problem is now resolved. You will now have got to the stage where the right staff have been selected, and you will have ensured that in the interests of both the law and yourself as employer the new members of your staff have a simple and clear guide as to the terms and conditions of their employment. They are ready to begin work.

So far, so good. Wouldn't it be terribly disheartening, however, if, having methodically and conscientiously completed the recruitment process this far, you now found that within a few weeks or months the newcomer was to leave you? Possible? Of course. Likely? Well, it greatly depends on you. Let one statistic speak for itself: the Hotel and Catering Economic Development Committee (Little Neddy) published a report called *Staff Turnover* a few years ago, and this report disclosed that, throughout the industry as a whole, about 70 per cent of all newcomers to the industry left their employment within the first few weeks or months. At least this gives the size of the odds against you.

What can you do to reduce these odds? This really can be answered only by asking an even more fundamental question. Why do so many staff leave so soon after starting work?

Try answering the question from your personal experience. Recall the last time you started a new job—your present job. You arrived on the first day, keen, enthusiastic, ready to please and show that your selection was the right one. Most people approach a new job in this way. No doubt, however, you were also anxious; the place would be strange, people would be unknown to you, and perhaps even the work was new to you. Again this is the experience of every newcomer in employment. If these anxieties are not laid to rest quickly, then the keenness and enthusiasm will quickly wane and the newcomer will be announcing his departure. He will become part of the 70 per cent of leavers referred to.

You have now identified the nature of the danger: the failure to ease the normal anxiety of any new employee and to make him feel useful and part of the company as speedily as possible. To achieve this is the function of what is commonly called 'induction' of new staff. It is more than simply 'introduction', because it implies a positive attempt to integrate the employee into his new surroundings and work in a very constructive manner.

4.2 INDUCTION OF NEW STAFF

Let us look at the newcomer and yourself as employer from the point of view of what each of you wants. The newcomer has the following aims:

1 To do a good job.
2 To be accepted by other staff.
3 To become part of the organization.

You, as employer, want the following sort of person:

1 One who will learn the ropes quickly.
2 One who fits in with the staff quickly.
3 One who will give you work or service in line with what you pay him.

The whole purpose and usefulness of induction is to reconcile all these wants. You could therefore say that induction is the process of changing a new employee from an accepted applicant into a satisfied and productive worker. To achieve this you need to consider four questions:

1 What sort of information does a new member of staff need to start work and to settle down properly?
2 How can this information best be given?
3 When should it be given?
4 Who should be responsible for giving it?

No one is capable of absorbing all the necessary information at once. Your guiding principle in terms of time span should be that enough information and reassurance is given to the newcomer at any one time to alleviate his anxieties, and at the same time to indicate to him that you, as the employer, are really interested in his settling down to work quickly and happily. Of course the newcomer will already be familiar, at least in outline, with certain information:

some will have been covered during the selection interview, and some may appear in the letter of appointment, if used; and in any case, provided you believe as an enlightened employer that there is no sense in waiting for weeks before issuing the written statement outlining the terms and conditions of employment, the newcomer will have on paper a number of the matters referred to.

With the best will in the world, however, such written statements are likely to be too brief for the starter to obtain a detailed view of everyday matters affecting him. Why not consider using at the same time a *Staff Handbook*? This should be designed to provide staff with information about the company and your particular establishment, and to give him a 'reference book', as it were, in which he can find details about anything affecting his employment.

What Might a Handbook Contain?

The short answer must be anything you see as giving staff information affecting their employment, letting them know what is expected of them and what they can expect of you. It can, therefore, be used to amplify some of the items already mentioned on the written statement: for instance, how to resolve a grievance. Be free with the information. Put yourself in their shoes and decide what will help them to become improved members of your team.

Here are some suggestions as to what you might include: brief history of the company, absence and timekeeping, dismissals, accidents, first aid, fire prevention, hygiene, holidays, lockers, lost property, overtime, jury service, loans, staff discounts, meals, pension schemes, promotions and transfers, personal savings plan, protective clothing, smoking, suggestion scheme, social activities, telephone calls, and trade unions.

No list can ever be comprehensive, but this should give you a start. Do write the *Handbook* in easy-to-read language. Even though you have issued the written statement and a *Handbook* to the newcomer, you would be wise to include all these items in your formal induction process, so as to ensure that each is fully understood.

A variety of methods are in use in the industry for carrying out induction. In some cases newcomers are given a formal off-job period of induction, in others they are shown immediately to their work-place and given information from time to time piecemeal, and yet others contain a mixture of both these approaches. Individual unit circumstances tend to dictate the best approach in any one case. Another, as yet relatively little tried, method is to cover the induction process by a form of do-it-yourself induction (see Appendix 8, p. 71). On the whole, the 'how' of induction is intricately tied up with the next question.

When Should Induction Take Place?

If you agree that 'first impressions matter' and that they are often the lasting ones—indeed this can be a separate and compelling reason for the induction process—then this must dictate a chronological sequence of some sort.

1 *At the Interview.* Apart from dealing with all applications promptly and courteously, this really is the first formal contact with the company or unit. Induction starts here. Those who are unsuccessful at this stage should leave you with an impression of having had a fair deal and with regret that they have been unlucky enough not to have been selected by a worth-while employer. As for any who subsequently begin work with you, you will have covered a number of things at this stage: something about the company or unit, an explanation of the sort of work they will be doing, some details about the terms and condition of employment and, if you let them know at this stage of their successful application, details of where and when to report for work.

2 *The First Day.* Of special importance here is that someone meets and welcomes the new starter; failure in this area will simply aggravate the anxiety. Appropriate introductions to other staff should now follow, and the newcomer should be shown over the place where he is to work. His immediate boss should take the opportunity on this first day to make sure all the essential information is given to enable the newcomer to settle down to his work quickly and happily. Such things as the following spring to mind: main features of the job and its standards, health and safety requirements, and procedures. Perhaps it is best to see this as the minimum requirement of the first day. Doubtless our newcomer will himself have a number of questions to ask. Since it is unlikely that his superior will be able to spend all day with him, you might consider that everyone's interests will be best served by attaching the newcomer to some 'sponsor'. This really means a trusted employee who can befriend him, show him what he needs to know geographically, supply him with the additional information required at this early stage, and answer his questions. Before the first day ends, a chance should be made

for the newcomer to have a chat with his superior or manager, so that the day can be reviewed, and perhaps more information and explanation given.

3 *The First Few Days*. Like most things, if allowed to drag on needlessly, the induction process can lose much of its impact and value. Your aim should be to complete it within the first week of starting work. Again this requires looking at with flexibility, because of the varying nature and needs for training in different jobs. However, by and large, you should have completed the main process within a week. This is where an induction checklist can pay handsome dividends (see Appendix 9, p. 73). Throughout the week you should allow for the new member of staff to have informal talks with either yourself as staff manager or his immediate superior, so that you can get useful feedback, help resolve any problems that he may have, and encourage him in his settling in and in his approach to the job.

4 *The First Few Weeks*. The formal induction process may well be completed within a week, but you must remember that until staff have worked for some time they will still experience a sense of newness and rawness, and their anxieties will remain, though to a lesser degree. On the other hand, you should by then be looking for something worth while from them. On both counts then it is as well to allow in the induction programme for newcomers to be visited regularly by the department head, and further, to arrange for follow-up interviews with you as staff manager. In this way a sense of belonging is quickly built up, a feeling of 'someone is interested in me' is encouraged, and you are able to reassure yourself about the correctness of your selection, about the standard of work being done and about the further development needs of the newcomer.

Who Should Carry Out Induction?

Once more the answer here will be determined by the size and nature of your hotel, restaurant, canteen, pub or whatever catering concern you are in. At one end of the scale, in the smallest units, the responsibility for induction may lie on one person's shoulders. In the larger establishments responsibility may be shared at many levels, from the manager who lays down the policy to the sponsor who has a part to play in its implementation. In all cases it is important (1) to determine what the responsibilities are, and (2) to make sure that, if other staff are used, each knows what his particular responsibility is.

Here is an outline of the main responsibilities in induction:

1 The drawing up of induction plans and programmes.
2 Deciding when, where and how induction will be carried out.
3 Allocating responsibilities for various parts of the programme.
4 Training staff to carry out their responsibilities.
5 Reviewing progress.

If you already have an induction programme for staff at all levels, and if it is successful—a measure of which will be the number of staff who leave your employment within the first few weeks or months—then this chapter's value to you may be in helping you to review and refine your programme. On the other hand, if you are troubled by a turnover of staff in the short period after coming to work for you, or you are not actively encouraging your staff to settle into their jobs by means of a definite programme of induction, then this chapter can help you get started. The rewards of a successful induction scheme are enormous. The cost of failing to provide one can be appalling.

CHECKLIST

1 Have you considered issuing all staff with some sort of handbook as an aid to their induction?
2 When a new member of staff starts work, do you make sure someone is detailed to meet him/her?
3 Have you considered the value of using a 'sponsor' for all new staff?
4 Have you considered the value of using a D.I.Y. approach to induction?
5 Is an induction checklist used to make sure the beginner is given the best and fullest start to his work with you?
6 Do you personally try to see every new starter, at least towards the end of his induction period?
7 Have you clarified the individual responsibilities of staff for the induction process?

CHAPTER FIVE

Keeping the Records Right

As staff manager you will be required to plan, advise and decide about matters affecting staff. To do these things you need *information*, which a sound record system can provide you with quickly and easily.

Now that you have reached the end of the part on recruitment, and hopefully have some new staff settling into their work, you will have a certain amount of information about them that can be very useful to you from time to time. This raises the question of how best to record this, and other information, about staff so that, whenever you need to, you can quickly turn up the answers to such questions as, how long has John Blaney worked for me now?, When did Mary Bloggs become a registered on-job trainer? Which of my staff are likely to understand basic French?, How many staff have left my employment in the last 12 months?, and so on.

Keeping records is often a boring part of a staff manager's job. It can also be time-consuming and therefore costly—if it is overdone. This chapter is in no way intended to encourage or demonstrate a paper-building exercise. Quite the contrary. Whether in your case it is a question of setting up a system of staff records from the start, or whether it is seizing the opportunity to review your present system, the advice that follows, in line with the manual's express intention to be simple and practical, is to help you decide what records to keep and how to set about keeping them.

There is no one ideal record-keeping system. The larger companies in the hotel and catering industry already have comprehensive recording systems and the appropriate forms may well be in your office already. Small boarding houses, pubs, and clubs may, on the other hand, rely on individual managers to keep whatever records they wish in any form. But in all cases this chapter asks the following questions:

1 What information should be recorded about staff?

2 How quickly can you find out what you are looking for?
3 To what use do you put this information?

If you cannot provide answers to questions of this sort that you are happy with, then this chapter may help you to set up a simple and practical system or to review the one you already have.

5.1 THE PURPOSE OF PERSONNEL RECORDS

This must be the first point to settle. Your answer will guide you as to *what* information you need. Another way of determining the purpose of records is to ask, What are the uses and likely uses I will have for the information recorded?

Every staff manager will answer this question in a different way, but here are a number of reasons, or uses, for recorded information:

1 To learn something about staff as individuals.
2 To provide information for labour turnover analysis.
3 To help select staff for promotion.
4 To check on the effectiveness of the recruitment process.
5 To give information on wage progression.
6 To decide on redundancy or dismissal liabilities.
7 To record training or staff development.
8 To check on staff attendance at work.
9 To note applications of any disciplinary procedure.

Of course there can be many more uses. In the end only you can determine the value of staff records, which in turn will dictate what information you will wish to collect.

5.2 METHODS OF RECORDING

There are several methods to choose from, depending on what decisions you have made about the uses you will have for this information, and on how sophisticated a system you want to have. Perhaps the best advice is that, whatever method you use to record information about staff, it should pass two tests:

1 Is it simple to understand and use for recording purposes?
2 Does it provide you quickly and easily with any information you are likely to want for statistical, analytical or simply record purposes?

Whatever the size of your unit, you should consider it essential to have a *personal file* system, which allows information about each member of staff to be recorded on his own file. In larger units you might consider, as an addition to this, the use of a *personnel record card* for each member of staff.

Personal File

A file allows you to accumulate documents and correspondence relating to a member of staff, which can be valuable for all sorts of purposes. What sort of information might the file contain? Here are some suggestions:

1 Application form/letter of enquiry.
2 Letter of offer/acceptance.
3 Copy of written statement issued under Employment Protection (Consolidation) Act, 1978.
4 Letters of reference.
5 Sickness/absence notes, certificates.
6 Record of disciplinary warnings given.
7 Subsequent applications for transfer of job.
8 Applications for grievance hearings.
9 Records of issues from company: for example, uniform, cars, buying cards.
10 Copies of notices of changes to written statements.
11 Appraisal forms and records of interviews.

Personnel Record Card

In a way this card can be used as a synopsis of all the information that is contained in the personal file of each member of staff. The cards can be filed alphabetically, and kept in a ring-binder, giving you a very quick method of establishing basic information about staff.

What information might be stored on such a card? The following list of possible items should help you draw up your own list:

1 Name, address and telephone number.
2 Sex.
3 Date of birth.
4 Marital status.
5 Nationality.
6 National Insurance number.
7 Job title.
8 Disabled persons registered number.
9 Aliens number.
10 Work permit expiry date.
11 Department.
12 Date started.
13 Interviewer/notes from interview.
14 Date contract issued.

15 Wage/salary: amount and date.
16 Education.
17 Qualifications.
18 Promotion potential.
19 Training record.
20 Date of leaving.
21 Reasons for leaving.
22 Disciplinary record.

Of course this is not necessarily comprehensive, but it should help to trigger off thoughts on what you want recorded, especially if you have decided earlier why you want the records anyway. An example of a Personnel Record Card is given in Appendix 10 (p. 75).

Preparing a Record Card

Your first decision about the form of record card, once drafted, is likely to be whether to have it printed or just duplicated. Both have their advantages in terms of cost and flexibility. On balance, once you are happy that the layout of the card and the type of information to be recorded is what you want, you might do better to have it printed.

The layout will naturally depend to a large extent upon what items are included. However, there are some practical tips to consider, whatever the information to be recorded:

1 If not printed, use good quality paper to withstand frequent handling.
2 For ease of storage use a uniform standard size of form.
3 Arrange items for speed and accuracy of entry.
4 Leave room for subsequent amendments. Here you will have to decide whether in some cases—for instance, the address block—you allow for a pencil entry that can be erased from time to time, or whether in other cases—for instance, in recording wage progression—you wish to keep a permanent record of wages, so that initial and subsequent entries can be recorded.
5 Consider the use of ballot-box type of entries that require only ticking.
6 Leave a margin to allow for filing without obscuring any of the recorded information.
7 Consider arranging for the bare personal facts of name, address, job title, etc. to appear at the foot of the form if you intend to use a visible index type of storage.

Further Considerations

1 Once you have prepared records for all your staff, and built up a

personal filing system, you must then consider the need for confidentiality of all that has been recorded. Treat all records of staff as privileged documents that you alone, as staff manager, have access to in the normal course of events.

2 Records that are out of date are not worth maintaining. If the records are to be valuable, they must of course reflect the true state of affairs at any time. This calls for consideration as to how you are going to be sure they are kept updated. In many ways this will be your personal responsibility, for you will record all the relevant information, but for such things as changes of address, marital status, added qualifications and so on, it will be necessary occasionally to refer to the staff themselves. Do not rely on them to keep you informed voluntarily. Perhaps it might be possible to send each of them, say annually, a questionnaire to complete, and that will allow you to update your records. Alternatively, and preferably perhaps, you might do this through the supervisors or heads of department.

3 How long should personal records be retained once someone leaves your employment? One thing is certain, no one wants to end up with a mountain of paper-work. However, for practical and in some cases legal reasons, it may be advisable to keep some records for a time once staff have left your employment. The Limitation Act 1939 and the Law Reform (Limitation of Action) Act 1954 provide, in brief, that any action that is founded on a simple contract (such as the employment contract) or tort, cannot be brought if six years have passed since the date on which the cause of the action happened. The following recommended periods of retention are worth considering:

Personnel files	7 years
Attendance records	7 years
Medical records	7 years
Clock cards	3 years
Overtime records	3 years
Employment applications	1 year

Testing your System

Once you have prepared your system of staff records, or if you have one and wish to review it for efficiency, try this random test for speed and ease of obtaining the necessary information:

1 How many married women do you employ?

2 How many new starters have you had in the last 12 months?
3 How many staff have been in your employment for at least 3 years?
4 Which of your staff are registered on-job trainers?
5 How many days' work have been lost as a result of sickness in the past 6 months?

Naturally the speed with which you can answer these questions accurately will depend upon the number of staff you employ. However, how easy was it for you to obtain the relevant information? Does it indicate a simpler and easier way in which to record the information?

With all staff records your aim should be to obtain whatever information you require easily, quickly and accurately. Your staff records should be designed or redesigned with these ideals in mind.

CHECKLIST

1 Can you describe your principal uses of staff records
—for statistical purposes,
—for analytical ends,
—for simply recording purposes?
2 Do your staff records enable you to plan, advise and decide on staff matters easily and quickly?
3 Are your records simple but sufficient?
4 Are your personnel records an accurate reflection of things as they are today?
5 What system do you employ to ensure they are updated?
6 How do you maintain the confidentiality of staff records?
7 How quickly can you retrieve information relating to staff?
8 Are the headings you use simple to understand?
9 Have you the basic information about all staff employed by you within the last 7 years?
10 Does each member of staff have a personal file for correspondence and other documents?

Appendix 1   Job Descriptions

J.D.1

JOB TITLE, DEPARTMENT AND LOCATION	Housekeeper, the Tartan Hotel, Glasburgh
JOB SUPERIOR	Hotel manager
JOB SUBORDINATES	4 room maids 3 part-time cleaners 1 laundry maid
RELATIONSHIPS WITH OTHER PEOPLE	Contract maintenance staff All departmental heads and reception staff Fire inspectors and fire equipment contractors

MAIN DUTIES

1 Organize the daily cleaning and servicing of all bedrooms and public rooms.
2 Supervise the collection, laundry and distribution of bed and table linen and staff uniforms.
3 Organize room service for early morning teas and breakfasts (up to 11.00 a.m.) daily.
4 Requisition and control the following stock:
   cleaning materials,
   linen,
   room service crockery.
5 Inspect staff accommodation with the hotel manager weekly.
6 Liaise with reception staff on accommodation services and security.
7 Plan and implement training of departmental staff in all relevant craft skills, social skills, fire drills and induction.
8 Assist and advise the managers in planning, repairs and maintenance work, replacement of furnishings, fittings and equipment.
9 Assist and advise in the selection of housekeeping staff.

OCCASIONAL DUTIES

Holiday relief housekeeping duties in the company's Blue Arrow Hotel, Waverly Square.

LIMITS OF AUTHORITY

Cash—up to £25 on any one purchase.
Discipline—recommend dismissal of staff to hotel manager.

J.D.2

JOB TITLE, DEPARTMENT AND LOCATION	General Catering Assistant, Works Canteen, Alpha Woollen Fabrics, Bradchester.
JOB SUPERIOR	Canteen manager
JOB SUBORDINATES	None
RELATIONSHIPS WITH OTHER PEOPLE	Delivery staff (dry goods) Food service staff in directors' dining room

MAIN DUTIES
1 Assist daily in the initial preparation of kitchen.
2 Prepare cold snacks as required by the chef.
3 Assist with preparation of lunch.
4 Pass to wash up or return to equipment store all utensils used in preparation work.
5 Clean and tidy the dry goods store.
6 Assist with the unloading of all kitchen supplies.
7 Check quality and quantity of dry goods delivered by suppliers.
8 Complete stock control records when dry goods are transferred to the store.

OCCASIONAL DUTIES
1 Assist with counter service as required.
2 Assist chef with stocktaking (quarterly).
3 Assist with wine service at special functions in the directors' dining room.

LIMITS OF AUTHORITY
The job holder is not authorized to sign orders for goods or supplies. Deficiencies and damaged goods must be reported to the chef at the time of delivery.

Appendix 2 Staff Specifications

S.S.1

JOB TITLE: HOUSEKEEPER

	Essential	*Desirable*
1 *Physical make-up*		
(a) Sex		Female
(b) Age	Over 23	25–35 years
(c) Height	Over 5′ 2″	
(d) Health	No serious disability	Sound health record over past 5 years
(e) Eyesight	Normal vision	
2 *Educational attainments*		
(a) School certificates	Be able to express him/herself effectively	GCE English, maths, domestic science
(b) Further education		IMA or supervisor training
(c) Recognized skills training		Registered HCITB 5 day trainer
3 *Work experience*		
(a) Experience in this part of industry	3 years' experience in housekeeping in medium sized hotel Some laundry experience	Supervisory experience in housekeeping
4 *Personal characteristics*		
(a) Affability		
(b) Honesty	Good reference regarding honesty from previous employer	
(c) Stability		
5 *Personal circumstances*		
(a) Live in/out	Live within 5 miles of hotel	Live in
(b) Children		None under 10 years of age

S.S.2

JOB TITLE: GENERAL CATERING ASSISTANT

	Essential	*Desirable*
1 *Physical make-up*		
(a) Sex		Female
(b) Age	Over 18	20–45
(c) Appearance	Clean	Smart and well groomed, particularly hair and hands
(d) Health	No history of notifiable diseases Good hearing	Energetic
(e) Speech	No serious defects	
2 *Education and Training*		
(a) School	Be able to read, write and do simple arithmetic	Be able to calculate invoice value from unit costs
(b) Skills training		Food prep. and cooking training either GCE or CSE. Wine service training
3 *Work experience*		
(a) In this industry	Any post in kitchen work	Canteen kitchen work for at least 6 months in one job
4 *Personality*		
(a) Affability	Polite and not easily flustered	Cheerful temperament
(b) Honesty	Evidence of high standards of honesty from past employers	
5 *Personal circumstances*		
(a) Marital status	Not married to shift worker	Single
(b) Children		None under 14 years
(c) Stability		Unlikely to move out of district during coming year

Appendix 3 Application Forms

A.F.1 SPECIMEN APPLICATION FORM FOR MANAGEMENT POST

PRIVATE AND CONFIDENTIAL

NAME AND ADDRESS OF ORGANIZATION

Application for the job of ....

1 *Personal particulars*

SURNAME (BLOCK LETTERS)	FIRST NAMES
ADDRESS TELEPHONE NUMBER	ADDRESS FOR CORRESPONDENCE IF DIFFERENT TELEPHONE NUMBER

DATE OF BIRTH	PLACE OF BIRTH	MARRIED ☐ SINGLE ☐ WIDOWED ☐ DIVORCED ☐ SEPARATED ☐

MALE ☐ FEMALE ☐ Tick the appropriate box	NATIONALITY	DO YOU HOLD A WORK PERMIT (WHERE APPLICABLE) YES ☐ NO ☐

DO YOU HAVE ANY CHILDREN? IF YES, GIVE AGES

NAME AND ADDRESS OF PERSON TO BE CONTACTED IN EMERGENCY

TELEPHONE NUMBER BY DAY BY NIGHT

WHAT SERIOUS ACCIDENTS, ILLNESS OR DISABILITIES HAVE YOU HAD?

ARE YOU PRESENTLY UNDERGOING MEDICAL TREATMENT? YES ☐ NO ☐
IF YES, DESCRIBE BRIEFLY

ARE YOU A REGISTERED DISABLED PERSON? YES/NO
IF SO, GIVE YOUR REGISTRATION NUMBER ——————————

DO YOU HAVE A CURRENT DRIVING LICENCE? YES/NO

HAVE YOU EVER BEEN CONVICTED OF A CRIMINAL OFFENCE? YES/NO
IF SO, PLEASE GIVE DETAILS

WHEN COULD YOU START WORK WITH US IF WE OFFERED YOU A JOB?

....

2 *Education and Training*

WHAT SCHOOL(S) DID YOU ATTEND?

FROM	TO	NAME OF SCHOOL	CERTIFICATES RECEIVED

WHAT OTHER COURSES OF EDUCATION HAVE YOU UNDERTAKEN?

FROM	TO	NAME OF COLLEGE/UNIVERSITY	QUALIFICATIONS RECEIVED

WHAT TRAINING COURSES HAVE YOU ATTENDED?

FROM	TO	WHO RAN THE COURSE?	QUALIFICATIONS RECEIVED

3 *Employment*

PLEASE GIVE DETAILS OF THE JOBS YOU HAVE HAD IN THE LAST FIVE YEARS

FROM	TO	NAME AND ADDRESS OF EMPLOYER	JOB TITLES. BRIEF DESCRIPTION OF DUTIES	SALARY INC. BONUS AND FRINGE BENEFITS	REASON FOR LEAVING

Please comment on the experience you have gained and say how it will help you in the post for which you have applied.

What particular aspects of the job for which you have applied interest you most?

4 *References*
Please give the names, status, telephone number and addresses of two referees. At least one of the referees must know you through your employment.

5 *This application*
Please make any other comments about yourself, experience or interests, which are relevant to the application. Also ask any questions about the job for which you have applied.

I declare that the information I have given is correct.

Signature .... Date ....

A.F.2 Specimen application form for craft/operative type of job

Private and confidential

X.Y.Z. Company

Application for employment

Type of work applied for ....

PERSONAL PARTICULARS

Surname: (block letters)	Christian Names:	MALE / FEMALE
Address: ....Tel. No.	Nationality	Do you hold a work permit (if applicable) Yes ☐ No ☐
Date of Birth: Day Month Year	Single/Married/Widow/Widower/ Divorced/Separated	
Age now:	No. of Children	

Are you a Reg. Disabled Person? YES/NO
If so, give Reg. No. ....

Name/Address of person to be contacted in emergency ....
....

Are you presently undergoing medical treatment? YES ☐ NO ☐ If yes, describe briefly ....
....

EDUCATION

Last school attended:

Type of school:	Highest class reached:

Examinations passed:

Details of any special training or qualifications: ....
....
....
....

Do you hold a current driving licence? YES/NO
Details of any current endorsements and dates ....
....

HOBBIES/INTERESTS

What are your hobbies/interests outside work? ....
....
....

PRESENT OR LAST EMPLOYMENT

Name and address
of last employer:

Occupation:	Wage/salary

Date started:	Date leaving/left:

What are your reasons for desiring
to leave (or for having left)?

PREVIOUS EMPLOYMENT

(1)
Name and address of employer:

Occupation:	Wage/salary:

Date started:	Date left:

Reasons for leaving:

(2)
Name and address of employer:

Occupation:	Wage/salary:
Date started:	Date left:

Reasons for leaving:

(3)
Name and address of employer:

Occupation:	Wage/salary:
Date started:	Date left:

Reasons for leaving:

FOR COMPANY USE ONLY

Date interviewed:	Job offered:
	To commence work on:
Wage/salary:	Wage dept./clerk notified? YES/NO
....	Interviewed by:

Appendix 4 Sample Advertisements

Display

Tartan
Hotel
Glasbrugh

HOUSEKEEPER

45 BEDROOMS

This interesting and responsible post will become vacant when our housekeeper retires in two months time.

The duties include organizing and supervising the cleaning and servicing of bedrooms and public rooms, training departmental staff and control of laundry services. Applicants should be over 23 years of age with a minimum of three years experience in housekeeping preferably in a supervisory role. Registration as an HCITB trainer would be an advantage.

The hotel is situated ½ mile from the city centre and has high occupancy rates throughout the year.

Salary - £?,000

Our excellent conditions include:-
Living-in accommodation available for single person.
5 day week.
3 weeks annual holiday.
Staff bonus scheme.
Life insurance cover.
Regular salary review.

Please contact Secretary, Tartan Hotel, Glasbrugh for application form and job description. Tel. Glasbrugh 1234.

Semi-display

NORBRIDGE RESTAURANTS

RESTAURANT SUPERVISOR

For our new Restaurant opening shortly in the City Centre Shopping Precinct, NORBRIDGE.

Duties include full responsibility for Dining Room Service, Supervision and training of ten food service staff.

Some experience as a Supervisor in a similar establishment is essential.

We Offer

5 Day Week
Meals Provided whilst on duty
Profit bonus Scheme
3 weeks Holiday.

Please apply to the Manager, Norbridge Restaurants.
Tel: NORBRIDGE 1234

Classified

Catering Assistant (Canteen) Alpha Woollen Fabrics, Bradchester. We offer an interesting and varied job as a Catering Assistant in our Main Works Canteen. If you are over 18 and have some experience in kitchen work, you are invited to apply to Personnel Officer, Telephone Bradchester 1234 for application form.

Appendix 5 Typical Interview Questions

Here are examples of typical questions used in an interview. They exemplify the way to ask questions and *must not* be used as a checklist of questions for an interview.

PHYSICAL MAKE-UP AND FAMILY BACKGROUND
Tell me about your family.
In what ways do you differ from your family?
Will you bring up your children in the same way as the family did you?
What changes will you make, if any?
What view would your husband/wife take if you were offered this post?

EDUCATION AND JOB HISTORY
How did you come to study ....?
What were your best/worst subjects at school?
Given a free choice and the benefit of hindsight, what would you have liked to study, and why?
Describe the main difficulties you found at school/college etc.
How did your career come to take this shape?
Looking back, what changes would you make?
Tell me about the main problems you have faced during your career.
What do you regard as your main achievement?
Tell me about things you really do not like doing at all.
For what precisely are you responsible in your present job?
What do you like most/least about your job?
What sort of relationship do you have with your present boss/colleagues.
(If difficult)—How do you deal with these problems?

LEISURE ACTIVITY
What do you do in your off-duty hours?
What part do you take in clubs or local groups?
How much time does that occupy on average each week?
Do you have one particular friend or just lots of acquaintances?
What sort of books do you like best?
What kind of people do you get along with best?
What interests do you share with your wife?
How do you normally spend your holidays?

GENERAL
Who have been the most influential people in your life and why?
What have been your most satisfying experiences?
What have been the most unpleasant experiences you have had?
What do you regret in your life so far?
What would you like to have accomplished in your life ten years from now?
What are the most important lessons you have had to learn in your life so far?
Describe the best boss you have ever worked for.
Describe the worst boss you have ever worked for.

Appendix 6 Interview Rating Form

INTERVIEW RATING FORM

NAME Miss Y. Brown

AREA	EXCEPT.	ABOVE AVGE	AVGE	BELOW AVGE	POOR
Physical make-up		x			
Education/work attainments			x		
General intelligence		x			
Special aptitudes				x	
Interests			x		
Disposition/temperament					x
Personal/domestic circumstances		x			

NOTES

She is a brunette, average height, wearing a green outfit and carrying a large shoulder-bag.

Haven't selected her for this post—too easily flustered, inclined to be short-tempered.

INTERVIEWER A. B. Smith

Appendix 7 Written Statement of Terms and Conditions of Employment

Name of employer/employee

In welcoming you to the staff of 'The Seaside Hotel', Blackton, we, Mr and Mrs I. M. Hotelier, as proprietors, hope that you, John Smith, will enjoy your work with us. To help all of us at the hotel to achieve and maintain a happy working relationship, a

Grievance procedure:

minimum number of rules have been drawn up and these are set out in this statement, together with your particular terms and conditions of employment. If, at any time, there is anything you do not understand or any problem you would like resolved, speak to your departmental head about it; he/she will be glad to listen to you and has been specially trained to help with any query you may have. If by chance he cannot resolve your difficulty, then speak to the manager with special responsibility for staff and lastly, if as occasionally happens, a problem persists and you think it requires further consideration, you should seek an interview with one of the proprietors, who will endeavour to see that a fair solution is reached.

Date of employment, job title, mobility clause

Your employment started with us on 1 January 1976, when you began work as a commis waiter in the hotel's main restaurant. Occasionally staff are required to work in our sister hotel, 'The Countryman' in Whitetown, and you may be required to work there at any time.

Wages, interval of payment, overtime, accommodation, meals

Your starting pay with us will be £X, including a proportion of the service charge for the standard 40-hour week. This will be paid to you weekly, one week in arrears. Sometimes it may be necessary for you to work overtime, in which case you will be paid at the overtime rate of Y pence per hour, or time off in lieu offered. In addition to your wages you will be provided with free accommodation and free meals.

Hours of work

The 40 hours of work, which excludes meal breaks, must be worked at such times and on such days as designated by your head of department, who will publish a weekly rota for staff. You will be entitled to 2 days of rest each week, exclusive of normally recognized public holidays, or time off in lieu.

Holidays

You will be entitled to 4 weeks' paid holiday each year once you have been employed for 12 months, increasing to 5 weeks after 5 years' employment. Provided you have worked for a minimum period of 12 weeks before 31 December in your first year you will be entitled to holidays on a pro rata basis.

In addition, you will be allowed all public holidays or time off in lieu.

Sickness

If you are absent from work through sickness, then, on production of a doctor's certificate before the end of the third day's absence from work, you will be allowed sick pay on the following scale:

1 week's sickness pay after 6 months' employment
2 weeks' sickness pay after 1 year's employment
3 weeks' sickness pay after 2 years' employment
4 weeks' sickness pay after 3 years' employment

These periods may be extended in certain cases at the discretion of the manager.

Pension

We do not operate any pension scheme for our staff.

Training/promotion

Throughout your employment you will be offered suitable training not only to help you in your present job but to prepare you for other work in keeping with your abilities. It is our policy to offer promotion to all suitable staff when vacancies occur.

Discipline

Your job is considered a position of trust, and staff regulations are designed for your protection. They explain your responsibility for the care and safe-keeping of the company's property and money. If any of the following regulations are not clear, you must ask your head of department for further explanation, since a failure to observe them will result in disciplinary action.

Fires/smoking

Hotel fires endanger the lives of both customers and staff. Smoking is a fire hazard and is therefore permitted in the staff room and your own bedroom only. Anyone found smoking elsewhere in the hotel, or staff who break any of the special fire precautions (displayed in the kitchen), will be considered for instant dismissal.

Conduct/dismissal

It is not our policy to list the offences for which you may be dismissed. However, if you are guilty of any act of such gravity as to be inconsistent with your continued employment, you may be asked to leave your employment immediately. Every case that could end in dismissal will be referred to the proprietors, who alone will make the final decision.

Disciplinary procedures

Our full disciplinary procedure is displayed on the staff notice board. You may appeal against any disciplinary decision to one of the proprietors.

Suspension

While investigations leading to possible dismissal are being undertaken, you may be suspended without pay at the proprietors' discretion.

Search

If there is a grave reason, the proprietors may authorize the searching of your person, your room and your effects.

Notice

Should you wish to leave our employment at any time, you are required to give at least one week's notice. If, however, the proprietors wish to terminate your employment and you are normally employed for at least 16 hours per week, you will be offered one week's notice for each year of your employment up to a maximum of 12 weeks' notice after 12 years' service.

Where you work for less than 16 hours a week normally, then the notice period will be halved until you have been employed for a minimum of 5 years, when the above notice periods will apply in full.

In either of these cases pay in lieu of notice may be offered.

Payment in lieu of holidays

Should you leave our employment for any reason other than being instantly dismissed, you will be paid in lieu of any entitlement you may have for any holidays that are outstanding.

The proprietors do not hold a contracting-out certificate in respect of staff, under the Pensions and Social Security Act, 1975.

Employment Protection (Consolidation) Act 1978

This statement of your main terms and conditions of employment is issued to you in accordance with Section 1 of the Employment Protection (Consolidation) Act, 1978. It is effective as from the date of your employment.

DATE OF ISSUE: 10 January 1978

Appendix 8 Do-It-Yourself Induction Programme

INDUCTION PROGRAMME FOR FOOD SERVICE STAFF
IN MEDIUM-SIZED RESTAURANT

Day 1 9.00—10.00

Meet and welcome new member of staff.
Introduce him to his immediate superior.
Explain the basic pattern of work.
Issue and go through the items on the written statement of the main terms and conditions of employment.
Issue *Staff Handbook*.
Issue a job description and a note-pad, and give staff a questionnaire to be completed by him before lunch.

10.15—Lunch

New staff to spend time finding out the following information:

1 List the colleagues who will be working with him in the restaurant.
2 Who is the restaurant manager?
3 Who is the chef?
4 What menus are used in the restaurant?
5 Where does he obtain uniform?
6 What are the arrangements for uniform cleaning and exchange?
7 How many tables are in each station?
8 Who are the station waiters?
9 Who is the staff representative?
10 What impresses him most/least about the staff rest-room?
11 What shift system is in operation?
12 What rules apply to working overtime?

LUNCH

2.00—2.30

Review of answers obtained.
Issue further questionnaire.

2.30—4.00

The following information to be sought by new staff:

1 Where and when are wages paid?
2 How does the tronc system operate?
3 How does he apply for holidays?
4 What does he do if he wishes to air a grievance?
5 What is the procedure for reporting an injury?

	6	Where is the nearest first-aid box in the restaurant?
	7	Where is the nearest fire exit?
4.00—4.30	Review with staff manager of first day's induction.	
(Day 2 etc	Designed along similar lines to suit the establishment.)	

Appendix 9 Induction Checklist

NAME J. BROWN

ITEMS	INTERVIEW	FIRST DAY	FIRST WEEK	INFORMAL FOLLOW-UP INTERVIEW
TERMS AND CONDITIONS				
Wages/salary	x			
Method of payment			x	
Overtime rates and conditions	x			
Bonus scheme	x			
Pay review				x
When and how paid			x	
Hours of work	x			
Shift system		x		
Breaks		x		
Holidays			x	
Holiday pay			x	
Sickness pay scheme			x	
Pension arrangements			x	
Grievance procedure			x	
Notice period			x	
CLOCKING PROCESS				
Number		x		
Clocking position		x		
Penalties		x		
Issue of written statement EP(C) Act, 1978			x	
Issue *Staff Handbook*		x		
HEALTH/SAFETY/WELFARE				
Medical examination		x		
First-aid regulations		x		
Reporting of injuries			x	
Fire precaution procedures			x	
Smoking		x		
Uniform issues		x		
Lockers		x		

ITEMS	INTERVIEW	FIRST DAY	FIRST WEEK	INFORMAL FOLLOW-UP INTERVIEW
Catering arrangements for staff		x		
Recreation facilities			x	
Sport and social clubs			x	
Car parking		x		
REGULATIONS AND PROCEDURES				
Disciplininary procedure			x	
Absence			x	
Certificate requirements			x	
Hygiene regulations			x	
Trade union membership			x	
Company rules			x	
WORKING ENVIRONMENT				
Immediate work areas		x		
Immediate department		x		
Whole unit			x	
Head of department		x		
Working colleagues		x		
Other staff, as appropriate			x	
Description of job requirements		x		
Standards		x		
Equipment		x		
GENERAL				
Company background etc.			x	
Education and training				x
Promotion and transfer				x
Purchase facilities			x	
Saving schemes				x
Suggestions schemes			x	
Personal problems				x

Appendix 10 Personnel Record Card

SIDE 1

DATE STARTED	D	M	Y	REFERENCE	YES	NO	IN'VIEWED BY:	DISABLED PERSONS REG. NO.

WAGE/SALARY	AMOUNT	DATE	SPECIAL NOTES:	CONTRACT ISSUED	D	M
COMMENCING						
AMENDED				LEAVING DETAIL	D	M
”						
”				REASON		
”						
”						
”						
”						
”						
”						
”						
”						
”						

EDUCATION	QUALIFICATIONS

RECORD OF SERVICE

OCCUPATION

FROM	TO	PAY	D M Y

PROMOTION POTENTIAL

GRADE	D	M	Y
A			
B			
C			
D			
E			

NAME	SEX	MALE / FEMALE	MARITAL STATUS	NATIONALITY	P	JOB TITLE

ADDRESS	TEL:	PLACE OF BIRTH	D	M	Y	NAT INS. NO.	DEPT.

SIDE 2

TRAINING RECORD	NAME JOB TITLE

OFF-JOB Activity	Cost/fee	Date	*ON-JOB* Activity	Date

ABSENCE RECORD

S—Sick H—Holiday
A—Accident U—Unauthorized absence

Type	Dates	Type	Dates	Type	Dates

DISCIPLINARY ACTION

Date	Details

PART II

THE ART OF KEEPING STAFF

CHAPTER SIX

Staff Turnover

6.1 HOW TO RECORD STAFF TURNOVER

It might seem somewhat strange to you at first sight that, immediately following the part dealing with recruitment of staff, you are now faced with a chapter dealing with loss of staff. The fact is that we do tend to have figures of staff turnover strikingly higher than in other industries. Instead of accepting this 'as a fact of life', which it must emphatically be said *not* to be, let us analyze the figures and determine what staff managers can do to reduce the number of leavers to an acceptable level. The chapters that follow in Part II are designed specifically to show staff managers what methods will help them retain their staff.

Staff turnover is the term used to describe the movement of staff into and out of work with a firm or an establishment. Theoretically it covers every person who comes to work for you and then leaves your employment, but in practice you might want to narrow its meaning. For instance, if you take on a student for, say, three weeks and he then leaves you as planned, you might not wish to record his departure as part of your turnover figures. He has fulfilled a specific function over a predetermined period. Likewise, you may sometimes want to take on some extra waitresses to cope with a definite function and no more. These categories of staff are quite different to those you looked at in Part I, for you took time to recruit them carefully for long-term employment. These will form the backbone of your staff turnover statistics, should you lose their services.

Cost of Staff Turnover

Too many managers in the catering industry seem to accept, almost fatalistically, that a high turnover of staff is inevitable. Worse than that, too many resign themselves and say that there is nothing they can do about it anyway. Dare we call such people managers?

How important do you think staff turnover is? Let us put it like this: today it is becoming increasingly difficult for businesses to make reasonable profits; one certain way is to cut costs, and this can be done even in inflationary times—by reducing staff turnover. Do you know how much it costs you each time you have to replace a member of staff? Few staff managers have troubled to cost this part of the business, but if you do so, you are almost certainly in for a shock.

Let us look at a simple example: a barman, employed for two years, has left because of a misunderstanding caused through poor communications on the part of management, and has to be replaced. The *direct* costs could be as follows:

1	Advertising and associated paper-work	£20
2	Recruitment time (interviewing and selection)	£30
3	Training of new recruit	£30

The *indirect* costs could work out as follows:

1	Time spent training previous barman	£10
2	Lost customers	£ 5
		£95

All these costs are of course fictitious, certainly not completely comprehensive, and likely to be under- rather than over-estimated. Indeed, the latest research findings in *Manpower Policy in the Hotels and Restaurant Industry*, published by the Hotel and Catering E.D.C. in 1975, mention that one figure quoted in 1973 was an average of £100 per recruit.

However, suppose in the course of a year the bar lost four barmen; it will have then cost the owner £380. Not too much? But consider it in the way in which it should be considered and ask yourself, how much business does that bar have to do before it recovers that £380 and starts to make a profit again? The answer is likely to be a staggering £12,000+.

If you want to be thorough in your costing, you will find that the following factors demand recognition:

1 Cost of recruitment, selection and engagement. This will cover costs of advertising, the use of agencies, associated paper-work, travel expenses, and management time discussing vacancies, reading applications and interviewing.
2 The cost of induction.

3 The expenses incurred in training and supervising new entrants.
4 The relatively low standard of service of the newcomer.
5 The cost of training the staff who have left.
6 The overtime that may have to be paid during staff shortages.
7 An increase in wastage/losses etc.
8 Lower staff morale if staff turnover is high.
9 Loss of customers.

When you put things in this way surely staff turnover must be of significant concern to any staff manager. How readily do you take out your chequebook and write a cheque for £200/£1000, or how easily do you get company permission for capital expenditure of this sort?

It is strange that we take so long to consider spending money on material items such as furniture and equipment, and yet, without worrying too much, allow even greater sums to be spent through the cost of staff turnover. Peter Drucker rightly put it this way: 'People decisions take less than one-tenth of the time top management give to capital appropriation decisions, yet the two, capital and people, should rank equally as key resources'.

Preliminary Work on Recording

One of the immediate difficulties is finding managers who keep records of staff turnover. And the first and fundamental step you must take, if you have not got a year by year record of staff turnover, is to set up a simple but reliable staff record system.

Start by opening a file entitled Staff Turnover and, at whatever date you start the file, list all the staff for whom you are responsible. Against each of these note in columns sex, job title, full-time or part-time nature of employment, department and date of starting in your employment. Finally leave two further columns headed Date Left and Period of Stay. An example of such a page is shown in Appendix 11 (p. 153).

Once this file has been brought into use, you will have the basis for making the calculations that will present you with a true and accurate picture of your staff turnover. More importantly, if the remaining part of the system is implemented, you will be able to answer the questions relating to staff turnover that will guide you into taking the right decisions to help cut down avoidable losses. As staff come and go, keep your file updated with the relevant information, including whatever you feel will be helpful from the exit interviews, which are discussed below.

Measuring Turnover

Once you have collected factual information for a period, you are in a position to make some calculations. There are three main measures to apply.

1 *Staff Turnover Rate*. This is a measure of the *number of leavers*, expressed as a percentage of the average number of staff employed. This measure can be taken annually or at lesser periods to suit your needs, and it can be worked out on the basis of the unit (all staff) or by departments, or by job and so on. All this information is available from your file. The formula to use is this:

$$\frac{\text{Number of leavers} \times 100}{\text{Average number employed}}$$

Suppose in your housekeeping department you employ a total of 24 staff, and in a year you lose 15 of them; then to find your turnover rate for the year, using the formula, your calculation would be as follows:

$$\frac{15 \times 100}{24} = 62.5 \text{ per cent}$$

On the other hand, if you suspect that a particular period of the year, for some reason, accounts for a higher loss of staff, you can work your staff turnover figure on a period basis. For instance, to find out the rate at 31 March in an establishment employing an average of 15 staff, when you have suffered comings and goings of 30 staff in that time, your formula would be:

$$\frac{\text{Number of leavers} \times 100}{\text{Average number employed}} \times \frac{12}{4}\text{(months)} = \frac{30}{15} \times 100 \times \frac{12}{4}\text{ (months)}$$

$$= 600 \text{ per cent}$$

2 *Survival Curves*. The figures obtained above may be helpful in giving you a picture of your staff turnover, and can be useful as a point of comparison with other similar establishments. However, a much more useful method of measuring turnover can be obtained from a survival curve. As its name implies, this chart can tell you accurately whether your problem is one of retaining staff in the early periods after employment. It is therefore a measure that concentrates on *new entrants* (see Appendix 12, p. 154.

3 *Length of Service Charts*. The final chart can be used to illustrate how long staff have been in your employment. It serves as a measure of the extent to which you have been able to build up a steady core of employees (see Appendix 13, p. 156).

Practical Tips

1 When you have set up your staff turnover file, resist the temptation to add more information than you need. These files frequently resemble a duplicated version of a personnel/staff record system.

2 Set as your objectives the obtaining of enough information to provide you with answers to the following questions:
   (a) What percentage of entrants left within the first 13 weeks of starting work?
   (b) What percentage of them left within one year?
   (c) What percentage have remained beyond two years of starting work?

3 Decide whether you are going to include every leaver, no matter for what reason, or whether you will record only 'avoidable' leavers; thus you may decide not to count those who die, or retire. On the other hand you may decide to keep separate calculations to cover all leavers.

4 Once you have started your system, continue making these calculations in respect of entrants joining in each successive year so as to indicate how more or less successful you are becoming in retaining staff.

5 If your unit takes extra staff on for a season, it will help you interpret your figures more accurately if you show these additional staff in brackets against each of the main calculations.

6 Should you be a manager in a totally seasonal establishment, which is open for part of the year only, then a number of adjustments should be made:
   (a) Length of service distribution would not need to be calculated.
   (b) Your staff turnover rate is worked out by totalling those who leave during the season and expressing this figure as a percentage of the average number employed during the season.
   (c) Your survival curve should be based on the total number of staff with whom you start the season.

7 Do not keep figures for figures' sake! Once you have them, analyse them and make decisions that will help retain staff in the future.

Part I Bibliography

Ansley, E. and Mercer, E. O. *Interviewing for the Selection of Staff* (Allen & Unwin, 1956).

Barber, D. *Basic Personnel Procedures* (I.P.M., 1974).

Boella, M. J. *Personnel Management in the Hotel and Catering Industry* (Barrie & Jenkins, 1974).

Bowley, A. and Lupton, T. *Job and Pay Comparisons* (Gower Press, 1973).

British Institute of Management *Induction,* Management Checklist No. 7 (B.I.M., 1969).

—— *Filling a Vacancy,* Management Checklist No. 8 (B.I.M., 1969).

—— *Selecting Staff,* Management Checklist No. 9 (B.I.M., 1969)

Bull, F. J. and Richardson, C. *Hotel and Catering Law* (Barrie & Rockliff, 1962).

Cronbach, L. J. *Essentials of Psychological Testing* (Harper & Row, 1960).

Cronbach, L. J. and Gleser, G. C. *Psychological Tests and Personnel Decisions* (University of Illinois Press, 1965).

Dunnette, M. D. *Personnel Selection and Placement* (Tavistock Publications, 1967).

Finnigan, J. *The Right People and the Right Jobs* (Business Books Ltd., 1973).

Frazer, J. M. *Employment Interviewing* (MacDonald & Evans, 1966).

—— *Interviewing* (Pitman, 1956).

Gough, J. S. *Interviewing in Twenty Six Steps* (B.A.C.I.E., 1961).

Guion, R. M. *Personnel Testing* (New York: McGraw-Hill, 1965).

Holdsworth, R. *Personnel Selection Testing – A Guide to Managers* (B.I.M., 1972).

Hotel and Catering E.D.C. *Manpower Policy in the Hotels and Restaurants Industry,* Research Findings (N.E.D.O., 1975).

—— *Staff Turnover* (N.E.D.O., 1969).

Hotel and Catering I.T.B. *A Manager's Guide to Staff Induction* (H.C.I.T.B., 1975).

Industrial Society. *Design of Personnel Systems and Records* (Gower Press, 1969).

Mager, R. F. *Preparing Instructional Objectives* (Fearon, 1962).

Marks, W. *Induction – Acclimatising People to Work* (I.P.M., 1972).

——*Preparing an Employee Handbook* (I.P.M., 1972).

McGehee, W. and Thaser, P. *Training in Business and Industry* (Wiley, 1961).

Mepham, G. J. *Equal Opportunity and Equal Pay* (I.P.M., 1974).

Miller, K. (ed.). *Psychological Testing* (Gower Press, 1976).

Pollard, W. B. (ed.). *Reference Book for Employers* (Croner Publications Ltd., 1976).

Ray, M. E. *Practical Job Advertising* (I.P.M., 1971).

Redgraves, A. *Factories Acts* (Butterworth, 1966).

Sidney, E. and Brown, M. *The Skills of Interviewing* (Tavistock Publications, 1961).

Taylor, E. A. *A Training Officer's Guide to Selection* (B.A.C.I.E., 1966).

Wainwright, D. *Race and Employment* (I.P.M., 1970).

8 Finally, remember the cost of losing staff. Carry out an exercise to cost as accurately as you can the unavoidable loss of a member of staff. When you have done that, motivate yourself by then asking, How much business do I have to do to recoup that loss?

6.2 USING STAFF TURNOVER INFORMATION PRODUCTIVELY

Let us suppose that you now have a system of recording staff turnover and that you have prepared a number of easily readable charts. This section is now designed so that you may 'read' the charts with a view to drawing accurate conclusions, leading in turn to decisions on your part to reduce your avoidable number of leavers to an acceptable level.

Exit Interviews

However, before that, let us also take into account other information you can use, which is obtainable through another common personnel practice—that of interviewing staff who are about to leave you. Combining this information with that obtainable from your own interpretation of statistical charts should go a long way towards finding out the real causes of staff turnover.

The purpose of the exit interview is to probe leavers' views of your organization, and if possible to discover the reasons for their leaving. Naturally, you will not rely too greatly on the reasons given, since often the real reason may be personal or be based on personal animosity towards a supervisor; indeed, the leaver may not himself be clear why he is leaving or he may be leaving for a combination of reasons. If this is so, then you might consider that in conducting exit interviews you are likely to find them more useful as a survey of attitudes rather than providing accurate reasons for leaving.

It can be useful to divide up the many and varied reasons why staff leave into those which are 'avoidable' and those which are not. No list can be comprehensive, but you might consider the following:

1 *Unavoidable causes of leaving*
Retirement
Illness
Marriage
Pregnancy
Death
Leaving the area

2 *Avoidable causes*
Pursuit of a career
Personal development
Material betterment
Nature of work
Dissatisfaction with the job
Dissatisfaction with wages, hours, etc.
Dissatisfaction with fellow employees
Dissatisfaction with the boss
Transport difficulties
Accommodation problems

Of course you may think of other general reasons why people leave you. The important thing for you as a staff manager is to get as near as you can to the real reasons for departures of staff and to discover if they show a trend or highlight something that you can put right in the organization.

The principles of good interviewing, as described in Part I, are equally valid when conducting an exit interview. However, the big difference you are likely to encounter in this sort of interview is in the attitude of those who are about to leave you. It all depends on the reason they have for leaving. Use this to your advantage, and let the mood they demonstrate guide you in deciding the real causes for their departure. From your point of view you are likely to find such interviews beneficial if you conduct them along the following lines:

1 Prepare for the interview by finding out as much as you can in advance about the interviewee, and have his personal record with you.
2 Express genuine regret, if that is appropriate, at his departure.
3 Explain immediately that your purpose is not to get him to change his mind about leaving, but rather to provide you with the opportunity to put things right in the unit if his leaving is on account of some weakness there.
4 Use open-ended questioning to encourage the leaver to talk openly and frankly about his reasons for leaving.
5 Adopt a friendly approach throughout the interview and do not be drawn into an argument.
6 End by expressing thanks for his service, if they are due, and good wishes for his future employment.

Interpreting the Information

All the work that has been described up to now has had one purpose only: to provide you with the necessary information from which, by analysis, you can make decisions that will enable you to reduce staff turnover. Some turnover is unavoidable and some of it is even desirable, but what you are now concerned with is to reduce avoidable turnover.

What information have you now got? Basically, in this section it is suggested that you have information derived from (1) staff turnover rates, (2) staff survival curves, (3) length of service charts, and (4) exit interviews. You may indeed have much more if you have carried out an analysis based on jobs, departments, sex, age and so on. What interpretation can be placed on information derived from these sources?

1 *Staff Turnover Chart.* You will recognize that this gives you a crude, usually annual, rate; it provides you with a general picture of the situation. While recognizing this limitation, you can interpret this chart in three ways:

(a) It will tell whether the number of those leaving is causing a large number of occasions when you are faced with having to replace staff.

(b) It can pinpoint for you whether certain jobs or departments are responsible for the bulk of your turnover.

(c) It gives you a measure for comparison with previous periods in your establishment, or with other, similar, units in your area.

The changes you wish to effect as a result of your analysis will clearly depend upon your own figures in this chart. Perhaps the best example to illustrate its value is to say that if you find your rate to be, say, 90 per cent but further analysis shows that 80 per cent of this is accounted for by one department, or even by one job category, then clearly you can start probing to find the particular cause and remove it. If a certain job keeps losing staff, you might ask yourself, Is there really a job to be done there? The job may be designed in such a way that no human being could last in it for any length of time.

2 *Staff Survival Curves.* This chart, probably the most useful in our industry, indicates your success or not in retaining staff for, say, two years or more. A number of surveys in the industry have shown with remarkable consistency that the vast majority of staff who leave their employment do so within the first few

weeks or months of starting work and that around 65 per cent of staff have less than 2 years' service with their employer. What do your survival curves indicate?

Supposing you have drawn your chart on the basis of quarterly periods, if you find that by far the majority of staff leaving are shown to have done so within the first quarter, you can draw one of three conclusions: (a) your recruitment of staff was not all it should have been, with the obvious remedies in your own hands; (b) your induction of your staff was not up to the mark; or (c) your unit or establishment has something fundamentally wrong with it. These first few weeks find the relations between new staff and the organization at its most brittle. Again the remedy is an obvious one. Staff who leave in this period are usually, in business terms, the most wasteful and costly to you.

Normally you should expect to find comparatively fewer leaving in the period 6–18 months after entrance; many who do have given your business a try and found it lacking the long-term prospects they sought. Your exit interviews with such staff should help clarify the reasons. What you can do to reduce the turnover in this period will depend, of course, on your findings. However, it is likely that you may deduce the reasons within your control to be ones related to job content, job satisfaction, poor training, indeterminate prospects, and comparatively poor wage rates or conditions of work.

3 *Length of Service Chart.* This chart should show you how successful you have been in establishing a stable core of staff. Such stability is essential in the successful running of your business and, hopefully, you will not find anything more than a healthy minimum turnover of staff here. Usually the most telling pointer, if you do suffer from turnover in this area, is a feeling of low morale in the unit. The reasons for this can be diverse, but it will be worth your considering such things as promotional policies, working conditions, salary structures and welfare facilities, to determine if any of these or a combination of them are causing a deterioration in morale.

4 *Exit Interviews.* Little need be added to what already has been covered under this heading. If you have completed an analysis of the statistical data above and drawn realistic conclusions, then you might expect to find your conclusions supported by the evidence obtained at these interviews. Why not go a little further and use the information you have got to probe during

the interviews for substantiation or not of your findings, rather than accepting the half-truths given by leavers as reasons for their departure, or trying to guess the real reasons for their leaving, which may not be clear even to them.

The Way Ahead

Everyone in catering recognizes that our industry has certain peculiarities and features that some people cannot stomach. To mention but two, we are an industry in which there is a very close contact between customers and staff, and we provide services during hours when most of the rest of the population are no longer working. To prevent people from bolstering our turnover figures, it is clearly necessary to recognize at the recruitment stage those who, by temperament or background, are unlikely to succeed in a service industry, or whose interests and social way of life is such that they are unlikely to accept the normal hours of work.

Nonetheless, you must recognize that staff turnover is a management responsibility. You can do a tremendous amount to reduce it to an acceptable level.

One of the principal findings of the Hotel and Catering E.D.C. in 1969 was that the high turnover of staff is attributable to what they describe as a 'management vacuum'. This term is used to describe the tendency of many managers in our industry to isolate themselves from their staff, to know little of what goes on in their establishment and, in general, to avoid responsibility for their staff. You will agree that this is quite an indictment but one which has so much evidence to support it that it must be the first area for you, as staff manager, to examine with all honesty. Is your 'management style' such that you can be said to have abdicated your responsibilities for staff at all levels? The remainder of this Part is devoted to certain areas of good management practice that can help you to develop as a staff manager in such a way that no part of your staff's turnover can be attributable in your case to 'a management vacuum'. Development of good human relations is the very foundation on which you must base every effort if you are seriously interested in reducing staff turnover.

Practical Tips

1 Allow staff to get on with their jobs without interference, but at the same time develop in them the realization that they are not being left in isolation and that they will have your full support when needed.

2 Get to know staff as individual persons, and learn enough about their work to appreciate the sort of stresses they are likely to meet.
3 Hold informal meetings with staff to allow wide-ranging discussions about their work and all that affects it.
4 Review your recruitment processes regularly so as to avoid recruiting the wrong sort of people.
5 Pay special attention to all new staff during their first few weeks and months of employment with you.
6 Maintain a simple but accurate method of recording the movements of staff into and out of your employment, analysing these figures and acting to remedy any weakness in your unit that is shown to cause staff to leave.

CHECKLIST

1 Have you prepared a list of all staff employed at a predetermined date, showing each one's name, job, department and starting date, with columns for entering dates of departure and periods of stay?
2 Have you considered keeping the list in alphabetical order?
3 Does your record system enable you to extract quickly and accurately the names and number of those who started work in each period?
4 At what periods have you decided to prepare staff turnover charts, survival curves and long service bar-charts?
5 Have you established a routine system for exit interviewing?
6 Have you considered seeking appropriate assistance in interpreting the statistical data allied to the reasons given by staff when leaving?
7 What action have you taken to implement changes your findings reveal as necessary to reduce loss of staff?

CHAPTER SEVEN

Working as a Team

7.1 UNDERSTANDING YOUR STAFF

'Here at any rate is a section I can skip through quickly. If there is one thing I am good at it is understanding staff.' Are you one of the majority of managers who might express such a thought? If you are, you are one of the many managers who believe that understanding staff is a skill they are born with; perhaps there are such a lucky few but most people have to learn the ground rules. So be honest with yourself. Do you *really* understand staff? You cannot afford to delude yourself. In a way this subject forms the kernel of the whole manual: your day-to-day dealings with staff. Nothing is more important than getting this right.

No matter what the size of your business or establishment, no matter how sophisticated your equipment and furnishings, no matter how modern your staff systems, in the end the question of whether you are successful or not depends entirely on how you and your staff operate *as a team*. This is the secret of success. In your role as a manager of staff, no matter what your job title may be, you are the team leader and your staff form the team. The weight of this responsibility is a heavy one, because it ultimately depends upon you and your attitudes as to whether everyone works as a team, pulling together to the same ends, or whether you simply head up a number of people whose sole interest lies in what each can get out of the organization.

It is a sad fact of business life that so few managers realize the potential for success that lies in understanding the people who work in the business, and deal with them accordingly. After all, when a machine is working to capacity, you cannot get greater productivity from it; every machine, from the vending machine to the computer, has its limitations built within it at the manufacturing stage. Not so with people! When they are working with heart and will, there seems no end to their abilities. But, unlike machines, they have to be managed effectively. A machine will never go off in a huff and sulk, but people will. A machine will never make a mistake, but people will. A machine will never arrive late for work, go absent, leave early or disagree with you—but people will.

Understanding staff is probably the most difficult part of a manager's job, no matter how experienced he is. You really do need to work at it. Its importance lies in the fact that unless you do understand staff you have no hope of arousing their interest or of being able to influence them. Without being able to do that, you must rate as a failure as a staff manager.

Actually, there is no secret formula for success. Good staff management may be defined as increasing people's *interest* in their work, and trying to make it a more *satisfying* experience for them through making their jobs a greater *challenge*. If you succeed in this, you will find a marked increase in effort and co-operation on their part in whatever they undertake. How successful you become as a staff manager depends largely upon how soon and how thoroughly you master this 'secret'.

Getting staff to co-operate as willing and fully productive members of the team depends first and foremost on your understanding what the goal of your efforts must be. In a nutshell it is this: to deal with staff in such a way that they need no outside stimulation but rather, through their self-generated impetus, *want* to give of their best. All the suggestions that follow are designed specifically to help you reach this goal.

How to Stimulate People to Give of Their Best

From birth a person accumulates experience and becomes a personality of his own. All his experiences are interwoven around a central core—the 'I' or 'ego'. Everything he wants or does must serve that self in the broadest sense or it will simply not survive.

This is the starting point for understanding people, no matter how different they may appear to be. If you want to succeed in influencing staff, you must be able to get an insight into the hidden world that makes each of us 'I'. Fortunately, because each of us is a card-carrying member of the human race, we have basic resemblances; this is what enables you to look into another's hidden self and understand what makes him tick.

In practice, understanding staff requires that you want to and are able to put yourself into your staff's shoes and look at things through *their* eyes, to understand what they need and strive for. Once you do that and begin to see things from their viewpoint, you must then develop the skill of harmonizing these yearnings with the goals of your business in such a way that they will act as levers to raise their performance to a higher level.

In summary, a staff manager's role is basically to deal with people in such a way that he can harness their *self-interest* to become better and more efficient members of staff. People will work more willingly when they feel they have a personal interest or stake in what they are doing. Motivating staff by appealing to their own 'selfish' self-interest is nothing more than common sense. It is far stronger than any monetary reward as a means of getting the work done well.

Many managers, if asked, would answer that their staff's main wish is for 'more money'. This is true in a sense. Cash is what enables us to buy material things, from the basic necessities to the more luxurious material things in life. But it is far from being the whole truth; what we are all seeking is 'satisfaction', and money can only take us part of the way towards full satisfaction and happiness. We all know miserable people who seem to have everything that money can buy. So the true answer to the question is likely to be that staff want sufficient money to buy the material things in life that matter to them, but they also want much more than money can buy to be really satisfied, such as recognition by you that they are people in their own right and that their work is appreciated. Money is important in the sense that it is often the cause of much dissatisfaction, but it can never provide full satisfaction.

Provided staff are happy that they are being reasonably paid, satisfaction in the job matters most of all. This can be obtained from the job itself and the feelings people have about their job. In general they will be more satisfied where the tasks being carried out are to them challenging, and where the actual process of working is interesting. So a waiter's job can be very satisfying if he finds that looking after six tables successfully is challenging but possible, and the process of attending to people's needs is stimulating. Another factor in providing for job satisfaction is in producing something tangible and something that is recognizably complete. Part of the job of a chambermaid in effecting a change in a bedroom so that it is clean, fresh and inviting is an example of how a tangible result can be achieved.

Completing a task and being able to see results generates a feeling of achievement. This is not confined, however, to making something. For instance, a receptionist may gain a lot of satisfaction from a set of ledger figures that show an accurate state of affairs, or by dealing with a customer's complaint. A pub manager can feel a pride in his job when he sees the joy on a face of the customer who drinks the ale which his cellar-management has ensured is in peak condition. Likewise there is a great deal of job satisfaction for all staff when customers acknowledge their pleasure, by word or gesture, for any service willingly and cheerfully given.

Practical Steps

How then can you influence staff so that they will willingly give of their best? Here are some practical ideas which will make a vast difference:

1 *Recognize Staff and Their Work.* No single person does not feel a little dissatisfaction if he fails to get proper recognition when he deserves it. Even when he asks for criticism, he is also looking for praise and recognition for the things he does well.

Praise, not flattery, when given properly is probably the most effective way to motivate anyone. Everyone thrives on it, even if they fail to show it in their faces. The fact of the matter is that no one will do a better job simply because he has been asked or told to do so. No one is going to do a better job merely because he is expected to, or is being paid to.

There is only one way to get staff to do a *better* job and that is by appealing to their self-interest. One of the best ways is through encouragement, recognition of what they have done, praise. There is no danger of people becoming conceited through receiving praise. On the contrary, it is discouragement, belittling and fault-finding that causes conceit.

Praise must not be indiscriminate, otherwise it becomes meaningless. Moreover it should always be directed at the performance and not the person himself. Far better to tell the hall porter, 'The hall is looking most attractive this morning', than to say, 'Well, John, you are a marvellous Porter'.

2 *Make Staff Feel Important.* Whether people would admit to it openly or not, all human beings want to feel important. We all have a strong craving for prestige. Let us go back to the question of money again. It is a vital necessity in life but much of the importance we attach to it is not due to our desire for it as such, but rather to what it can bring us in the way of luxuries of life. Staff want to *be* somebody, they want to be *considered* somebody.

If you agree with all this, then it immediately points another way for you as staff manager: to give the work of your staff an added significance or importance. How can you do this? There is simply no cut and dried formula, you will have to play much of it by ear, but you can go a long way towards making staff *feel* more important by taking a serious personal interest in their work and by letting them know that the measure of their success is also the measure of the success of your establishment.

One practical way in which you can apply this step is, for example, in relation to job titles. Give each job the most honourable yet properly descriptive title you can think of—most people would like to describe their job with pride. Indeed most people exaggerate their job title when asked about their work. Why? In an attempt to feel important, of course.

3 *Listen to Staff*. You will often hear people say: 'I like my boss, you can talk to him. He listens to me'. Yes, it is a fact that one of the most favourable influences you can have upon staff is to take time out to listen when they come to you with problems or complaints, or simply when they want to get something that is bothering them off their chest. Listening attentively and sympathetically is one of the most important attributes of a good staff manager.

One of the hardest things in the world is to listen to others without constantly interrupting. But if you do listen, not only do you learn what's on people's minds (and then perhaps be able to solve their problem), but you also give the person a chance to cool down if he is really badly upset.

4 *The Art of Criticizing Constructively*. Even if you were to do everything so far suggested, there will still be times when staff will have to be 'told off'. This usually means two distinct actions on your part: (1) criticizing what has been done or not been done, and (2) giving directions as to what should be done. Fortunately if both are handled properly, they can become tools to influence staff to improve their work and with better will. Let us look at each factor more closely.

Even the best criticism is a blow to a person's morale and self-esteem, but it should never be fatal. The secret of success is to criticize constructively—the outcome will then raise and not lower morale.

The only justification ever for criticism is to correct errors that otherwise impair a person's work or behaviour, with a view to prevention of future errors. Criticize so as to teach, not to release your hurt feelings by resorting to mere scolding—that is the road to loss of respect for you only.

Start by giving some deserved compliment before quickly pointing out the shortcoming and how it can be overcome or prevented, and end with a smile and a reassurance of your support. Morale should suffer no serious setback and staff will usually accept the criticism, however serious, in the spirit in which it is given. Make sure you mean what you say—be sincere in telling the man or woman of your willingness to help him or her overcome the difficulty and that you hold no grudge. In short, show the one criticized how to improve, and support his or her effort.

It is already implied in criticizing constructively that you will give orders or directions. What matters most here is how you do it. No human being likes taking orders, for we work much better if we believe we are acting under our own volition. Here is a clue then to the art of giving orders: make it appear to staff that you are allowing for compliance, not demanding it. The best managers go so far as to get staff themselves to suggest remedies and actions, and if these appear to meet what is required, then staff are not so much 'under orders' as self-directed—a far happier and more motivating state than complying with the strict orders of another.

When you have to criticize, make sure you do so out of earshot of other members of the staff or of customers.

5 Greet all your staff with pleasant 'Good mornings' etc., even if, or perhaps especially if, you are feeling anything but pleasant about it yourself.

6 Remember the first and last names of all your staff and always call them by one or the other. A person's name is all that distinguishes him from the three billion other people on the earth, and using it makes him feel that you think enough of him to be willing to distinguish him from the faceless mass of the rest of the human race.

7 Without prying, get to know something about each member of your staff—their backgrounds, their hobbies, their families. You can chat to them quite informally when occasion permits. You will be amazed at how much goodwill is built from such tiny foundations.

8 Be complimentary now and again, even if there is no particular need to do so. 'You're looking smart this morning' said to a chambermaid can lighten her load for the day.

9 Stop fault-finding and start 'good-finding'. So many managers write staff off for what they are not or have not before they take the trouble to find out what they are or have. Rate people on their successes rather than on their failures and you will soon

find that working with the staff is friendlier and pleasanter, and from a business point of view much more profitable, because staff will work with a will.

What makes staff tick has been the subject of much research and writing for many years. For those of you who wish to pursue the subject in greater depth the Bibliography attached to this Part may help. This section has set out to show you some of the ways in which you can influence the attitudes of staff so that they have both the heart and the will to improve their performance at work. In this area you are truly dealing with the art of management—being sensitive to the needs and wants of staff and trying to satisfy them so that in turn they act as their own generators of better work performance. Deal with staff as people. See what a difference it makes in their work when you are prepared to smile, to respect them, to praise good performance and to give them that feeling of importance which is so fundamental to all of us.

7.2 JOB SATISFACTION

It is worth repeating what was said earlier in this section: satisfaction in a job comes from much more than pay, which must be considered reasonable to prevent dissatisfaction. We in this industry do not need to check on all the research that has been done to establish the truth of this. There are many people working in catering who know they could earn more money by moving into another job, even within the industry, but refuse to do so. Their reason? They like their present work—it gives them job satisfaction.

When staff are doing work that they find satisfying, the staff manager's job is an easy one: for the most part the staff are self-starters, with the desire to do their work well. Unfortunately, of course, not everyone finds this sort of satisfaction in their work, and hence this section sets out to provide some guidelines for the staff manager who wants to remedy this situation, knowing full well that to obtain feelings of satisfaction in doing a job is one of the greatest motivators of all.

You probably need little reminding that when staff find no joy in their work, because they are human and still reach for satisfaction, they will tend to look for this fulfilment elsewhere. Meanwhile the job suffers. Here are some of the symptoms whose presence should immediately spur you into a reassessment of jobs to see how they can be restructured or changed so as to provide the job holders with the basic need for satisfaction:

Lackadaisical approach to the job.
Poor quality of work.
Higher rate of staff turnover than normal
Absenteeism.
High degree of lateness.
Lack of co-operation.
Petty complaints and grievances.
High accident rate.
Disputes and disruptions.

Any one or a combination of these symptoms should cry out to you for investigation of the jobs your staff do.

Setting Jobs in Context

Take any job you like to consider and you will find that many factors have a bearing on it. Basically you can divide them into two categories: (1) the conditions in which the job is set, and (2) the content of the work and the attitude shown to its performance.

1 *Job Conditions*. Under this heading you can list such items as the following:

(a) Physical working conditions.
(b) Wage or salary allotted to job.
(c) Status that goes with the job.
(d) Relationships necessary with superiors, equals and subordinates.
(e) Security of the job.
(f) General company policy and administration.

If any of these items cause dissatisfaction, then staff will complain, since all of them are to do with the needs of human beings, and people react to their dissatisfaction with them as readily as they cry out in physical pain. These conditions must therefore conform to a high or, rather, a satisfactory standard to prevent annoyance. However, the most you can say is that if you get these factors right, they will restrain dissatisfaction; of themselves they will not create satisfaction. This is the role of the next category of items affecting a job.

2 *Job Content and Management Attitude*. What this category concerns itself with are the following:

(a) The nature and challenge of what the job entails.
(b) The growth and learning associated with the work.

(c) The achievement and creativity allowed for.
(d) The responsibility associated with the job.
(e) The recognition and feedback on performance.

In these factors is the very stuff of job satisfaction to be found. If any of these factors are missing, it is unlikely that your staff will complain about it as such; instead you will find symptoms of bloody-mindedness, apathy, unrest, discontent, laziness, carelessness and all the other problems usually ascribed to 'poor morale'. The message from them must be clear: treat staff as well as you can by paying attention to the conditions of their work as described, thus keeping dissatisfaction to a minimum; but use staff so that they get a sense of achievement, recognition for achievement, interest in their jobs, responsibility and opportunities to advance in their work, all of which are the positive contributors to job satisfaction.

How to Provide Job Satisfaction

If your establishment shows signs of low morale, as described above, you could call in a firm of consultants, who would probably set about instituting what they would call a 'Job Enrichment Programme'. Many companies have indeed set about things in this way and it has paid handsome dividends—at a cost, of course. However, there is much that a staff manager can do himself, with the collaboration of other managers and indeed of the staff themselves. He can take the following steps:

1 Select jobs in which lack of job satisfaction is evident, and study the relevant job descriptions.
2 Consider each job in turn and apply the following questions to see if the jobs themselves can be altered, added to, or even done away with as they are:

 (a) Can the boundaries of the job holder's responsibilities be extended by adding other duties naturally associated with it?
 (b) Can the job holders be given more freedom to set their own objectives, and at the same time are they likely to accept increasing accountability for what they do?
 (c) Can the individuals be subject to less supervision?
 (d) Can the job as such be so changed as to really become a more challenging and exacting one?

Many managers will answer these questions after insufficient consideration. Of course you must recognize that it is not always feasible or economic to alter a job so that it provides more personal satisfaction. However, consider the matter further. Every job can be looked at as consisting of three separate stages, as follows:

1 Planning and organizing: use of people and equipment, standards of quality, quantities needed, work layout, and so on.
2 Doing: waiting at tables, serving drinks, cleaning, cooking, etc.
3 Control: evaluating what is done, correcting, inspecting, adjusting, measuring, etc.

Most jobs in the catering industry are concerned only with the Doing stage. To help make jobs more satisfying, it is worth a lot of thought as to how and how much you can change this position so that the job holder can be brought into the other two stages of the job.

Practical Tips

If you are seriously interested in helping staff to achieve a greater satisfaction in their work, then you will find that some or all of the following suggestions will bear fruit:

1 Introduce new and challenging tasks not previously handled.
2 Provide positive standards against which results can be measured.
3 Allow as much autonomy as possible.
4 Provide opportunities for learning and increasing ranges of skills.
5 Show trust in your staff by removing certain controls—for example, clock-cards.
6 Delegate to staff as much responsibility and decision-making as possible.
7 Provide a variety of tasks.
8 Let staff know how their job contributes to the whole.
9 Give them a chance to look after and develop new staff.
10 Give individuals jobs they can improve.

If you decide that you would like to reorganize jobs as suggested, recognize immediately that, despite the fact you know it will be to your staff's advantage, you are likely to meet resistance—from the staff! People dislike changes. However, you can take steps to reduce resistance:

1 Get the staff affected to realize they have a problem with the job as it now stands.
2 Consult the staff throughout, seeking their opinions.
3 Show how changing the work will lead to an increase in their satisfaction.
4 Give a complete picture of the nature of the change and its effects.
5 Let the staff air their views freely, and show sympathy for any fears expressed.
6 Find the person who is really the 'opinion' leader and concentrate your 'selling' on him.
7 Give as much notice of the change as possible.
8 Provide the necessary training to allow the staff to undertake the changed responsibilities.

If you tackle this as suggested in the guidelines, you can expect to find staff slowly realizing their identity and getting a feeling of belonging, and perhaps after a few months achieving your final aim of having staff who realize their contribution to the establishment as a whole. As satisfied staff, they are more likely to stay.

7.3 BEING A TEAM LEADER

Whenever a group of people get together to work towards a common end, invariably someone has to 'take charge'. This is true in any field of human endeavour, whether the pursuit be recreational, like soccer, or has a business purpose. No matter what title the group gives the person who 'takes charge', he is being called upon to exercise what is generally described as 'leadership'. It used to be fashionable to study this subject by examining what qualities a good leader possesses and from this to derive the practical steps a manager should take to acquire such qualities. However, this has proved a negative type of approach, and nowadays it is considered much more fruitful to look at what good leaders do, with a view to emulating their approach as a team leader.

What is your approach as a team leader? Here you must be honest with yourself if you sincerely want to improve your way of acting as the leader of your staff, and ask the following questions: (1) do you want to dominate staff, or inspire them? (2) do you give staff reason to fear you, or reason to like and respect you? or (3) do you get your way by fighting, or by winning the support and goodwill of staff so that they want to get behind you and your plans for success in business? Your answers will determine to what extent you are a team leader or a driver.

Before going further, here is a maxim that many studies have shown to be true. Managers who have mastered the basic principles of knowing how to deal with people by appealing to their self-interest get almost twice the co-operation and twice the productive efficiency out of their staff as the old-time driver did.

You can categorize the manner adopted by managers towards staff leadership as follows:

1 They make a decision—issue instructions—and expect it to be carried out without question. This approach is generally described as *autocratic*, and our industry abounds with managers who see this and no other method as the only true way to deal with staff.
2 They make a decision—and expect compliance. You could describe this approach as a *persuasive* one, and again many managers in the catering industry adopt this approach in the firm belief that in doing so they are in line with modern thinking about the best way to manage.
3 They make decisions but put their ideas forward for discussion among the staff and perhaps modify them, or they seek the views of the staff and then make decisions, taking account of the staff's views. This is the *consultative* approach.
4 They bring staff into a problem, share views, and then accept the view of the majority as the basis of the decision reached. Today this approach is called *participative*.

Which approach is best? The answer is that no one of them is right in every case. After all, much depends on the subject of the decision. For instance, it may be more correct for you as a staff manager to decide autocratically that in future all candidates for the job of unit manager will have a minimum qualification of an H.N.D., while at the same time using a participative approach to deciding what sort of television set should be installed in the staff rest-room.

To manage successfully you must be flexible in your approach—at times, or with certain staff, you may have to be quite autocratic in your manner as their team leader, while in other cases you may act more successfully in a consultative or participative role. In the catering industry your staff are such a vital resource in the business that if you are not presently as successful as you should be, or as you would wish to be, in your relations with staff, then you might be best advised to change your approach so as to become much more staff-centred. Here are some practical steps to take in this direction:

1 Treat all your staff as individual people in their own right first, and not as 'staff' in general.
2 Build up self-respect in all staff.
3 Look at things through staff eyes.
4 Protect the interests of all your staff.
5 Do not supervise their work too closely.
6 Avoid falling into the trap of becoming 'one of the boys'; rather maintain your position as a helpful team leader.
7 Keep all staff informed of their progress.

None of this means you should become 'soft' with staff—there is no question of trying to adopt an approach that can be summed up as 'Keep them happy at all costs'. It does mean that, as their manager, you treat them fairly and with respect, bringing them as much as you can into the business of achieving whatever targets you have set.

A team that succeeds is a team that pulls together—all the individual efforts are combined to reach a goal. It is your task as their manager to co-ordinate this effort, to direct their energies and to control the way in which the team works. Quite a task! Enough has already been said about your need to look after the interests of each individual in the team, but as their manager you also have the team needs to take care of. This means building up a team spirit.

Practical Tips

1 Give your team a set of targets to achieve and make sure the targets are understood by all.
2 Set working standards for the group—timekeeping, quality of work, hygiene, etc.—and be fair and impartial in enforcing them.
3 Look at the variety of jobs staff do and try to constitute groups of them so that they can work together as sub-teams.
4 Look out for matters that may disrupt the group and put them right: for instance, uneven distribution of work-load, unjustified differences in pay.
5 Let your team know that their ideas and suggestions are always welcome.
6 Hold regular discussion meetings with your team and consult them before making decisions about matters that affect them, such as work plans and methods.

7 Keep your staff informed about how the firm is doing financially, its current plans and future developments.

CHECKLIST

1 Do you know all your staff by name?
2 Do you know enough about each member of your staff so as to see them as individuals other than as mere employees?
3 When you meet staff in the course of the day, do you take the trouble to smile, nod or pass the time of day with them?
4 When a piece of good work has been done, do you go out of your way to congratulate the staff responsible?
5 How do you help each member of staff to feel important in his own right?
6 Do you make it easy for staff to see you at any time?
7 When you have to correct errors, do you adopt the teaching role and help staff to improve and yet save face?
8 Do you know which jobs are presently found to be least satisfying, and why?
9 What steps have you taken to re-examine such jobs with a view to making them more interesting or more challenging?
10 Have you considered how to allow staff more responsibility for planning and controlling their work, and not simply allowing them to get on and do their work?
11 Do you allow the staff an opportunity to express their views on things which affect their work, before making decisions?
12 How often do you get the staff together as a team to discuss work and inform them of their progress, the way things are going financially and the plans of your establishment?

CHAPTER EIGHT

Keeping Your Staff Informed

8.1 THE PROCESS OF COMMUNICATION

'No one tells you anything around here.' 'Why didn't he say?' 'I just work here!' These *cris de coeur* indicate that all is not well in the communications field. Unfortunately examples like these are daily occurrences in many catering establishments up and down the country; and in many cases managers are not concerned. Indeed many even adopt the attitude, 'So what! Why should staff know?'

This manual does not set out specifically to lay blame for poor staff-management attitudes; instead its aim is to point out the value, to the business, management and staff, of sound practices. One such crucially important practice is to keep the staff abreast of what is happening if it in any way can affect their work or their morale. Of equal importance is the encouragement needed for the staff to speak freely to management. In this way a continuous dialogue is built up within the team for the benefit of everyone. Such is the stuff of a good communications system.

How important is good communication? Perhaps the easiest way to find an answer here is to look at what can and does happen when readiness to keep others informed is overlooked or ignored. The most common effect of 'not knowing' is a build-up of frustration—sometimes leading to anxiety, perhaps even to anger and providing a breeding ground for rumour. You must exclude from consideration here what is often called 'blissful ignorance'; the only reason it can be called 'blissful' is because you do not know that you do not know. What should concern you here is the occasion when you are conscious of questions in your mind while those who are in a position to do so are not providing you with the answers. 'How well am I doing?' 'Should I go ahead with this before they tell me about that?' 'Am I going to be allowed my holidays at the time I've asked for?' These are some of the questions. The longer you are without the answers the greater the problem appears, and sooner rather than later the emotional effects of 'not knowing' will be translated into action ranging from becoming bloody-minded, disloyal and disgruntled, to the ultimate action of packing up and leaving. That is the negative answer to the question of how important it is to communicate.

On the positive side a ready flow of information up, down and across builds up a spirit of trust and mutual respect, which is the very foundation of good teamwork. In practice it amounts to this: staff are content when they have the knowledge needed to do their work, know what their supervisors think of them and their value to the organization and know that when questions arise on matters affecting them, they can find the answers quickly by asking in the right quarters. Equally, management know that they will be informed by staff of anything that affects the running of the unit, and staff are confident that others will keep them in touch with events which may affect their work. This free flow of information makes for a contented team and is an essential element in the art of keeping staff. However, it will not just happen. You have to plan and work for it. Before you consider means of improving the ways in which you keep staff informed, it is worth while stopping for a moment and clearing the mind as to what communication really means. Many managers believe that passing information, whether by word of mouth or in writing, is what is meant by communication. Your practical experience, however, probably contradicts this; after all, how many times have you found yourself saying to a member of your staff, 'But I told you a dozen times not to do that!', or 'I put a notice up on the staff notice board a week ago about it'. If these meet with blank stares or a denial that your instructions were ever heard or seen, does it necessarily mean that the staff are stupid, forgetful, or plain cussed? Not at all. It might simply mean that in fact, although you passed the information on, it was not received or, at any rate, not received in the manner you expected. To use a hackneyed phrase, 'Communications have broken down'.

Ancient philosophers argued at length as to the correct answer to this question: 'If a tree crashes down in the middle of a forest, does it make a noise?' You can discuss this at length as a conversation piece, but for our purposes here we can agree the answer as 'No, unless there is someone there to hear it'. It illustrates an essential element of communication, that passing information and ideas to others becomes true communication only when these ideas are received in the way we intended. Basically, therefore, the process of communication entails a giving and a receiving.

Even then the process of communication cannot be left to appear that simple, however basically true that definition may be. Take a practical example: suppose you say to a receptionist, 'I'd like to see you in my office at 2 o'clock, O.K?' To you the words you have used are simple, can mean only one thing and only an idiot could misinterpret what you mean. But wait! The receptionist, on her part, not only interprets the words you have used but also listens and gives meaning to the inflection of your voice, the expression on your face, the thought in your eyes and the drumming of your fingers on the desk. All these factors will influence the meaning she takes from your verbal message, and if she does turn up in your office as requested, at the time suggested, she may do so expecting to be 'carpeted' or to be told of her promotion—it will all depend on how she interprets the many other signals she received when you passed the message. Not only that, but her own internal stimuli will affect the message she receives—her emotions, past experience and many other factors that cause us to perceive actions and words in specific ways.

No wonder communication is so difficult! No wonder that in many ways it is the most important activity in managing staff!

However, there are means that you can use to develop a more effective way of communicating with staff; but before looking at them let us look a little closer at the barriers to good communication. After all, when you know the enemy it is always easier to defeat him.

Barriers to Good Communication

1 *Differences in Perception.* Our past experiences determine to a large extent how we react to various stimuli. We all use our learning, our culture and our experience to interpret what we see or hear. Here are the housekeeper and the general manager walking along the corridor on a daily inspection, and as they pass the service room the floor-maids break out into laughter. Mrs Stearn, who has been having trouble getting co-operation from some of her staff, hears derisive and insulting laughter directed at her. Mr Abel, on the other hand, who prides himself on running a good hotel with high morale among staff, hears good-natured steam being let off. If a customer had been passing about the same time, he might not even have heard the laughter at all, being engrossed in thought about the after-dinner speech he is due to make that evening. Of course it is impossible to see every situation as the other person does, but an

honest effort to appreciate his point of view goes a long way to helping achieve effective communication.

2 *Lack of Knowledge*. Just as it is impossible to discuss a problem with a member of the staff who only speaks, let us say, Greek without the knowledge of that language, so it becomes a real barrier to communication if you lack the background to understand the basic concepts being discussed. This raises the whole question of selecting the words you believe are readily understandable by the listener. How many people entering the industry have wondered about the politics of the young man whom he first hears referred to as 'the commis chef'! Words aside, it is best not to make assumptions about the depth of knowledge of the recipient. Try to determine in advance how much knowledge of the subject he already possesses.

3 *The Emotions*. Whether expressed by the giver or receiver of a message, strong emotions cause real distortion. Unfortunately it is often the case that when we are subject to deep emotions, we are strongly motivated to communicate. In most cases when you have strong feelings of hate, fear, anger or love, you find it difficult to communicate anything other than the emotions. On the other hand, emotions can often engender enthusiasm, which aids good communication. The lesson is to recognize the part emotions can play in either sender or receiver in terms of its effect on the communications process, and to act accordingly.

4 *Appearance*. This barrier to communication can be seen in either the person or the means he uses to pass on information. Most staff react more favourably to a manager who is neat and tidy in his appearance, just as a notice put up on the board is more likely to receive favourable attention if some thought has been put into the way in which it is laid out. A lack of eye-catching headings, some messy erasures, etc. detract from the message as much as a scruffy personal appearance. The removal of this barrier should be easier than most.

5 *Distractions*. Because it is very difficult to 'switch off' any of our senses, passing ideas to others becomes a hazardous operation when other things are clamouring for our attention at the same time. How can the commis chef be expected to hear and understand what you are saying when his sense of smell is warning him that the pastry is ready, his ears are being pounded by the shouting of other staff in the background and the hissing of the steamer, and his eyes are taken by the comely waitress who is passing his corner! Being aware of this barrier

will help you make sure that you eliminate as best you can the danger of distraction when you wish to communicate effectively.

6 *Lack of Interest.* Whether it is present in the speaker or the listener, a lack of interest is a real deterrent to the reception of ideas. The blank face, fidgeting, gazing aimlessly around, all are signs that the body may be present but the mind is likely to be far away. To succeed in breaking down this barrier, you need to use words or statements that are provocative or unexpected—always provided of course that you avoid arousing animosity or antagonism, which simply replaces one barrier with another. Perhaps the best way to overcome this barrier is to structure your message in such a way that you arouse the listener's desire to pay attention. Once again it is a question of appealing to the self-interest of the listener—letting him see what is in it for him.

Of course there are many other barriers to effective communication, but these few main ones should help you recognize the difficulties we all experience, and being aware of them lead you to take whatever steps are necessary to avoid blocks to effective communication.

8.2 EFFECTIVE COMMUNICATION

Let us immediately identify now what it is that effective communication means, by describing the basic objectives of all communication:

1 You would like to be understood exactly as intended.
2 You would like the staff to agree and accept the message.
3 You would like to receive a favourable action or response to your message.
4 You would like to maintain favourable relations with all those with whom you communicate.

That is your target and you recognize the blocks that must be surmounted in order to reach it. Now let us look at some of the problems you must surmount if you are going to succeed in reaching your target.

The Importance of Feedback

How do you know when you get through to staff, or, perhaps even more importantly, how do you know when you fail to. Perhaps the only way to determine whether you have been successful is to secure a response, or 'feedback'.

The word 'feedback' owes its origin to the science of cybernetics. There it is used to describe the ability in men or machines to detect an error or deviation in an operation and feed back that error to a control mechanism, which then makes the necessary correction. A simple example is the thermostat in our central heating system, which records a temperature that is too low, feeds back a signal to the boiler, and thus operates as a corrector. The similarities of feedback in this techinical sense are immediately apparent in the context of communication between people.

If you ask the canteen assistant to open a window and she does so, then her action, her response, tells you that you have communicated successfully. The type of response you get to any message is an indication of the success or failure of your communication skill. Of course responses can be made in many different ways—by a reply in words, a raised eyebrow, an angry expression or a smile. It may be no response at all, which, paradoxically, is a response nonetheless, indicating that this message was not heard, not understood, or not accepted. However you look at it, it is only through the feedback that you can know whether you have communicated your ideas.

Whatever the response, even the negative one, it is the returning signal that should immediately help you decide whether or not you have been understood. It is the opportunity, if need be, for you to revise or rephrase your message and present it again. Of course there will be occasions when you cannot obtain immediate feedback: if you are talking to a group of people, for instance, it is very difficult to gauge the success of your communication with each individual.

There is also the problem of gaining accurate feedback. It is no answer to the problem to ask after each instruction, 'Do you understand?' Most people will immediately say they do, some in the firm belief that they really do understand, even if they do not, while others will do so because of a reluctance to admit they do not understand; there is a feeling of loss of face or embarrassment in admitting a lack of comprehension. What is certain is that unless you take the trouble to check return channels, you cannot find out what is happening to your information. You cannot tell how it is being used or even if it is being used at all.

There is only one practical message for you here: test the understanding of those with whom you communicate. Check out their interpretation of what you have said, either by asking questions, the answers to which will indicate correct interpretation or otherwise, or by checking on the actions which follow. Remember, you can tell that you have successfully communicated with someone if their response or reaction is in accord with your message to them.

The Art of Listening

Communication is a two-way street. Not only is it necessary for you to be alive to the need for a response from staff to your communications, but it is equally important to encourage and to be open to communication from staff. Managers are not the only people with ideas. But whether it is a question of looking for and accepting the response to your messages or being the receiver of ideas and information from staff, a vital area of effective communication is developing the skill of being a good listener.

Perhaps as much as 60 per cent of our normal day is spent in listening, though many people do not do so very effectively. If only we could hear our own staff's assessment of the situation, we would probably be told: 'The problem is not getting us to talk, the problem is one of getting managers to listen.'

What is the secret of listening? The good listener makes a determined effort to distinguish three different areas in any statement: facts, feelings and fancy.

Your first attempt should be to establish the theme of the discussion or conversation. It may be stated right at the beginning, be repeated in different ways throughout, and serve also as a concluding statement. Once you have grasped this, you should then seek to recognize the major ideas; these invariably enable you to recall specific *facts*. This sort of listening is hard work and requires your complete concentration. Most people speak at the rate of 140 words a minute but we can assimilate around 500 words in the same span of time. It is no wonder then that the listener's mind begins to wander. Learning to concentrate is the first step in good listening.

You cannot speak without expressing your *feelings*. Listening to another person, then, means paying attention to the words he uses, and interpreting them as far as you can within the meaning that he gives them. You must also try to understand his ideas, feeling and biases—recognizing his point of view and his frame of reference. Just as important is the need to listen to his non-verbal communication—his gestures, the look in his eyes, the confusion in the lines of his brow. When he finishes by saying 'Well, it's not all that important to me anyway', but his posture is rigid, his knuckles white, his eyes hopeful and his forehead awash with sweat, then his non-verbal communication is what matters and not his words. You must listen to his feelings if communication between you is to be effective.

How can you separate facts from fancy? At times our previous experience of the person will help us evaluate the validity of what he says. But only careful listening can tell you what 'facts' given are substantiated and which ones are mere figments of the imagination.

Practical Tips

1 Listen actively: decide what is the theme and look about for specific facts; concentrate, remain alert and ask questions.
2 Do not do anything unrelated to the discussion while the speaker is talking.
3 Sit up straight and look directly at the speaker.
4 Listen objectively: put aside for the time being your own ideas; he may have new ideas, new concepts, new ways of approaching things.
5 Listen to his words and try to understand them in the way he uses them.
6 'Listen' to the speaker's non-verbal communication: does it support what is being said, does the hope in his face, the fear in his voice, the twisting of his fingers indicate a different meaning?

Finally, to encourage you in the effort it takes to become a good listener, think of the following benefits:

1 Listening carefully promotes better understanding—of the way the speaker thinks, his reasoning and what is important to him.
2 This deeper understanding can in itself improve relations as well as engender an appreciation of your interest in really listening to him.
3 You can add to your knowledge content.
4 Knowing that he has a ready listener often helps another to see his problem more clearly.
5 We are all keen to be understood, and this can be achieved best by sensitive listening; disagreements can then be quickly resolved.
6 Good listeners stimulate others to become better listeners.

What to Communicate

If you could reach into the hearts of your staff, you would find that what they really want to know are the reasons for management decisions and whether someone cares about their needs. This of course means in practice that there is a whole range of information staff would like to have and, indeed, should have. Your guiding principle should be to tell staff all they need to know to do their job and to be contented as a member of the team. In practice there should rarely be any need for secrets, except where the information could damage your company if competitors were privy to it, or in cases where personal privacy is concerned. You might therefore say that staff should be given information not only on what they need to know but also about what they want to know. What sort of information then should we be ready to give to staff?

1 *Information that Can Affect Them Personally*. Under this heading you might consider:

(a) Wage/salary.
(b) Status and immediate superior.
(c) Where and when they can eat.
(d) Grievance and disciplinary procedures.
(e) Prospects in terms of training and promotion.
(f) Holidays.
(g) The sick-pay and pension scheme.
(h) Any changes in personnel policy.
(i) Any projects or experiments that can affect them.
(j) Any changes in the physical place in which they work.

Of course this is not comprehensive but merely indicative of what sort of information they should be given. Many of these items must be covered anyway under the Employment Protection (Consolidation) Act, 1978.

2 *Information about the Job*. You might consider the following as representative of the kind of information under this heading:

(a) Work standards and who checks them.
(b) Hygiene and safety standards expected, and the reasons for them.
(c) How the job holder will be measured in terms of success.
(d) His effect upon costs.
(e) Where to obtain any materials needed.
(f) Any changes affecting the job and the reasons for them.

3 *General Information*. At last it is becoming generally agreed that staff have a greater role to play in business than simply turning

up for work each day; they are as much a part of the business as the shareholder or proprietor, and want to be 'in the know'. So under this heading consider:

(a) The broad position regarding the company's finance.
(b) Plans to expand or contract.
(c) Changes in top management.
(d) How the company is doing generally.

Finally it is interesting to note that in a recent survey of a large company an attempt was made to discover the amount of information staff received from various sources and compare this with the information they would have preferred to receive from the different ones available. A significant finding was that the 'grapevine' provided 45 per cent of the information obtained, while only 29 per cent came from managers/supervisors. Asked about the preferred sources of information, two-thirds of the staff said they would have liked management to be the main source, and only 2 per cent preferred the grapevine. There is surely a significant message here for you.

Practical Tips

1 Take as your motto, Information-giving is a fertiliser not a pesticide.
2 Tell your staff of anything that affects them directly as quickly as possible.
3 Tell the truth.
4 If facts have to be given, do so in writing, but give reasons verbally.
5 Never use the bush telegraph; inspired leaks never achieve the sort of response you want.
6 Check that your staff understand the message and information given.

In the end the importance of good communication can never be over-stressed. Your staff are much more likely to stay if they feel they matter, that they are being kept in the picture and are always given the truth. To feed them work instructions only is to treat them as if they are machines, and their work is likely to be even less satisfying. Even more importantly, when staff are able to express their views and feelings and know that you will take account of them in reaching your decisions, they are much more likely to become active team members and want to remain with you.

CHECKLIST

1 Have you decided *what* you are going to say?
2 *When* is the best time to say it, since timing is always of importance?
3 *How* will you say it—can your words be misinterpreted or seem emotive?
4 *Where* will you do the telling? Privately? At a meeting?
5 *Why* are you saying it? What are your motives?
6 Have you checked out with the receiver to ensure his understanding?
7 As the listener, do you give full attention?
8 Are you prepared to seek clarification or repetition, if necessary?
9 Are you prepared to look for non-verbal signs of communication?
10 Are you being truthful?
11 Do you plan/prepare what you are going to communicate?

CHAPTER NINE

A Fair Deal for Your Staff

9.1 MONEY MATTERS

Remember that the whole purpose of this Part is to identify what you can do to retain staff and cut out the unnecessary waste and cost of a high turnover. You will recall that on numerous occasions the subject of money has been mentioned, and an attempt made to put its value to staff in perspective. Now let us look money straight in the face, weigh up its real importance as a means of keeping your staff, and bring to bear on the subject all legal requirements and the demands of equity so as to find a sound answer to the question, 'What is a fair wage?'

Be honest with yourself in answering this question: 'Do you regard the cost of labour as a burdensome expense on your business, or as an investment?' Your answer will indicate an outlook that will make the implementation of this chapter an absurdity or an attractive proposition. The factual answer to the question really is that the cost of employing staff is both an expense and an investment. Unfortunately some unenlightened managers may regard it consciously only in the light of its being a drain on the business.

What a difference it would make to you, your business and your staff if you began to look on wages/salaries as an investment. Suppose your annual wage bill is £10,000, or £100,000; if instead you were to invest these sums annually on capital equipment, would you not be going to tremendous lengths to make sure you got value for money? Of course. But where is the difference when you are spending these amounts on people? Are they not equally resources of the business? Your business aims must be to earn maximum returns on your investment—*in people* as much as in material items.

If you buy cheap goods or cheap machines, you cannot expect superb products. Buying cheap labour cannot be expected to be any different. Give staff second-class treatment and you will get second-class attitudes. It can never be sound economics to pay low wages, because it invariably results in poor quality of staff, low morale and a high labour turnover—all of which are very expensive.

Let us start by taking a look at the structure of your wages system. It might be better if we examine it not to see how 'fair' it is, since that word is quite meaningless and certainly emotive, but rather to judge how logical and systematic it is. You offer 'rewards' so as to attract, retain and motivate staff; these are both financial and non-financial (such as the status and job title associated with the work). Now any remuneration given as a result of deliberate managerial policy is already the basis of your official reward system. What is worth keeping in mind is that there can also grow up an unofficial reward system. Under this heading you can count anything which, unplanned, provides pleasure and satisfaction at work; the range of such unofficial rewards may stretch from the friendship established at work to petty pilfering.

It is an established fact that if the official reward system is inadequate, then, like it or not, staff will create an unofficial system. The more adequate the official system, the less time and effort will be spent by your staff in seeking unofficial rewards.

Here is a simple way to start looking objectively at your present wage structure to determine if in any way it is a cause of your inability to retain staff. Carry out a check with your wages clerk or on your own payment system: it can be an enlightening experience that may well show up inadequacies or inequities. You can find that you have just as many problems in overpaying as underpaying staff.

Why are your chambermaids paid X pence per hour, whereas your waiters receive Y pence per hour? How do you justify paying your catering supervisor £X per annum and your catering manager £Y per annum? What accounts for the difference in payment to a hall porter and a kitchen porter, or are they paid the same?, and why?

The bases used in most catering establishments are the relevant Wages Council Orders adjusted to meet the local market for labour, and totally subjective judgements on the part of management. Stop right here and ask yourself if this is the best way to do it. Should it be otherwise, and, if so, on what should wages be based?

Look at it from a different angle. Perhaps the reason you are reading this particular chapter is because you have completed an analysis of staff turnover, and discovered that a basic cause of people leaving you is that they believe your payment system is 'unfair'. Could it be that you know cases where a newcomer in a job is being paid more than staff already employed? Or are there cases where staff have been promoted, say from chambermaid to trainee assistant housekeeper, which means for them, in fact, a reduction in pay? These anomalies do exist and must feature highly in the thinking of many who claim that there is not a fair system of payment in our industry. If you agree that there is even a modicum of truth in all this and that the whole system should be rectified and put on a fairer basis, then this chapter is designed to point the way.

Erecting a Sound Wage Structure

If you are earnest about putting your wage system on a sound footing, your first step must be to determine a wages policy. It should be based on the principle that you will pay a fair and competitive rate for every job adequately performed. You may consider adding that you are prepared to pay, additionally, an amount over those rates that is entirely dependent on individual performance. In other words, it is worth thinking about some sort of incentive system.

Here are some of the benefits you can expect from overhauling your present system and erecting a structured wage system:

1. It will provide you with a better control system of manpower costs.
2. It should ease your recruitment problems by ensuring you pay competitive rates.
3. It will give staff more satisfaction, because promotion paths will be clearly defined and will provide rewards for above-average performance.
4. Any anomalies should quickly be brought to light and quickly corrected.
5. It will help you to plan the cost of your organization and of any necessary manpower changes.

If you intend to review your present wage system and either amend it or replace it with a new approach to rewarding staff, a number of factors have to be taken into account. Here are the principal ones:

1. Wages Council Orders.
2. The 'going-rate' in the industry and in your locality.
3. Other legislation that may affect pay.
4. The value of the work to your business.

Each of these will now be considered in turn and the last of them, dealing with the value you put on jobs, will be dealt with separately in section 9.2.

Wages Councils Act 1959

In many industries the terms and conditions of employment are fixed by collective agreements, by voluntary methods. Where such agreements do not exist, as in our industry on the whole, the force of the Wages Councils Act is applied. Under this Act various statutory regulations of wages have been introduced to ensure minimum standards are observed in the absence of adequate organization on the part of either management or staff.

A Wages Council may make orders that stipulate minimum remuneration, holidays and any other terms and conditions, as well as declaring the date from which payments must be made. Since the passing of the Employment Protection Act any employer who fails to pay the minimum wage rates is subject to a fine of £100. Your responsibilities under the appropriate Wages Order are, in brief:

1 Not to pay less for work and holidays than the rates laid down in the appropriate Wages Regulation Order, under penalty of £100 fine for each offence.
2 To keep certain records (for instance, wage, time and holiday records) for a period of three years.
3 To inform all staff of the Wages Regulation Order that affects them.

The Wages Inspectorate is charged with enforcing the Orders and investigating complaints of breach made by staff.

Clearly, then, your wage structure must take account of the current requirements of whatever Wage Regulation Order applies to your establishment. Unfortunately, in their effort to be comprehensive, these Orders end up as rather complex documents, and your best plan is to make a friend of your local Wages Inspector to help you understand what is the minimum requirement. Remember, however, these Orders specify the minimum and should be viewed in that light alone. If you sincerely want to build a sound wage structure, it is only the first factor to be considered. An outline of the Wages Councils affecting our industry will be found at Appendix 14 (p. 157).

Local Market Conditions

What rates of pay are being used by your competitors in the local area? This must have a bearing on your wage system. To your staff their wages are a tangible measure of comparison. Money means more than the goods it will buy. A man who can say he earns £5,000 a year says so in a different fashion to the one who tells you he is 'on £25 a week'. In just the same way, if a waiter in your establishment can speak at home or in his club of being on Grade 3 or earning £37 a week, when another waiter from another local restaurant can claim to be Grade 2 or earning £28 per week, the sense of difference in status is very real. In this sense money is more tangible, and is seen as more genuine than a pat on the back or a fancy job title.

Nothing of what has been said should make you think you ought to pay well above what everyone else does. Rather, just as you must consult the appropriate Wages Order to ensure you are within the law, so you must look around you to help you determine what wage rates will be competitive in order to attract and retain the right staff.

Apart from the Wages Councils Act 1959 there are a number of other legal statutes affecting pay. Let us look at two in particular.

The Equal Pay Act 1970

The purpose of this Act is to remove discrimination between men and women in respect of their pay and other conditions of employment. This is to be accomplished by establishing a legal right for women to be treated equally when their work is the same or broadly similar to that of men, and even when their work is quite different but given equal value under any form of job evaluation exercise.

In order to establish a basis for comparison the men and women concerned must be employed by the same person or company. Moreover you will only be concerned in comparing women with their male counterparts in the same establishment when the other establishments are owned by the same employer, and the terms and conditions of employment are common to the different establishments.

The Equal Pay Act, which came into force on 29 December 1975, should have been seen as a golden opportunity to review the whole of your present wages system. The whole of this chapter is an encouragement and an aid to your review.

The Employment Protection Act

In the context of this chapter's consideration of a wage system, you will want to be aware of Schedule 11 of the Act. This replaces Section 8 of the Terms and Conditions of Employment Act 1959.

Specifically, Part II of this schedule makes special provisions under which the pay of staff in Wages Council industries can be brought up to the lowest rate negotiated by a union in that industry through voluntary collective bargaining with an employers' association or employers at a significant number of establishments in a district or the industry. This means in effect that in erecting your wages system you must also consider what other employers in the industry, and specifically in your district, are paying staff who have similar jobs. The Act does not define what is meant by 'district', but in accordance with normal practice you should consider it as having its normal sense, i.e. a territory marked off for special administrative purposes (like a District Council Area) or a 'tract of country with common characteristics' (such as the Yorkshire Dales). Claims against employers under this part of the Act will be dealt by the Central Arbitration Committee.

Since 6 April 1977 all staff are entitled to receive a statement of pay showing both gross and net wages, and listing both variable and fixed deductions, although you may cover the latter by issuing an annual statement only.

Summary

Money does matter. It is the basic attraction for people to leave home and give of their time and effort to others in a situation that is generally known as work or employment. If the rewards offered are to attract the right staff and to make them want to go on working for you rather than for someone else, then they must be constructed on a sound basis, be seen by all to be fair or equitable and have a built-in system that allows for periodical review, as well as a means of increasing the rewards in proportion to the efforts made.

To build such a structure requires a conscious effort to formulate a wages policy based in the belief that staff wages/salaries are an investment in people and not simply an inevitable drain on the business. With such a policy you can then begin to build a wage structure that gives all the staff a fair deal. A wages policy statement is given in Appendix 15 (p. 159).

The wage system must take appropriate legislation into account and be competitive. However, if your business is to remain competitive, what you pay staff must be proportionate to the service they render you. Hence we now need to look at the final factor in erecting the wage structure: the value of each job to your business.

9.2 PUTTING A VALUE ON JOBS

It is outside the scope of this manual to give full coverage to what is generally described as 'Job Evaluation'. It is a subject that is comprehensively covered in many other books, and the serious student of the subject is referred to the Bibliography attached to this Part (p. 151).

Basically job evaluation is a rather sophisticated technique of analysing jobs and assessing their relative importance and responsibility by means of common criteria. Once a scale is completed on this basis, you have a foundation for a fair pay structure. It does not supply you with a complete wage scale in itself; as you have seen, other factors need to be taken into account, such as the Wages Council Order, local market conditions and any collective agreement that may apply. However, what it does give you is a fair comparison of the relative value of each job, which should form the foundation for your pay structure.

Provided you carry out a thorough and, as far as possible, totally objective investigation of the various jobs in your establishment, and determine the relative value of each, there are distinct advantages for both management and staff to compensate for the amount of work undertaken. Here are some of the main ones:

1 It will provide you with factual data upon which you can base a fair system of remuneration.
2 It can reveal duplicated or unnecessary work.
3 If it is combined with an appraisal system, it will provide you with a logical system for promotion and transfers.
4 It can give you a basis for identifying training needs.
5 Because it establishes the relative value of various jobs, it can form the basis for collective bargaining.

If you wish to make serious use of this valuable technique for evaluating various jobs, you must immediately recognize what is entailed. It will not be easy and it will take time, but, on the other hand, the reward awaiting the company or establishment that takes the plunge can be enormous. Here is an outline of what you must do:

1 Collect detailed information about each job.
2 Decide which evaluation system you intend to use.
3 Prepare detailed job descriptions.
4 Obtain full co-operation of all staff.
5 Carry out job interviews.

6 Decide on the criteria for evaluation.
7 Evaluate each type of job.
8 Allot remuneration on the basis of your evaluation.

Job Evaluation Systems
A number of different systems have been evolved. Here is a brief description of the main ones:

1 *Job Ranking*. This is probably the simplest system of all, but it can produce very good results, especially in the smaller establishment. It consists in comparing one complete job with another and assessing which one has a heavier 'weight' or is of greater value to the business. No individual factors are used, but a good deal of knowledge of the job make-up is needed.

The first stage consists of making a series of job-to-job comparisons from which a preliminary rank order list is built up. Suppose, for instance, the following jobs exist in the 'Royal Restaurant': dispense barman, cashier, chef, commis cook, restaurant manager, plateman, salad hand, and waiter. A job-to-job comparison might result in the following rank order being established:

Restaurant manager
Chef
Cashier
Dispense barman
Waiter
Commis cook
Salad hand
Plateman

The final stage might then be to group these jobs into four grades:

Grade 1	Restaurant manager and chef.
Grade 2	Cashier, barman and waiter.
Grade 3	Commis cook and salad hand.
Grade 4	Plateman.

Whilst this system may appear very rough and ready, it does provide a sound basis for job comparisons. What is essential is that it achieves results that broadly relate to market values, since this is the ultimate measure of effectiveness of any system of job evaluation.

2 *Job Classification*. This is another relatively simple system, but, unlike job ranking, it establishes a number of grades to begin with and then fits the job into the most appropriate grade. The difficult part of this system is in establishing the various grades or classifications, which are determined by general statements of job difficulty. Here is an example of a six-grade system:

Grade A	Simple tasks that are subject to close supervision.
Grade B	Tasks that require a limited amount of knowledge, those that require simple manual dexterity, and those that carry a low level of responsibility and where the work is subject to frequent checking.
Grade C	Routine type of work but with more responsibility than Grade B; checking of Grade B work.
Grade D	Work requiring a little initiative where routine may alter, and where little supervision is required.
Grade E	Special knowledge/skill is required, with responsibility for own sequencing of work and for small number of staff.
Grade F	Work requiring special experience, discretion and judgement; in contact regularly with management; responsible for supervision of a complete section of work.

Once you have established this series of grades, you then allocate pay rates to each grade before allocating jobs to them. If you implement this system, it is usually necessary to review the grades after an initial run and to have an adequate appeals procedure.

Job ranking and job classification have one thing in common: they make a comparison on a whole job basis. The next two systems, however, use an analytical rather than an assessment approach, since they break the jobs down into a series of headings or factors applicable to all jobs being considered; these factors are then given a monetary value, which add up to the cash rate for the job.

3 *Job Factor Comparison*. This system takes a variety of forms, but at heart it is concerned with identifying and using those factors specially relevant to the job being evaluated. The first decision to be reached is the list of factors. Usually these will consist of items such as the following:

1 Experience, knowledge and skill.
2 Work complexities.

3 Working conditions.
4 Contacts.
5 Responsibilities.

The most practicable approach here is to select some key jobs representing various wage levels you believe to be correct and fairly related to one another, and to rank each one factor by factor. To check the accuracy of your ranking, break down the total wage rate into monetary units and allot them in the order of importance of each factor. If your ranking is accurate, this should coincide with that produced by the allocation of the money units. Once you are satisfied that you have the basics right, you take all the other jobs, comparing and ranking them among the key jobs under each factor. Finally a comparative money value is then established for each factor in each individual job. The total of the factor value of each job gives you the total wage rate for the job.

While this system is still of a general nature, it does have the advantage of great flexibility in adaptation to the individual requirements of evaluating any group of jobs. It is especially effective when ranking groups of heads of departments. Variable 'weightings' may be applied, or other steps towards points evaluation taken, as seems best to suit your own situation. An example of a factor assessment is shown in Appendix 16 (p. 161).

4 *Points Rating.* This is perhaps the most commonly used of all evaluation systems, since it appears to provide the greatest accuracy. Once again the starting point is to draw up a list of main factors or characteristics common to the jobs under review. In many cases this will result in four or five broad characteristics, such as:

Skill.
Knowledge and aptitudes.
Responsibility.
Performance or effort.
Working conditions.

Each of these factors is then broken down still further into basic categories. So, for instance, under the factor of 'skill' you may have the following subdivisions: previous learning needed, learning/training period, mechanical ability, numeracy, and social skills.

Once this has been completed, a number of points is allotted to each factor. This can be in any range to suit your requirements but usually a workable scale of 0–30 for each factor will be found suitable. Generally you would provide a different range of points (weighting) for each factor since some will be considered to have greater significance than others. So, for instance, you might decide that 'skill' merits a range of 0–30, 'responsibility' 0–20, and 'performance/effort' 0–25. At this stage your evaluation sheet might look something like the accompanying table.

		Job Title					
Factor	*Areas*			*Degree*			*Points*
		1	2	3	4	5	
SKILL	Education Experience Training period Initiative						
RESPONSIBILITY	Materials Machinery Cash Work of others						
EFFORT etc.							

A further refinement in this system is also illustrated in the table, when each area is still further broken down into degrees in an attempt to arrive at an even more accurate allocation of points. Having allocated the number of points to each factor, you then add them together to provide the total points value of each job.

That is the broad picture of the points-based scheme, an attempt to arrive at some sort of mathematically accurate grading of jobs. However, before launching into what might be a lengthy and difficult exercise in the firm belief that eventually you will arrive at a totally objective and mathematically accurate evaluation of jobs, recognize also the weaknesses in this system. It may give the appearance of providing a scientific measurement of job value compared to the others, which allow so much subjectivity of judgement, but the extent of its inadequacy must not be underestimated. The difficulties you will meet with are in finding the balance between the factors, of allocating weightings and defining points along the scale. Each decision in the end is quite arbitrary, and the total number of possible inaccuracies should counterweigh, in your mind, the apparent scientific basis of the points rating system.

A Final Thought

Now that you have looked at the outline of what a methodical approach to establishing fairness of pay entails, you have reached the stage of having to balance two considerations:

1 Carrying out a job evaluation exercise is demanding in terms of time and effort, with no guarantee of achieving complete success.
2 The value to you of implementing a pay structure based on a real effort to achieve fairness will place you among the very few in the catering industry who show that, despite the effort, you are anxious to establish a fair system, and so remove one of the biggest causes of staff leaving to work elsewhere.

Even if you do decide that a full evaluation cannot be undertaken at the moment for any reason, the principles outlined here could be applied usefully so as to achieve a disciplined and conscious approach to equitable rewards for your staff. There is no need for it to become an elaborate and inoperable structure.

Practical Tips

1 Do not rely on copies of job descriptions that have been previously prepared or ones designed for other purposes, such as for the recruitment of staff.
2 While making sure that you use concise sentences as far as practicable, complete the job descriptions required by allowing a free-ranging approach to describe not only what is done in the job but its every aspect, from the type of equipment used to special aptitudes needed, and from a description of the standards to be achieved to the kind and amount of responsibility.
3 Remember that it is the job that it is being evaluated and never the job holder.
4 Bring into the study everyone who can be affected by it, so that they know precisely what you are doing and for what purpose.
5 Be prepared for minor disagreements about your weighting, and institute an appeals system.

6 Concentrate completely on achieving fairness.
7 The Department of Employment will give advice and assistance in implementing a job evaluation scheme.

9.3 INCENTIVES

In most other industries you will find that many wage systems incorporate a vast array of different incentive schemes, from payment by results through measured day work to premium pay plan. Perhaps the most appropriate incentive scheme operable in the hotel and catering industry is one based on 'merit rating', a method of payment based on management's judgement of an individual's qualities and aptitudes. Like all incentive systems it has its strengths and its weaknesses.

The advantages of the system are as follows:

1 It provides for supervisors to consider each subordinate's contribution regularly.
2 The interview between supervisor and supervised provides an opportunity to plan the future constructively.
3 The method of payment is flexible.
4 Staff are made to feel they are being treated as individuals.

The disadvantages are the following:

1 The assessment is usually subjective.
2 The supervisors are expected to make personal judgements about individuals when they may not have such refined abilities.
3 Economic pressures often result in the system being weighted so that everyone ends up at the top end.
4 There is always a danger that it may become an employee right.

Applying Merit Rating

Before making a decision as to whether an employee is to receive a merit increase, you must review his performance. This will mean using some kind of appraisal system, which will be looked at in Chapter 10. However, performance alone is not the only factor to be considered in determining the size and timing of a merit increase; you must also consider the relation between the employee's performance and his position on the salary grade.

When you measure any human characteristic over a large number of people—be it weight, height, or anything else—by far the largest proportion of the group will tend to be around the average, with a small percentage significantly above or below that point. This is just as true when you are measuring job performance as anything else.

The consequence of all this is that you will find the biggest proportion of staff will be assessed as 'satisfactory' and 'satisfactory plus', a small number assessed as 'satisfactory minus' and 'excellent', and an even smaller number still as 'very unsatisfactory' and 'outstanding'. To reward people fairly must be the objective of any wage system. It follows then that staff on the same grade rated as 'consistently outstanding' should, over time, achieve a higher reward than those rated 'consistently excellent', and those in turn rewarded higher than those rated 'consistently satisfactory plus'.

Suppose then that you have introduced a grading system and some sort of appraisal takes place annually; consideration for a merit increase must start with the worker obtaining at least a 'satisfactory' grade. Bearing in mind the need mentioned above for considering not only performance but also the relation between the employee's performance and the position of his salary in the appropriate grade range, your objectives for awarding merit increases should be as follows:

1 Wages of 'satisfactory' staff will be around the mid-way point of the range.
2 Wages of staff who are 'satisfactory plus' will tend to occupy the third quarter of the range.
3 Wages of those who are rated as 'excellent' or 'outstanding' will reach the fourth quarter of the range.

This use of a merit rating system appears to be fairest of all. A member of staff who never reaches the higher performance ratings can still achieve the maximum in his range, but, rightly, it will take him much longer than a colleague who consistently has higher performance ratings.

Remember that the whole purpose of merit increases is twofold: to reward good performance and to stimulate improved performance. You might well consider that, since the granting of a merit increase should have the maximum motivating effect on the employee you will time merit increases to take place throughout the year rather than at a predetermined date annually. This should also result in more evenly spread increase in payroll throughout the year. On the other hand, do not forget to make due allowance in the budgeted annual wage figure for such additional payments as incentives.

If you do introduce a merit increase type of incentive scheme, make sure your staff understand it fully. The important aspects to cover are these:

1 It is a system designed to reward performance and is not automatic.
2 It demands an honest appraisal of each member of the staff regularly.
3 It is aimed at rewarding in proportion to improvement in performance standards consistently.

No set of incentives, however good, will work if they are nullified by disincentives such as poor working conditions, lack of job security, inadequate communication and an uncongenial atmosphere. And they certainly will not work if the basic wage structure is faulty.

9.4 THE TOTAL WAGE SYSTEM

Now that you have completed a review of the major factors to be weighed in structuring rational and fair rewards, it remains for you to put the system into being.

Let us suppose you have carried out some form of evaluation of the various jobs and decided to introduce a grading system. It probably looks fine on paper. You will also have checked the wage scales to see that they are in line with local competition and that, in any case, they comply with current legislation. Finally you will also have considered how best you can build in some sort of incentive element. This will now form your total wage system. Here are some practical steps for implementing it:

1 Prepare a brief outline of the whole system for distribution to all staff.
2 Hold a meeting or series of meetings with your staff to explain the system in detail and to discuss the implications of the revised system.
3 Be sensitive to any constructive suggestions that may be made at these meetings and, where possible, amend the system to take account of these suggestions.
4 Check out with those staff concerned that the administrative machinery is geared up to the new system, and that, where necessary, appropriate staff receive the training to enable them to operate the payment system.

5 When you are happy that you have checked out all the arrangements, fix a date for implementation.
6 Institute an appeals and review system.

Major rewards await the companies in our industry who take the plunge and replace the wage structure that has existed until now by systems that reward staff fairly and are seen to operate fairly, thereby removing one of the commonest causes for staff leaving. But no wage structure, however good, can remain static; it needs to be reviewed regularly, and to take account of trends, in just the same way as any other aspect of your business planning. In this regard, therefore, it is worth ending this chapter by looking ahead at what must influence wage structures in the days to come:

1 The change away from manual to staff status.
2 A reduction in the hours of work.
3 Increased leisure requirements.
4 Increasing trade union membership.
5 Increasing importance of 'fringe benefits'.

CHECKLIST

1 How many different wage rates do you now have?
2 How do they compare with your competitors'?
3 What is your budgeted labour cost for the next 12 months?
4 Is there at least a 20 per cent differential between the pay of departmental heads and the gross pay of those they supervise?
5 What is the cost of your labour turnover?
6 What is the cost of absenteeism?
7 To what extent can you involve job holders in the job evaluation system?
8 Will you allow all staff to see the job evaluation system operate? If not, why not?
9 How can you ensure that your departmental heads make a contribution to restructuring your wage system?
10 What sort of image does your company have as a 'wage-payer'?
11 What sort of incentives are people used to in your work area?
12 What is your wages policy?
13 Does it cover equal pay?
14 How will you handle pay anomalies?
15 Is your supervisory structure adequate to handle any new pay structure you implement?

CHAPTER TEN

How to Develop Your Staff's Ability

10.1 COACHING SKILLS

Do you realize that if you were to recruit someone who was to spend his lifetime working for you as, say, a waiter or a chambermaid, this would be equal to an investment of something like £70,000? However, unlike investment in capital equipment, which begins to depreciate as soon as it is installed, investment in people can appreciate depending to a large extent on how you handle them. In short, to develop the latent abilities of staff is to make sure that your precious assets, people, do not stagnate but grow to provide you with a return worth much more than your wage investment.

But there is more to it than that. How many staff have you promoted in the last year or two? What was the basis of your selection for promotion—length of service, loyalty, best craftsman, hunch, or was it based on a judgement of worthiness and suitability? If you can honestly say it was for the last suggested reason, on what did you base your judgement? What criteria did you use to measure suitability? How do you measure potential? These are all questions the thoughtful manager must consider at times.

As we have already seen, your success depends very largely on your staff. A big part of your job demands that you harness and bring out the capacity resident in all of them. This must be a recipe for success in a service industry. On the other hand, again as we have seen earlier in this manual, your staff have an innate wish to grow in their jobs and to develop as individuals. So these two facts are complementary. They await but the opportunity of development, and it is your job as staff manager to see that this happens. This chapter sets out to suggest a practical approach to developing the ability of staff in the industry. Consider:

1 Hidden away in the hearts and minds of your staff may be a great wealth of undisclosed abilities—if only you made it your business to dig them out.

2 A recent research study by the Hotel and Catering Economic Development Committee showed that:

(a) There is no shortage of opportunity for promotion in the industry.
(b) Precious little evidence exists to show that promotion takes place as part of a planned system of staff development.
(c) Only 7 per cent of managers claimed systems based on annual assessment procedures.
(d) Where appraisal systems do exist, the emphasis is on management development and practically nothing is done for supervisory or other staff.
(e) At least one-fifth of all staff want promotion.
(f) Something approaching a quarter of all staff consider their prospects of promotion to be good.

3 Most managers take great care to avoid material waste, but very few consciously consider waste of human resources.
4 Managers of staff can experience few things as satisfying as being the medium by which another person is brought to glimpse new possibilities for his own achievement.

Here is a resumé of what is called for if you seriously wish to develop staff fully:

1 You must take on the role of counsellor and coach on a day-to-day basis.
2 You must take a realistic inventory of staff resources so as to maintain an accurate picture of present performance in jobs.
3 You must devise the most suitable measures for assessing the potential of all staff.
4 You must decide what training is required to improve the staff's present performance, and what training is needed to develop their full potential in the context of careers.
5 You must arrange for all the training needs to be met in time.

It looks at first sight like a frightening prospect, but remember the rewards, and then the price will appear reasonable. Even if the only result is a massive reduction in staff turnover—and you can really expect this with confidence—it must be the cheapest line in man-management today.

Coaching and Counselling

Whether you describe the activity of a manager in developing his staff as coaching or counselling does not seem to be important despite the difference in meaning given to these words in the dictionary. What does matter is agreement that the activity concerns itself with talking together with staff in a helpful and advisory manner, with the object of improving their present performance and stimulating the release of latent ability.

Most people are familiar with the idea of there being a coach in the field of sport. He is the person who watches the golfer or footballer exercising his native talents, spots the weaknesses in technique and, with the authority of experience and not of status, talks freely with the sportsman about his performance and his difficulties, exploring with him possible remedies and new approaches, and then, when watching future performances, intervening with cajoling and counselling, encouragement and advice. If that is how you see the work of an athletic coach, you will have no difficulty in accepting the idea of a manager acting in a similar fashion to develop his staff.

The essential ingredients of coaching are as follows:

1 Coaching includes 'talking things over together'. That is the first and fundamental element to grasp. It has nothing at all to do with 'telling' people what to do, nor of handing out cascades of criticism. An essential requirement in coaching is mutual deliberation.
2 Because the purpose of coaching is to help staff improve and develop, other necessary ingredients are to be keenly observant in your approach, to be sensitive to cues, and to be objective in seeing things as they are, so that strengths can be determined and weaknesses uncovered.
3 The final element lies in the skill of moulding together your findings and the prescription for improvement and development, and presenting them in such a way that your staff feel a sense of self-development rather than that they are 'being taught'.

While you can readily recognize what all this entails, the crucial questions are, How do I implement it; where do I start? Let us be clear about one thing: to develop staff through coaching is not a skill that can be learned from studying a list of 'dos' and 'don'ts'. Coaching is not a technique. Principles can be cited, examined and tested in practice, but proficiency is gained by constant practice. Treat the following suggestions as guidelines:

1 The starting point is clear: you must be determined to coach. Once you have made that decision, then the use of basic principles and the experience you gain in practice will lead, in time, to your carrying out your coaching role as a natural part of your daily work, so that it will cease to have any significance as a separate technique.
2 Leave aside your 'boss' or 'management' role when you undertake coaching; it should be a dialogue between equals in all respects except that you have greater experience. It is this greater experience you must call upon to short-circuit the time otherwise needed for staff to learn and develop.
3 Set out to coach on-job. Your whole approach must be job-related. This is the field in which not only can you help improve work performance but also discover hidden talents and ambitions and build staff into bigger individuals. Encourage them to rethink their ways of doing things—do not be afraid of even a restructuring of the work. You cannot do better than make work a challenge.
4 Coaching is not 'answer-supplying'. Remember it is a dialogue—a mutual discussion designed to encourage staff to think for themselves, and to put forward ideas. This means that you must be prepared to accept ideas that demand thought and enterprise on your part. If you are carrying out your role successfully, you too will learn from the experience.
5 You will not find one universal approach to coaching. Development is an individual matter, and what works for one person will not necessarily work for another.
6 Make sure, whenever a new idea, a new method or a novel approach is tried out, that you build in along the line some means by which staff can learn if their efforts are meeting with success. Feedback is a quality of coaching that can never be ignored.

Practical Tips

1 Visit staff at their work every day so as to establish your image in their eyes as a source of encouragement and help, and remove their natural tendency to see you exclusively in the role of critic, inspector and boss.
2 Talk with staff about their work and encourage them to put forward ideas and exercise their initiative.
3 Use questions to open up a discussion; design them so that they give staff an opportunity to express opinions and feelings, as well

as to provide you with facts. A useful start can be made with questions beginning with 'How' or 'What': for instance, 'How do you carry out your early morning call routine?' or 'What do you suggest might be a better way of doing it?'

4 Listen to staff, pick their brains, and be sensitive to any new idea or any suggestion made.
5 Watch what staff actually do. This will help you to understand their work better and to discuss the way things are done—something they may not be consciously aware of.
6 Having gathered information and opinions, and having watched what the work entails, make assessments of what needs improving and how best to implement improvements.
7 When criticism is necessary, make sure that it is constructive. Explain what needs improving by suggesting a different approach.
8 Summarize what you consider has been agreed on before moving on to coaching the next person.

You spend a lot of time considering how to use the financial and material resources of your business to good effect, and you may even spend quite a lot of time planning the workings of staff. If you don't already do so, add a daily coaching session. You will soon find that it becomes a way of life for you and not an optional extra duty. The reward? Developing your staff will make your job easier and more satisfying and your company/ establishment more profitable.

10.2 AN APPROACH TO APPRAISAL

A good manager keeps an eye on his stocks day by day, and then once in a while he is visited by the stocktaker to make a formal check. Likewise, through all sorts of daily financial controls, the manager sees to it that his trading is healthy, and yet at least annually he has a formal statement of financial information to prepare. So it should be with staffing. After all, as emphasized so often in this manual, staff are assets of the business. You have seen how, through constant counselling and coaching, you can help them to do their job better, but there is also a strong argument for setting aside time, say annually, for formally interviewing your staff in order to carry out an individual appraisal of their strengths and weaknesses. This lies at the heart of any appraisal system.

Many managers may argue that, because they are in constant touch with staff, their subordinates know what they think of them. They often add that, indeed, they operate an open-door policy for staff to come and discuss their careers and personal hopes and fears with them whenever they wish. If you are really honest about it, you will probably agree that the daily contact normally concerns itself with immediate work matters, and that discussions about a member of staff's progress and career rarely take place informally. Is it not tragically true that at times the first you have known about staff's feelings about their progress is when they come to tell you they are leaving. Appraisal can help to avoid this cause of staff departing and must therefore be considered as another facet of the art of keeping staff.

Here are some of the important benefits of introducing an appraisal system:

1 It should help you in manpower planning, it may be able to give you enough information on whether or not your present staff requirements would be able to meet expansion of your business or more simply in determining whether you need to recruit now or later.
2 Promotion and transfer decisions should have a more objective basis.
3 You will be able to plan your staff training more thoroughly and systematically.
4 It will give you more reasonable grounds for deciding on merit awards.
5 Your staff will benefit from being formally assessed as to their progress, and from knowing what is expected of them and how they will be judged.
6 Everyone will benefit from an opportunity to discuss how each can be developed as a person, both in terms of the job and in regard to personal development and career.

Before you take any positive steps to begin an appraisal system, make an honest appraisal of the establishment you are working in. Is the atmosphere such that it has a real chance of success? Is there a basic sense of trust between managers/supervisors and staff? Staff need to feel secure enough to know that if they admit to weaknesses or admit ones that were unrealized by superiors, they will be helped to overcome them. They also need to believe that there is a genuine sincerity of will to help them, and that the timing of their training and development will be arranged according to their needs and not by what costs least. Unless your establishment does have this basic openness and supportiveness, it will probably be better to work on these problems first, before entertaining the introduction of an appraisal system.

However sophisticated or simple a system you install, it should be able to perform the following functions:

1 Measure results achieved against targets set.
2 Pinpoint personal strengths and weaknesses.
3 Highlight training and development required.
4 Assess potential for promotion.
5 Provide a basis for rewarding according to merit.

In order to overcome most of the objections raised to appraisal you must spend time on deciding what criteria you will use for appraising staff. Ideally, if you can agree targets to be achieved by them in their work, then these will provide you with some objective yardsticks against which you can measure their performance. This is even more true if these targets can be made quantifiable. For instance, a departmental head may agree a target that in the year he will reduce his departmental staff turnover by 20 per cent. A wine waiter may agree to accept as one of his targets that he increases his sale of white wines by 15 per cent.

You will readily agree that it may not always be possible to be so definite in setting down targets of performance. This will be especially true of more junior grades of staff, when you may have to limit yourself to a general assessment of job performance. This does not denigrate the value of the appraisal, however; in discussing the general assessment you can take the opportunity of highlighting the strengths and weaknesses that have led to your assessment, and preferably doing so through examples.

You will need to prepare some sort of form on which you can record the annual appraisal of each of your staff. There is no such thing as a perfect form for this purpose, and indeed you may even require one sort of form for those staff who occupy supervisory positions and for whom you can set specific performance targets, and another for staff in more junior positions. Indeed, where performance appraisal exists in this industry, you will normally find that it is confined to 'managers'. You may well agree that all staff are entitled to know where they stand, and to have an opportunity for a formal annual interview to determine what needs to be done, and can be done, to improve their performance and to develop them as people. Examples of appraisal forms may be found in Appendix 17 (p. 163).

Practical Tips

1 Keep the appraisal form as simple as possible.
2 Avoid rating scales.
3 Word the form in such a way that it leads to proposals for action rather than for passing of judgements only.
4 Include a specific requirement for an assessment of:

 (a) Training/experience required in present job.
 (b) Development required for career advancement.
 (c) What other steps need to be taken to improve performance.

5 Allow space for recording an assessment of potential in terms of promotion.
6 Leave room for the appraisee to record any comments he wishes to make about the completed appraisal form before signing it.

The Appraisal Interview

However well you may design the appraisal form, there will always be a requirement for purely subjective judgements to be recorded. If for no other reason this demands that the appraisal should be completed by means of a formal interview; it allows staff to talk through the points made and to put forward their views. Even more important is for them to help in identifying what training they need and would like, to improve their performance and potential.

Like all interviews, if it is to be successful, then certain ground rules have to be applied. First and foremost it must be prepared for. Before the interview you should attend to the following practical matters:

1 Arrange a suitable time and place with staff for the interview.
2 Let them have a copy of the appraisal form in advance so that they will be better prepared to discuss the content of their appraisal. It may be possible to complete some parts of the form in advance of the interview.
3 Think of examples and incidents you will use to back up any written statements you may already have made.
4 Make sure that you are not interrupted during the interview.

Once staff arrive for their appraisal interview, you must realize that you have now reached the apex of the whole system; a formal interview with each member of your staff is the cornerstone of appraisal. All the interviewing techniques outlined in Part I, and all the skills emphasized then, apply as much to appraisal interviewing as to recruitment interviewing. Perhaps two aspects need particular highlighting: (1) because appraisal is so personal and likely to touch upon sensitive spots, an atmosphere must be created to allow the interviewee to unwind; and (2) the interviewer should ensure that most of the talking is done by the interviewee.

Your interview should be structured in such a way that it embraces the following stages:

1 An evaluation of performance in the job.
2 A review of potential and promotability.
3 A planning of future development.

Naturally these three phases require to be interlinked. Throughout the whole interview your aim should be to be constructive; use the appraisal interview as a jumping-off point for future action and not as a historical recording session.

1 *Job Performance*

1 Start by stressing the purpose of the meeting, making it clear that there is joint responsibility for its success and that you are there in the role of counsellor rather than judge.
2 Explain that you will take notes during the interview and complete the appraisal form later.
3 Begin by highlighting what you see as the person's strengths, using factual information to sustain your belief.
4 Encourage continuation in the good work, suggesting ways in which he can reinforce the strong points and asking him to suggest further improvements himself.
5 Do not wait too long before you bring up for discussion what you consider are the man's weaknesses in performance; after all, he will expect this to loom large at this sort of interview.
6 Centre your discussion on two or three main weaknesses only. That is the most you can expect him to cope with.
7 Relate the weaknesses to the person's job, making sure that they are capable of being remedied.
8 Be prepared to support your nomination of his weaknesses with facts and evidence.
9 If you have carried out your role as a coach, none of those weaknesses should appear for discussion as something new. Criticism should never be aired for the first time at an appraisal interview.
10 If staff counter your arguments, listen carefully and avoid

the temptation either to argue or justify what you have said for the sake of your own satisfaction. The points made may be perfectly valid. You must judge that.

11 Encourage the interviewee to discuss his weaknesses openly, and get him to suggest ways in which he can improve.

12 Listen to everything he has to say, including suggestions on how you can behave better towards him as his manager. He may well have a point.

2 *Potential and Promotability*

1 Stress that your estimate in this area, however accurate you believe it to be, is subject to ratification by your superiors (if such is the case).

2 Be honest and frank in stating what you believe the man's potential to be and how this affects the possibility of promotion.

3 Stress that, even if he has been unacceptable in his present job performance, this does not condemn him as an 'also ran'. Encourage him to discuss his potential, as he sees it, and you may unearth previously undisclosed traits or suggestions of other abilities.

4 Ask him to tell you what he would like to do most, and suggest activities that might help him to achieve his hopes.

5 If he gives an unrealistic opinion of his potential, try to assess the opinion and offer alternative advice.

6 Since a lateral move can broaden a person's experience, discuss this where appropriate; however, also ensure that if this is discussed, it is not interpreted by him to mean he is unfit for promotion.

7 Discuss promotability openly. Avoid giving false hopes or making rash promises, and allow for inclusion of a possible time span in fulfilling any hope that may be allowed.

3 *Future Development.* This is the key part of your interview. Until now you will be seen to have reviewed the man's past performance and to have assessed future possibilities; now, however, you should be pointing the way ahead through *action.*

1 Discuss what can be done to remedy present weaknesses; encourage suggestions from him as to how best he can tackle his problems and what help you can offer him in the way of further coaching, training, or by widening his experience.

2 Encourage this discussion and your subsequent discussion of personal development by letting staff know you are prepared to spend time and money to help.
3 Try to translate this discussion into action by coming to agreement with him on proposals for *doing* something to improve his present performance and to help him become a more developed individual.
4 Now you have reached the end of the interview, summarize the important points discussed, making sure there are no misunderstandings.

As soon as possible after the interview complete the sections on the appraisal form of your discussion with staff. You should then invite him to read the completed form and sign it, allowing him to add any remarks he wishes.

Few managers are enthusiastic about an appraisal system—it is often described as a paper exercise, most dislike having to sort out the factual from the subjective, none enjoy having to criticize, and it is often seen as something that tells superiors more about the appraiser than the appraised. Perhaps underlying all the objections you can detect resistance to it because it does not seem to be worth while. In other words it is demanding in time and effort but bears little fruit. With respect, that is a damnation of a system because it is not effectively used, not because formal appraisal is ineffective in itself.

How can you be sure that your appraisal system will produce the benefits it is designed to provide? The practical and simple answer, assuming that you and any others taking part carry out your part constructively, is that it will show real benefits to staff and your establishment *if it is followed through*. This means that you implement all the actions decided upon during the interview within, say, two months of each interview. That is the time scale to work towards. Until the first proposals for action are implemented, staff will not believe in the promises made or the good intentions expressed during the interview. If it should prove impossible for some reason or other to implement an agreed recommendation within that time scale, your staff should be given good reasons for the delay.

The success of your appraisal system depends on your willingness and ability to implement agreed courses of action for improving staff performance in their present work and in developing them as fuller people. Suspicions will die away, sincerity will be shown to be well-founded and motivation will take effect only when actions take the place of words.

CHECKLIST

1 Have you made a conscious decision to act in a coaching capacity as a manager?

2 Is your role as a coach one of 'helper' with experience to support you rather than exclusively one of 'boss' with status to uphold you?

3 Do you encourage staff to discuss new ways of doing things?

4 Do you see staff at work regularly—daily if possible?

5 Is your coaching approach one of questioning rather than telling?

6 Are the organization and climate of your establishment such that mutual trust between management and staff exists?

7 Have you considered setting targets to be achieved by staff, especially at departmental-head level?

8 What objective criteria have you devised against which you can measure staff performance?

9 Have you informed staff about your appraisal system?

10 How have you planned to carry out appraisal interviews for all staff?

11 Have you gathered all the evidence you need to support your appraisal of staff?

12 Have you geared your whole approach to appraisal so as to establish norms for action in the future rather than simply to review historical performance?

CHAPTER ELEVEN

How to Train Your Staff

Training and education are two terms that are frequently interchanged, and much argument abounds as to the real distinction between them. We do recognize that there can be a difference—for example, compare sex education with sex training! However, within the context of this manual you are likely to be concerned with the outcome of both processes.

As a practising staff manager you must be concerned with providing the opportunity for staff to learn to do their work better and to undertake other training that will fit them for new, perhaps more responsible, work. It is this area of training with which this chapter is primarily concerned.

However, before looking at what has to be done, it is worth reflecting on what training/education is available nationally for staff in our industry. A great deal of this work is carried out in colleges of further education and higher educational establishments. If you are to understand what staff may be capable of when they arrive with any one or more of a whole variety of qualifications, it is as well to have a working knowledge of what is available. A list of the main qualifications open to staff in the catering industry, entry qualifications and a resumé of what is covered, can be found in Appendix 18 (p. 165).

When you begin to take a serious look at how the training needs of your staff may be met, you may well find that you need the advice and assistance of professional training staff. Generally speaking this is available freely to all managers in the industry if they contact the local training adviser from the Hotel and Catering Industry Training Board, or from any of the professional bodies that look after your interests, such as the BHRCA or HCIMA as well as professional training bodies that could help with training itself. A list of useful names and addresses may be found at Appendix 19 (p. 170).

11.1 BE SYSTEMATIC

Companies that train staff tend to retain them. This is the reason why the subject of staff training merits its inclusion in this part of the manual dealing with 'The Art of Keeping Staff'. Generally speaking, such companies operate a sound personnel policy, but when their staff are asked what they like most about working there, the reply invariably places high on the list the fact that they are given every opportunity to be trained to do a better job, and to develop themselves for better positions in the future.

Since this is the case, why has 'training' been looked upon by many managers in our industry as something of a sick joke? The reasons are endless. Perhaps the most prominent of them are that some training has often proved remarkably ineffective in improving performance, there is often an over-emphasis on off-job courses as the best training in all circumstances, training has more often than not been regarded as a low-level function, and many managers lack formal training and consider qualifications as a relatively unimportant aspect of their staff's attributes. For those who recognize the value of training, and whose experience of its worth leaves them in no doubt about its importance as a management function, this is a sad state of affairs.

Precisely because of this jaundiced view of training the Industrial Training Act was passed in 1964 to give employers an impetus to provide, as part of their business activity, training for staff at all levels. This Act was replaced in 1973 by the Employment and Training Act, which seeks to remove the coercive aspects of the earlier Act, now that industrial training is under way on a much larger scale, and to provide greater emphasis on the advisory role of training boards, while still retaining a modified levy/grant approach.

However, as a staff manager you may feel that you have no need for the law to breathe down your neck to enforce training. While training is not the answer to all your problems, you will recognize that it has an important part to play, not only in helping you to keep good staff but also in enabling you to make your business a more profitable one.

This manual can only point the way towards helping you provide training for your staff. Volumes abound on the subject, and the Bibliography (p. 151) will help you study the subject in greater depth.

Unless you see training as an important part of your management role and plan your approach to it accordingly as a vital section of your whole business strategy, it is unlikely to provide you and your staff with the rewards it could achieve. It must be planned or, like most things, it either will not happen at all or it will take place in a haphazard fashion with limited results.

To plan your training effectively here are the steps of a systematic approach:

1 Determine what your training policy is.
2 Identify what training is required.
3 Plan your training to meet those needs.
4 Prepare programmes to fulfil your plan.
5 Carry out the training programme.
6 Review and evaluate the training completed.

This may look at first sight too sophisticated, too complex or too time-consuming to make it worth while. It need not be so. It really is a matter of commonsense, and, in any case, professional advice is obtainable from your local training adviser, whether or not you pay levy to the training board. Let us look briefly at each of these steps.

11.2 TRAINING, STEP BY STEP

1 *A Training Policy*. Many managers are loth to write anything down if they can avoid it. Resist the temptation to overlook this step, as the self-discipline required to think through and write out a training policy will be amply rewarded; you will have thoroughly considered the implications of instituting a systematic approach to training your staff. Staff are sure to have increased confidence in a company that has a declared policy about its training intentions. If you are a manager in a large company, you will no doubt be familiar with its policy statement, and therefore you can move straight on to the next step. But if you are managing in a business of your own or in a smaller organization, the benefits of drawing up your own policy statement cannot be over-estimated.

Briefly your policy should show a broad statement of training intent, covering not only the industrial training requirements of your staff but also your declaration to allow them the possibility of any further education that is appropriate to them. This last point is important, for education and training are sometimes difficult to separate. What really counts is whether your policy points towards development of staff, both in their present work and for their future careers, or whether you merely seek to use training to serve the immediate needs for improvement in job performance. Hopefully your policy will be the former; apart from anything else it will then provide the teeth of your appraisal approach and show that you are not simply paying lip service to that technique.

Finally, if it is to be seen by all staff as a serious statement, you should also cover, in a broad sense, where the responsibility for training lies and what resources, in terms of people and cash, you are setting aside for training. Naturally you can only prepare such a statement if you have the authority to cover all these items.

2 *Identifying Training Needs.* You will probably find this is the most difficult step of all, especially if you have not yet started an appraisal system, backed up by coaching. However, in one sense it is crucial: all the other parts of your system are built upon what you find in this stage.

Basically you can identify as a training need any knowledge or skill the staff require for their present or future work. Three broad areas can be considered:

1 Where present performance of staff is not up to the standards you expect.
2 When planned or actual changes affect staff's work.
3 When staff are or will be changing their jobs.

You should take the following action:

1 List accurately the staff who work for you and the jobs they do.
2 Prepare a chart showing how all those jobs fit together to meet your business purposes.
3 Sort out a list of the main duties each category of staff is responsible for performing.
4 Compare the performance of each member of staff with what you expect of them in their present work.
5 Consider what requirements for training will exist if you have planned to expand, introduce new equipment or make any other changes that can affect present staff work.
6 If you foresee changes in staff—either a need to recruit new staff or to promote others—consider what training they will require to do their job well.
7 Decide what kinds of career development among staff you would wish to encourage, and the implications of this for training or further education.

8 Draw together your complete list of identified training needs and, in the light of your decisions about those facets of your business that are critical for success, sort out a list of priorities.
9 Decide whether you have the resources available to carry out training to meet these needs, whether you should earmark some staff to be trained in instructional skills to support this training, or if you should explore what help is available to you from outside your establishment.

You should now have a fair picture of what training is required, both to enable your staff to carry out their jobs more efficiently, and to prepare for the future in the light of foreseen changes.

3 *Training Plan.* With a total list of training needs before you, your next task is to draw up a plan of training action. This need not be a complicated document, but unless you draw up a written plan of how you are going to satisfy the needs you have identified, you are likely to find difficulty in covering the training systematically.

1 Decide on the length of time to be covered by your plan—usually a 12-month period.
2 Consider the necessary resources in terms of money and people, and budget for them.
3 Be realistic in deciding how much of the training is possible within the time span of the plan, bearing in mind your earlier decisions about priorities for training.
4 Set down the categories of staff, and numbers to be trained, and note the kinds of training planned for each.
5 Remember to incorporate induction training for all new staff.
6 Describe against each type of training planned how it will be carried out: for example, on-job courses, guided experience, and so on.
7 List where you plan each kind of training will be carried out.
8 Where it is appropriate, fix dates by which the training will be completed, specifying also how long it is expected to last: for instance, a 5-day course to be completed by 10 January.
9 Plan who is to be responsible for doing the training.

You will probably find in most cases that this plan can be drawn up on a single sheet of paper, ruled in appropriate columns. Allow for changes to be incorporated, for no plan can ever be totally accurate. If you keep it amended, you will always be able to look on it as an up-to-date picture of your progress.

4 *Training Programmes*. There are no set rules for preparing programmes to meet each sort of training for which you have planned. Indeed, if your establishment is relatively small, this step could well be incorporated as part of your plan. However, on balance you will probably find it easier to keep a set of programmes separately. Follow these guidelines:

1 Set out briefly the results you expect to be achieved for the training—in other words, try to answer the question, 'What will these trainees be able to do after training?'
2 Draw up a timetable of events, covering dates, times and locations of the training, as well as the duration of each part.
3 Specify what subjects are to be covered.
4 Determine how the training is to be carried out—in other words, consider the methods of learning to be used.
5 Identify, by name, those people who are to carry out the training.
6 Build into each programme the way in which its success can be assessed—by practical tests, projects, coaching, assessments etc.

Once you have reached this stage, all those taking part should be given copies of the programme, and time allowed for anyone giving the training to prepare for it.

5 *Doing the Training*. All the hard work is now about to be proven in the furnace of actual training. You have done your part as a manager and now it is in the hands of those to whom you have entrusted the carrying out of your plans. However, your support and encouragement are paramount. There will be snags and difficulties, and who is better equipped than you to iron them out? No practical suggestions are listed in this step because of the tremendous differences between the various kinds of training. However, those who are to implement the training should be well versed in instructional skills. Still, as far as you are concerned, you might consider looking at the training that is being undertaken and satisfying yourself on three counts:

1 That the trainees want to learn. Are they totally committed and being shown the relevance and worth of the training given?

2 That the learning is geared to the trainees, at their pace and within their grasp.
3 That the training is not being done in isolation, but is suitably welded into the reality of work life and is wholly relevant.

Finally, since memories are fickle, you will want to be sure that you have a record of what training has been completed. Whether or not you need these to sustain a claim for a grant from the training board, the value of records to you as a manager should be clear. If you have a staff record system, as outlined in Part I, you can record for each individual what training he has received. Whatever form your records take, keep them simple and easy to use, so that, like staff records, they can give you the sort of information you may need to manage the training function of your work more successfully.

6 *Reviewing Your Training*. The cycle is now about to be completed. You are now in a position to draw up your training account, and to answer the basic question, Was it worth it? Equally importantly, however, this step in the process of systematic training should pinpoint areas that need more attention in planning future training. Check on the following:

1 You laid out a training plan. Determine how much was actually carried out, and why other parts failed to materialize.
2 Try to measure as objectively as you can what training met with the greatest success and what the least. Above all, try to discover the reasons.
3 Check on the type and methods of training used. Do they need rethinking about or perhaps replacing?
4 See if, in carrying out this review, you can discover other training needs that were not originally identified, such as a lack of training skill in some of the staff to whom you entrusted the training of others.
5 Make sure you incorporate all the lessons learned during your review in future training plans and programmes.

As you will have noticed, this systematic approach to training covers a circle of activities, with each step dependent on its predecessor and leading back to the starting point—your policy for the training and development of staff. Staff will always be the most important asset in your business. They will join your unit with certain skills and knowledge, however basic in some cases; if you are to reap the full benefit of their capabilities, then you must help to develop them. This is all part of the training function: to ensure that staff are enabled to do their present work more efficiently but also, with the help of further education, allied to their training, to undertake other work as part of their career development.

Training is one the the most satisfying activities of a manager, and it can also be one of the most profitable ones too. Whether you reap the rewards or not, and whether the staff benefit as much as they should, depends on how thoroughly you are willing to enter into a systematic approach to your training.

CHECKLIST

1 As a measure of your good faith, have you issued a written statement of your training policy?
2 Have you methodically drawn up a list of your staff training needs, and sorted them out in order of priority?
3 Have you committed to paper a plan of how you intend to meet these training priorities?
4 Has each training event been covered by a programme describing how it will be carried out and what its objectives are?
5 Do you take a live interest in and fully support staff before and after they undergo training?
6 Do you keep a record of all training carried out?
7 What steps do you take to review any training completed with a view to building on it and improving it?
8 Do you take into account training for future requirements as well as to meet immediate needs?
9 Do you remain conscious of your own training needs and budget for them to be met?
10 Have you established a working relationship with your local Training Adviser from the Hotel and Catering Industry Training Board?

Part II Bibliography

Arbitration, Conciliation and Advisory Service, *Job Evaluation*, Guide No. 1 (1975).

Argyle, M. *The Psychology of Interpersonal Behaviour* (Penguin, 1967).

Argyris, C. *Integrating the Individual and the Organization* (New York: Wiley, 1964).

—— *Executive Leadership* (New York: Harper & Brothers, 1953).

Bass, B. M. and Vaughan, J. A. *Training in Industry: the Management of Learning* (Tavistock, 1968).

Belbin, R. M. *The Discovery Method in Training* (H.M.S.O., 1969).

Bindra, D. and Stewart, J. *Motivation* (Penguin, 1971).

Birchall, D. *Job Design* (Gower Press, 1976).

Blake, R. and Mouton, J. S. *The Managerial Grid* (Houston: Gulf Publishing Co., 1970).

British Institute of Management *Merit Rating – a Practical Guide* (B.I.M., 1954).

—— *The Cost of Labour Turnover* (Management Publications, 1959).

—— *Job Evaluation* (B.I.M., 1961).

Brown, J. A. C. *The Social Psychology of Industry* (Penguin, 1953).

Buckingham, G. L., Jeffrey, R. G. and Thorne, B. A. *Job Environment and Organizational Change* (Gower Press, 1976).

Cattell, R. C. *Personality* (New York: McGraw-Hill, 1950).

Collingridge, J. M. and Ritchie, M. *Personnel Management: Problems of the Smaller Firm* (I.P.M., 1970).

Cooper, R. *Job Motivation and Job Design* (I.P.M., 1974).

Dept of Employment *On the 'Quality of Working Life'* (H.M.S.O., 1972).

Drucker, P. F. *Managing for Results* (Heinemann, 1964).

Fayol, H. *General and Industrial Management* (Pitman, 1967).

Fraser, J. M. *Industrial Psychology* (Pergamon, 1965).

Gagne, R. M. *The Conditions of Learning* (Holt, Rinehart & Winston, 1970).

Gowers, Sir Earnest *The Complete Plain Words* (Penguin, 1962).

Hague, H. (ed.). *Human and Industrial Relations – a Working Handbook*, Vols 1–3 (London: Kluwer Harrap Handbooks, 1974).

Herzberg, F. *Work and the Nature of Man* (World Pub. Co. 1966).

——*The Motivation to Work* (New York: Wiley, 1959).

Hughes, C. L. *Goal-setting: Key to Individual and Organizational Effectiveness* (A.M.A., 1965).

Ivens, M. *The Practice of Industrial Communication* (Business Publications, 1963).

Kelly, T. *Personnel Records and Manpower Planning* (H.C.I.T.B., 1973).

Klein, J. *Working with Groups* (Hutchinson, 1961)

Knight, I. B. *Patterns of Labour Mobility in the Hotel and Catering Industry* (H.C.I.T.B., c. 1972).

Likert, R. *The Human Organization* (McGraw-Hill, 1967)
—— *New Patterns of Management* (McGraw-Hill, 1961).
Lupton, T. (ed.). *Payment Systems* (Penguin, 1972).
Lupton, T. and Gowler, D. *Wages and Salaries* (Penguin, 1974).
McGregor, D. *Leadership and Motivation* (M.I.T., 1966).
Maslow, A. H. *Motivation and Personality* (Harper & Row, 1970).
Paterson, T. T. *Job Evaluation* (Business Books, 1972).
Pocock, P. (ed.). *Personnel Management Handbook* (Mercury House Business Publications, 1973).
Sigband, N. B. *Communication for Management* (Scott, Foresman & Co., 1969).
Singer, E. J. *Effective Management Coaching* (I.P.M., 1974).
Sprott, W. J. H. *Human Groups* (Penguin, 1958).
Stewart, R. *The Reality of Management* (Pan, 1964).
Taylor, L. K. *Not for Bread Alone – An Appreciation of Job Enrichment* (Business Books, 1972).
Thakur, M. and Gill, G. *Job Evaluation in Practice* (I.P.M., 1976).
Townsend, R. *Up The Organization* (Hodder and Stoughton, 1971).

Appendix 11 Staff Turnover Chart

STAFF SHEET, 1 JULY 1976

Name	*Sex*	*Job*	*F.T./P.T.*	*Department*	*Date Started*	*Date Left*	*Period of stay*
MALLOY	F	Chambermaid	F.T.	Housekeeping	12.6.74		
BROWN	M	Porter	F.T.	Kitchen	1.2.75	1.6.75	4 months
WHITE, A.	F	Waitress	F.T.	Service	11.1.75		
WHITE, P	F	Chambermaid	P.T.	Housekeeping	21.4.75		
CONROY	M	Chef	F.T.	Kitchen	21.9.65		
WHITMARSH	M	Porter	P.T.	Front of house	27.6.75	30.6.75	3 days
JONES, K.	F	Receptionist	F.T.	Front of house	2.2.74		

Appendix 12 Constructing a Survival Curve

Suppose in the year 1976 the York Hotel has had the occasion to recruit a total of 50 staff, of whom 30 left within the first three months; this can be charted as follows:

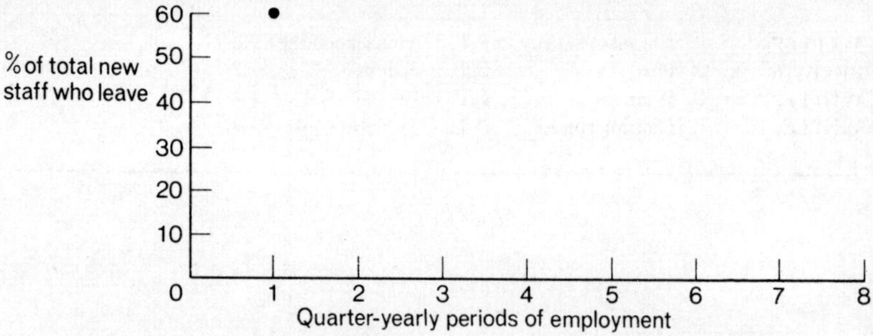

Out of the remaining 20, suppose a further 5 leave before they have been with the hotel 6 months; this can be added to the chart as follows:

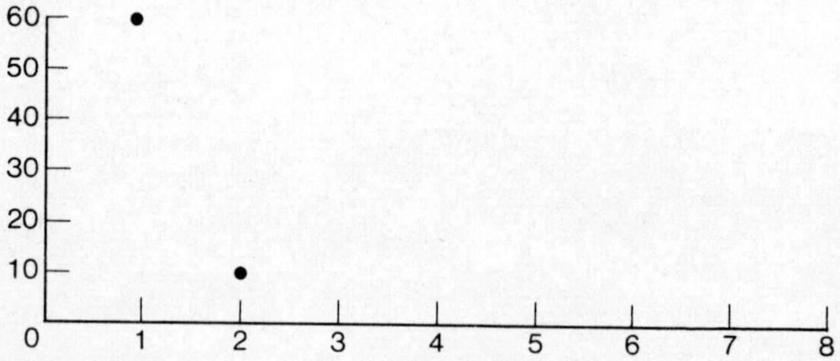

This check on the original entry of 50 is maintained quarterly over 2 years so that it eventually looks like this:

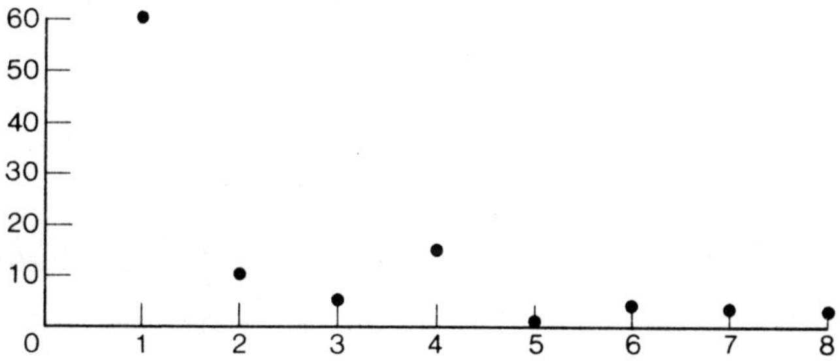

If you now join up these points, you will find that you end up with a curve:

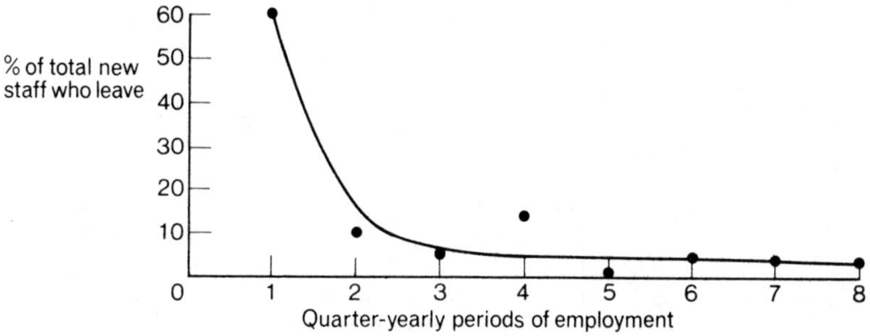

Appendix 13 Length of Service Charts

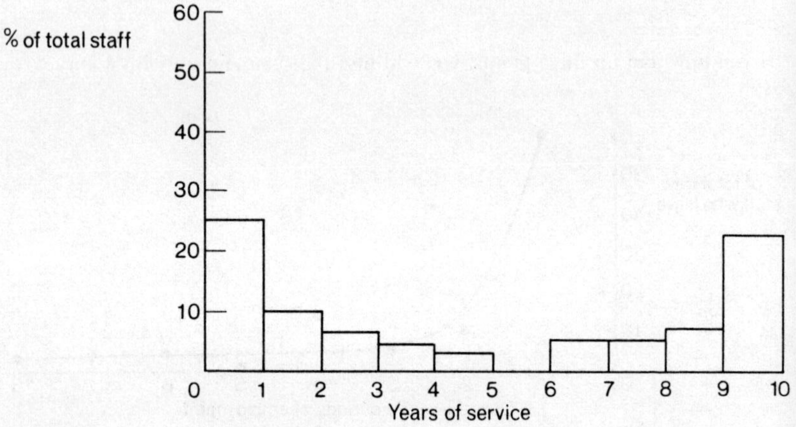

This chart can become even more significant if you show alongside it a similar bar chart covering staff in their first year of employment.

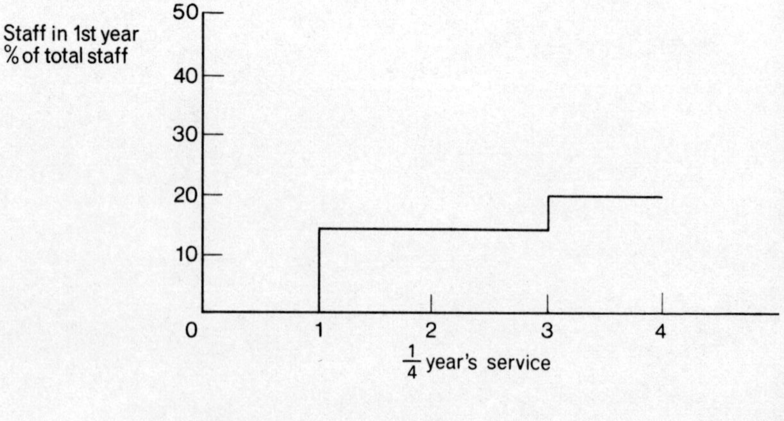

Appendix 14 Wages Councils

Of the forty-five Wages Councils in operation, the following three deal specifically with the hotel and catering industry:

1 Licensed Non-Residential Establishment Wages Council.
2 Licensed Residential Establishment and Licensed Restaurant Wages Council.
A variation order in 1965 excluded from the scope of this Council all workers employed in hotels and refreshment rooms by the British Railways Board or by British Transport Hotels Ltd.
3 Unlicensed Place of Refreshment Wages Council.

A distinctive feature of all legislation for the control of wages and working conditions is that the wage-fixing authority in all cases includes representatives of the employers and workers in the trade concerned.

The following are the current Wages Regulation Orders; you should have a copy of the one(s) which applies to your business:

1 Licensed Non-Residential Establishment (Bar Staff) Wages Order 1978 L.N.R. (131).
2 Licensed Non-Residential Establishment (Club Stewards) Wages Order 1979 L.N.R. (132).
3 Licensed Residential Establishment and Licensed Restaurant Wages Regulation Order 1979 (S.1 1975 No. 1571). L.R. 59.
4 Unlicensed Place of Refreshment Wages Order 1979 UPR 56.

The address of the Wages Councils is 12 St James's Square, London SW1T 4JB (Tel 01–214 6000).

Wages Inspectorate

The function of the wages inspectorate is the enforcement of the payment of wages in compliance with Orders under the Wages Council Act. The inspectors make routine checks on employers, and investigate complaints by employees that the statutory minimum rates are not being paid. In answer to a question in the House of Commons on 16 July 1975 the Secretary of State for Employment gave figures which indicated that many firms were found on routine inspection and on complaint to be paying below the statutory minimum rate. Make sure you are not one of them. Call on your local wages inspector to advise you; he is based in major offices of the Department of Employment. If you have difficulty, you can contact the Chief Wages Inspector at the Department of Employment, Steel House, 11 Tothill Street, London SW1H 9BR.

Appendix 15 Wages Policy Statement

We want everyone who works for us to have a copy of this statement. If you do not understand any part of it, you should ask for guidance from your immediate superior, and if you feel that any part of this policy is not operating, then you can raise it through the Staff Consultative Committee.

AIMS

The aims of this policy are:

1 To recognize the value of each job in relation to all others throughout the hotel.
2 To provide stability in earnings.
3 To allow for individuals to reach their full earning potential.
4 To ensure that all staff share in the hotel's prosperity through increased efficiency.

JOB EVALUATION

The basis of a fair wage structure is job evaluation. This is carried out by a joint management/staff team, and the grading system that results from their efforts will be reviewed from time to time.

WAGE STRUCTURE

In designing the wage structure the company aims to implement the belief that our labour costs are primarily an investment in staff to achieve both our long- and short-term objectives as a business. Attainment of these objectives will provide security of employment for all our staff.

WAGE RATES

No one will ever be paid less than the minimum required under the current Licensed Residential Wages Order. Our wage rates will be established through a grading system, based on job evaluation, and will be founded on the principle 'equal pay for work of equal value'. No discrimination will be made on grounds of sex, race, or creed. The only difference to be allowed for within grades is on a basis of merit. We do not plan to pay the highest rate in the Wondertown area but rather to place an emphasis on pleasant working conditions, job security and an atmosphere in which staff can attain their full potential. Nevertheless we aim to be in the top 10 per cent in this district as far as total earnings are concerned, covering all staff benefits.

NUMBER OF GRADES

The number of wage grades will not exceed 5 so that the differences between them are of a sufficiently high level to reward real differences in responsibilities and skills.

MERIT AWARDS

We do not believe that staff give of their best if their earnings fluctuate week by week. The wage rates are designed, therefore, to provide a regular weekly income without reference to any service gratuities. However, each member of staff will be appraised annually, and we will reward effort and worth with a system of merit awards.

MINIMUM EARNINGS

No member of staff will be paid less than £28 for a 40-hour week. This means that in order to maintain 'a living wage' for lower-paid staff it may not always be possible to maintain established differentials between pay reviews.

PROMOTION

We believe that as far as possible promotion should come from within our own hotel. When this happens, the person will then become eligible for the new grade and will be paid immediately at the new rate.

COST OF LIVING

We think it is right that our staff's purchasing power should be maintained in the same way as our shareholders' investments earn a fair return. We are, therefore, in favour of allowing 'cost of living' increases to all staff on an annual basis, to take place six months before general salary reviews are carried out.

WAGE/SALARY REVIEWS

A review of all wages and salaries will be carried out on 1 April each year.

Appendix 16 Factor Assessment Sheet

JOB TITLE .... DEPARTMENT ....

DATE ....

1 DESCRIPTION OF DUTIES
(Detail the type of supervision received or exercised, summarize the basic and distinguishing characteristics of the job and show general level of responsibility.)

2 TYPICAL DUTIES
(Give a detailed outline of the main duties in the job, considering what is done and how it is done, and list in order of importance. Give an indication of whether the work is carried out regularly or intermittently.)

FACTORS

A EXPERIENCE, KNOWLEDGE AND SKILL
(These will cover the minimum requirements in these areas that are essential for starting the job and performing the work.)

1 Previous experience required.
2 Specialized or technical education needed *(citing specific qualifications or recognized level of attainment)*.
3 Manual or physical skills needed.
4 Physical effort required *(such as continuous standing or lifting)*.

B WORK COMPLEXITIES
(This covers the extent and frequency of judgements in making and carrying out decisions, versatility and ingenuity of mind required, how serious would be errors and the degree of possibility of error.)

1 Complexity and difficulty of work *(degree of originality, judgement and developmental work involved)*.
2 Seriousness of errors *(types possible, consequences in terms of expense, reworking or loss of goodwill)*.

C WORKING CONDITIONS
(This factor is intended to cover hazards in the job, and conditions relating to location or physical conditions under which the job has to be done and over which the member of staff has no control.)

1 Hazards *(types, risk and frequency)*.
2 Adverse working conditions *(anything disagreeable, uncomfortable)*.

D CONTACTS

(Under this heading come all inside and outside contacts required of the staff. Outside contacts relate to customers, the general public and other companies—indicating the extent of the responsibility in the job for extending service to outside contacts or obtaining services from them. Internal contacts are those necessary in the job for receiving assistance and collaboration with other staff in order to complete work or achieve time schedules.)

1 Contacts with customers, general public or other companies *(level, type, difficulty and importance)*.
2 Contacts with other departments *(type, volume, importance and difficulty)*.

E RESPONSIBILITIES

(This covers everything from company goods to looking after other staff.)

1 For the safety of others *(staff and general public)*.
2 For company funds or property *(custody of, or personal accountability for, cash/goods, and amounts)*.
3 For confidential information *(nature, and extent of discretion for revealing the information)*.
4 For performance of work without immediate supervision *(who assigns the work, how frequently checked)*.
5 For the supervision of others *(number and kind of jobs supervised; amount of selection, direction, instruction and training of subordinates; amount by which the work of others has to be planned, allotted and supervised; and the percentage of time spent on work similar to that of subordinates)*.

Appendix 17 Appraisal Forms

A.F.1 APPRAISAL FORM FOR DEPARTMENTAL HEADS

(This indicates layout only and does not attempt to show spacing)

JOB APPRAISAL

NAME .... APPRAISER ....
JOB TITLE ....
DEPARTMENT ....

A PERFORMANCE

	KEY TASKS	STANDARD	ACHIEVED	NOT ACHIEVED	COMMENTS
1	*To increase total sales*	*15 per cent on 75/76 figures*			This space should be used for recording reasons why standards have not been met in any instance, for strengths to be highlighted and weaknesses to be noted.
2	*To reduce L.T.O. among staff*	*Maximum of 40 per cent*			
3	*To implement the new staffing structure agreed*	*By 30 November*			
4	*To train all staff in social skills*	*By 30 November with a 50 per cent reduction in complaints on previous year*			
5					
6					

Summary of Attainments

1 Main strengths:
2 Areas for improvement:
3 Action required to improve job performance: *(include here coaching, on-job, or off-job training, projects, further experience etc.)*

B POTENTIAL AND PROMOTABILITY

1 What is your estimate of his/her potential? *(consider here abilities, activities, career prospects etc.)*
3 Has he/she the potential to be promoted in present type of work?
If so, how soon?
3 Could he/she be suitable for a more senior position elsewhere?

C DEVELOPMENT

1 What training is required to help him/her to develop more fully in his/her present job?
2 What training and development are recommended to equip him/her to achieve good career prospects?

RECOMMENDED PRIORITY ACTION

1
2
3

Signature of Appraiser .... Date ....
Signature of Appraisee .... Date ....

Comments by Appraisee

A.F.2 APPRAISAL FORM FOR STAFF

JOB APPRAISAL

NAME .... APPRAISER ....

JOB TITLE ....
DEPARTMENT ....

A PERFORMANCE

AREA	COMMENTS
1 Attitude to job	(This space should be used to describe your assessment of each heading and to highlight strong points and areas for improvement)
2 Basic skills	
3 Knowledge of work	
4 Appearance	
5 Interest in work	
6	
7	

B POTENTIAL/PROMOTABILITY

1 What is your assessment of his/her potential for greater responsibility and development.
2 What signs are there that he/she is capable/incapable of being promoted at present?

C DEVELOPMENT

1 List the training required to improve present job performance.
2 Describe how he/she can be helped to develop to allow for a fuller career.

RECOMMENDED PRIORITY ACTION

1
2
3

Signature of Appraiser.............................. Date..
Signature of Appraisee .... Date..
Comments by Appraisee

Appendix 10 Résumé of Catering Courses and Qualifications

Title of course	*Anticipated career level*	*Nature and duration of course*	*Entry requirements*	*Broad content*
CITY AND GUILDS OF LONDON INSTITUTE				
CGLI 705 General catering course	Introductory	One-year full-time	College selection	Food production and service, accommodation services, applied science, business and general studies
CGLI 706/1 Basic cookery for the catering industry	Craft	One-year full-time, two years part-time	College selection	Basic cookery, theory and practice, related and general studies
CGLI 706/2 Cookery for the catering industry	Craft	One year full-time, two years part-time	Normally 705, 706/1	Cookery theory and practice, related and general subjects
CGLI 706/3	Craft		Normally 706/2	Advanced cookery theory and practice, related studies and elements of supervision
Kitchen and larder		Two years part-time		
Pastry 1 & 2		Each one year part-time		
CGLI 707/1 Food service certificate	Craft	8/12 weeks full-time;* part-time equivalent	College selection	Introduction to food service, related and general studies

Title of course	Anticipated career level	Nature and duration of course	Entry requirements	Broad content
CGLI 707/2 Advanced serving techniques	Craft	4/6 weeks full-time;* part-time equivalent	Normally 707/1	Advanced food service, social skills, elements of supervision and general studies
CGLI 707/3 Alcoholic beverage service	Craft	4/6 weeks full-time;* part-time equivalent	Normally 707/1	Service of alcoholic beverages, elements of supervision, related and general subjects
CGLI 708 Housekeeping certificate	Craft	8/12 weeks full-time;* part-time equivalent	College selection	Housekeeping, elements of supervision, related and general subjects
CGLI 709 Hotel reception certificate	Craft	One year full-time, 30 weeks block release	College selection	Hotel reception, business practice, book-keeping, calculations, legal aspects and general subjects
CGLI 710 Hotel uniformed staff certificate	Craft	Four terms part-time	College selection	Hotel organization, operational procedures, legal aspects, social skills and salesmanship (Introduction Part II)

* Often included in full-time courses

NATIONAL EXAMINING BOARD FOR SUPERVISORY STUDIES

Title of course	Anticipated career level	Nature and duration of course	Entry requirements	Broad content
Certificate in supervisory studies	Supervisory	One year part-time	College selection over 21	Elements of supervision, economic and financial aspects, personnel aspects, work organization and control

	career level	duration of course	requirements	
JOINT COMMITTEE FOR NATIONAL DIPLOMAS IN HOTEL, CATERING AND INSTITUTIONAL MANAGEMENT				
O.N.D. in hotel and catering operations	Supervisory	Two years full-time	4 G.C.E. 'O' Level passes	Food and beverage preparation and service, accommodation operations, applied science, business studies, English and social studies
O.N.D. in institutional housekeeping and catering	Supervisory	Two years full-time	4 G.C.E. passes at 'O' level	Catering, food preparation and service,, institutional housekeeping, applied science, business studies, English and social studies
O.N.D. in hotel, catering and institutional operations	Supervisory	Two years full-time	4 G.C.E. passes at 'O' level	Embraces subjects in the two courses above
H.N.D. in hotel and catering administration	Management	Three years sandwich	5 G.C.E. passes with 1 at 'A' level or appropriate O.N.D.	Food and beverage operations, accommodation operations, planning and maintenance of premises, accounting, economics, law, business administration, applied science and general studies
H.N.D. in institutional management	Management	Three years sandwich	5 G.C.E. passes with one at 'A' level or appropriate O.N.D.	Food services, house services, applied science, business studies, management studies and general studies
H.N.D. in hotel, catering and institutional management	Management	Three years sandwich		

Title of course	*Anticipated career level*	*Nature and duration of course*	*Entry requirements*	*Broad content*
HOTEL, CATERING AND INSTITUTIONAL MANAGEMENT ASSOCIATION				
H.C.I.M.A. Part A	Management	Two years part-time	4 G.C.E. 'O' level passes	Food studies, liquor studies, accommodation studies
H.C.I.M.A. Part B	Management	Two years sandwich part-time, one year full-time	H.C.I.M.A. Part A	Foundation studies, major studies elective studies
DEGREE LEVEL				
B.A. in hotel and catering management, University of Strathclyde	Management	Three years full-time	5 approved G.C.E. subjects with 2 at 'A' level, or 4 approved G.C.E. subjects with 3 at 'A' level	Hotel operations, catering, catering techonology, tourism, planning and development, service planning, accounting, administration, business economics, industrial administration and relations, operational research, languages, economic history, geography, law, marketing

Title of course	*Anticipated career level*	*Nature and duration of course*	*Entry requirements*	*Broad content*
B.Sc. in hotel and catering administration	Management	Four years sandwich	As for Strathclyde	Accounting, administration, economics, law, food and beverages, food preparation, food science, catering operations, business resources management, catering administration, food technology, hotel administration, modern languages, nutrition, environmental studies
B.Sc. in catering studies, Huddersfield Polytechnic	Management	Four years sandwich	5 G.C.E. passes with 2 at 'A' level, incl. maths and chemistry	Catering technology, nutrition, biological chemistry, food chemistry, behavioural studies, statistics, computer science
B.Sc. in catering systems, Sheffield Polytechnic	Management	Four years sandwich	5 G.C.E. passes with 2 at 'A' level incl. maths and a science subject	Food science, food preparation, quantitive methods, economics, psychology, operations analysis, food formulation catering technology, work design, accounting

This table appeared in *HCIMA Review* No. 2. Permission to reproduce it here is gratefully acknowledged.

Appendix 19 Useful Addresses for Trainers

BRITISH ASSOCIATION FOR COMMERCIAL AND INDUSTRIAL EDUCATION (B.A.C.I.E.)
16 Park Crescent, London W1N 4AP (01-636 5351)

BRITISH HOTELS, RESTAURANTS AND CATERERS ASSOCIATION (B.H.R.C.A.)
13 Cork Street, London W1X 2BH (01-499 6641)

BRITISH INSTITUTE OF MANAGEMENT
Management House, Parker Street, London WC2B 5PT (01-405 3456)

BRITISH TOURIST AUTHORITY
Queen's House, 64 St James's Street, London SW1A 1NF (01-629 9191)

CENTRAL OFFICE OF INFORMATION
Hercules Road, London SE1 7DU (01-928 2345)

CITY AND GUILDS OF LONDON INSTITUTE
46 Britannia Street, London WC1 X9RG (01-278 2468)

DIRECTORY OF COURSES
30 High Street, Kingston-on-Thames, Surrey (01-549 2256)

HOTEL AND CATERING INDUSTRY TRAINING BOARD (see map)
Head Office: P.O. Box 18, Ramsey House, Central Square, Wembley, Middx HA9 7AP (01-902 8865)
Greater London: As for head office
South and East Region: 170 High Street, Lewes, Sussex (07 916 77374)
North East Region: Stonebow House, Stonebow, York YO1 1·2NQ (0904 26134)
North West Region: The Graftons, Stamford New Road, Altrincham, Cheshire (061-928 2761/2)
Scottish Region: 10 Magdala Crescent, Edinburgh EH12 5BE (031-337 2339)
West and Wales Region: 3rd Floor, Prudential Buildings, Wine St, Bristol BS1 12PH (0702-24074)

HOTEL AND CATERING PERSONNEL AND TRAINING ASSOCIATION
c/o Butlins Ltd., 439/441 Oxford Street, London W1 (01-493 9636)

HOTEL AND CATERING PERSONNEL MANAGERS ASSOCIATION
Centre House, 57 Russell Square, London WC1 (01-637 1661)

HOTEL AND CATERING TRAINING ASSOCIATION
Strand Hotels Ltd., 12 Sherwood Street, London W1 (01-734 6755)

HOTEL, CATERING AND INSTITUTIONAL MANAGEMENT ASSOCIATION
191 Trinity Road, London SW17 7HN (01-672 4251)

HOTELS AND CATERING E.D.C.
Millbank Tower, Millbank, London SW1P 4QX (01-834 3811)

INDUSTRIAL SOCIETY
48 Bryanston Square, London W1H 8AH (01-262 2401)

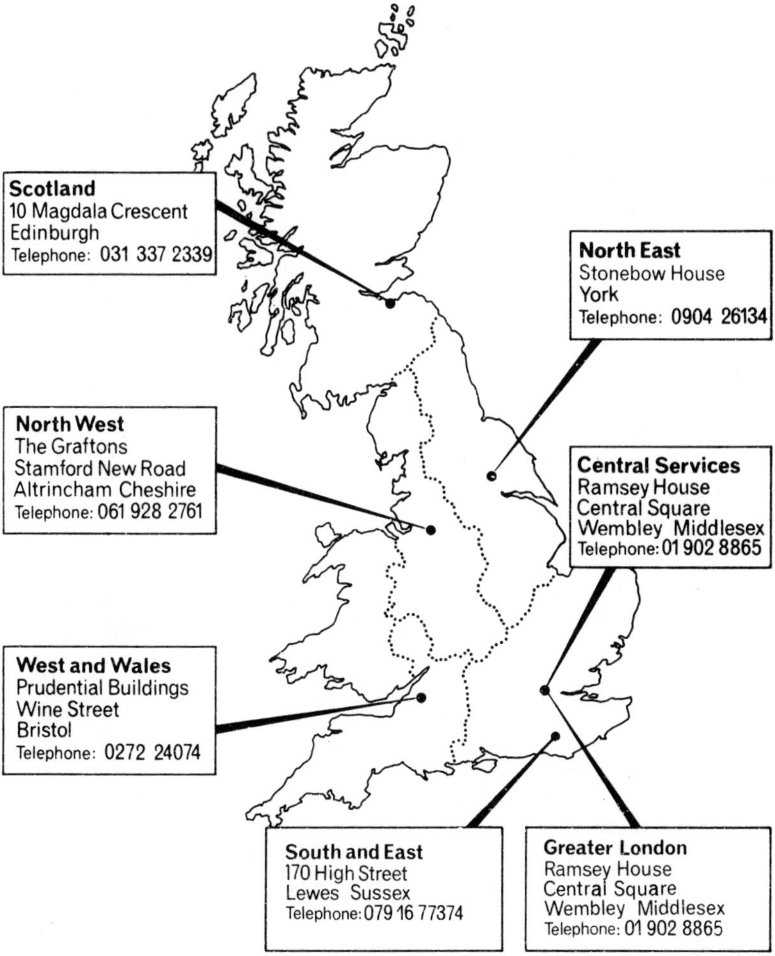

Hotel and Catering Industry Training Board

INSTITUTE OF PERSONNEL MANAGEMENT
Central House, Upper Woburn Place, London WC1H 00HX (01-387 2844)

INDUSTRIAL TRAINING SERVICE
53 Victoria Street, London SW1 (01-222 5421)

MANAGEMENT COURSES INDEX
Haymarket Publishing Ltd., Gillow House, 5 Winsley St, London W1A 2HG (01-636-3600)

NATIONAL TRADE DEVELOPMENT ASSOCIATION (N.T.D.A.)
42 Portman Square, London W1 (01-486 4831)

WINE AND SPIRIT EDUCATION TRUST LTD
Kennet House, Kennet Wharf Lane, London EC4V 3AJ (01-236 3551)

PART III

CARING FOR YOUR STAFF

CHAPTER TWELVE

Health and Safety

In the United Kingdom on any normal working day an average of three workers will die and about 3,000 will be seriously enough injured to lose at least three days' work. In fact millions are injured every year at work. By any standards this is quite appalling, and what makes it worse is that the majority of those accidents need never have taken place. There has always been an obligation on employers to take care of their employees' safety at work under common law, but over the years a body of specific statute law has emerged. Here are examples of such laws:

Young Persons (Employment) Act 1938
Shops Act 1950
Food and Drugs Act 1955
Occupiers Liability Act 1957
Factories Act 1961
Employers Liability (Defective Equipment) Act 1961
Offices, Shops and Railway Premises Act 1963
National Insurance (Industrial Injuries) Act 1965
Employers Liability (Compulsory Insurance) Act 1969
Food Hygiene Regulations 1970
Fire Precautions Act 1971
Employment Medical Advisory Service Act 1972
Health and Safety at Work etc. Act 1974

Clearly it must be outside the scope of this manual to look in any detail at all these Acts and their implications. What must concern you, rather, is having sufficient knowledge of the legislation and some practical guidelines to follow so as to create in your business a climate where everyone's safety is of paramount concern—where as an employer you can demonstrate that, to the best of your ability, you have established a set of working conditions conducive to the health, safety and well-being of your staff.

This Part will be kept deliberately brief, since so much has been written recently on the subject of staff health and safety. To support it, a comprehensive Bibliography (p. 198) is attached; this should enable you to read about particular aspects of the subject in greater depth, and show you where you will find help and advice, often freely available.

12.1 OUTLINE OF LEGISLATION

In May 1970 the Secretary of State set up a committee of enquiry under Lord Robens to review the safety structure of industry throughout the United Kingdom, with a view to making recommendations for changes required in legislation to help reduce the number killed and injured at work. The *Robens Report* was published in 1972 and briefly concluded that all employers needed to take specific action to improve the existing situation, through consultation with their employees; this, it was added, demanded new legislation to bring to fruition.

The Health and Safety at Work, etc. Act 1974 (H.S.A.W.)

This Act resulted from the Robens recommendations. It attempts to provide one comprehensive piece of legislation dealing with the health, safety and welfare of all staff. You have already seen that a whole host of laws exist on the subject of safety, and this Act may eventually replace all the fragmented legislation already in being. You must note, however, that the H.S.A.W. Act does not yet supersede any of the earlier legislation.

The H.S.A.W. Act is an 'enabling' Act—that is, it is a broad generalized piece of legislation, which does not spell out every detail. Instead, it authorizes the Secretary of State for Employment, through the new Health and Safety Commission, to draw up detailed regulations and codes of practice on specific health and safety matters.

It is laid out as follows:

Section 1 tells you the general purpose of the whole Act.

Section 2 lists some general duties of employers to ensure the safety, health and welfare of their employees at work, to consult them on joint action to improve safety standards, to establish safety committees in certain circumstances, and to prepare a written statement of their safety policy.

Section 3 places a general duty on you to make sure that none of your activities endanger anyone, including the general public.

Section 4 deals with your duty to see that your premises, plant and machinery do not endanger those who use them.
Section 5 provides for the need to see that no harmful substances, or smells, are emitted into the atmosphere.
Section 6 covers the duties of those who supply equipment or articles used at work.
Section 7 prescribes a responsibility for all staff to take care of their own safety and health.
Section 8 places a duty on everyone at work not to misuse anything provided for the safety of those at work.
Section 9 prevents you from charging staff for equipment or anything done in their safety interests at work under statutory requirement.

Since 1 April 1975, when the H.S.A.W. Act became effective, you are subject to the following legal obligations:

1 To ensure, as far as practicable, the health, safety and welfare of all your staff. To understand the full significance of this general obligation you must appreciate that (a) to fail to comply now renders you liable to a *criminal* conviction, and prosecution even if no accident takes place; and (b) the Act covers 'welfare', whatever its meaning, for the term is not defined.
2 To provide and maintain plant and systems of work which are safe and without risk to health; this obligation covers not only tools and machinery but also such things as safety equipment and clothing.
3 To make arrangements for the safety in use, handling, storage and transport of articles and substances—solid, liquid, or in the form of gas or vapour.
4 To provide such information, instruction, training and supervision as is required to ensure the health and safety of all staff.
5 To maintain your premises in a safe and healthy condition; this covers entrances and exits, and also 'premises' in the widest sense, so as to cover even your vehicles.
6 To provide a safe and healthy working environment and adequate facilities and arrangements for staff welfare.

The H.S.A.W. Act requires in almost every case that an employer prepares a written statement of his general policy covering the health and safety at work of all staff, and the organization and arrangements in force for carrying out that policy. The whole purpose of this statement is to let staff see that you have planned to keep at bay all unavoidable illnesses and accidents at work. You need not supply each member of staff with a copy of this statement, but they must have it brought to their notice. You can simply put it up on a staff noticeboard or put a note in the wage-packet telling them where they can see a copy of it.

The Health and Safety Commission has issued guidelines as to what the policy statement should contain (see Bibliography, p. 198, for details). Briefly it should contain the following:

1 A broad general statement of your intention, signed by the managing director, or equivalent, which names a senior executive responsible for health and safety matters, and emphasizes that your statement will be subject to regular review (this is legally required).
2 An explanation of your organization for health and safety matters, showing the role of line managers, specialists (if any), safety representatives and committees (if they exist) and individuals, and also the resources being set aside for this subject area.
3 A description of the main arrangements for implementing the policy, a list of the main hazards and the rules and regulations to be observed, and a note of the procedures for accident reporting.

The Act does not require you to have safety representatives, but an independent trade union, recognized by you, has a legal right to appoint safety representatives from among your staff. It will then be your legal duty to consult these representatives who can also legally demand that you establish a safety committee to keep all measures under review.

If you have no safety representatives at the moment, nor a safety committee, you are breaking no law. But why wait until the law forces you to do so? Common sense would seem to dictate that the appointment of such helpers in this field must be to everyone's benefit, not least your own.

The H.S.A.W. Act provides considerable power for the inspectorate in the hope of reducing the death and injury caused by accidents at work. Punishment is, of course, the last resort, but you must know what is the penalty for failing to carry out your legal obligations.

The penalties can of course fall on the company, but you must also note that every person in an executive role is liable to be punished for any offence under this Act committed with his *consent* or *connivance*, or attributable to his *neglect*. To *consent* means to agree to the commission of the offence, whereas to *connive* not merely calls for positive approval but some sort of active role.

Neglect covers a very wide range. You are negligent in your duties if you are guilty of some act or omission that has led, directly or indirectly, to the commission of an offence. If there was anything you should have done to ensure the Act was observed, and failed to do so, then the finger of accusation may be pointed at you.

How all this will work out in practice remains to be seen as case law is built up. Do not put yourself in danger of being a test case for the hotel and catering industry.

Other Legislation Affecting Health and Safety of Staff

You will remember that, although the H.S.A.W. Act is intended as an umbrella act that will eventually incorporate all the legal requirements in this field, it does not at the moment supersede the already existing statutes, many of which have an application in our industry. Here are thumbnail sketches of some of these Acts as they apply to hotel and catering.

1 *National Insurance (Industrial Injuries) Act 1965 (as amended by the Social Security Act 1975)*. This covers all staff employed, and provides benefit for anyone who suffers personal injury, disease or death in the course of employment. If you are proved to have been negligent and injuries result, staff can claim damages from you within three years.

2 *Factories Act 1961.* Among much else this Act requires the guarding of machinery, the supply of lighting and heating to certain standards, and the provision of toilet and washing facilities, and covers many other general aspects of safety and health.

3 *Offices, Shops and Railway Premises Act 1963.* This Act applies to much of the catering industry, since it covers any premises open to members of the public for the sale of food or drink for immediate consumption. Among the more important provisions for the health and safety of staff are these:

   1 The premises, furniture and fittings must be kept clean:

floors and steps must be washed weekly or, if that is effective, swept only.

2 There must be no overcrowding—a minimum of 40 sq. ft must be allowed per person.

3 The temperature must be reasonable, and a thermometer must be hung up on each floor so that staff can check it.

4 Ventilation must be provided to circulate supplies of fresh air.

5 Lighting must be effective, and therefore all windows must be kept clean and free from obstruction.

6 Sanitary provisions must be made, and lavatories kept clean, maintained, and provided with suitable lighting and ventilation.

7 Staff must have ready access to washing facilities, including a supply of hot and cold running water, plus soap and clean towels or other means of drying.

8 Drinking water must be made available for all staff.

9 Staff must be given suitable accommodation for hanging up clothes that are not worn at work.

10 Seating facilities must be provided for those staff who can use them without interfering with their work. This also means the provision of footstools for those who are normally employed on sedentary work, if they ask for them. Have you any short-legged receptionists?

11 All floors, stairs, steps and passages must be maintained and kept free of obstruction, and hand-rails provided for any staircase.

12 All dangerous machinery must be properly fenced, and staff who use items like bacon-slicers or dough-mixers must be fully instructed in the dangers and the safety precautions to be observed. Moreover staff below the age of 18 years are not allowed to clean such machinery if this exposes them to risk of injury from a working part of that machine.

13 A first-aid box or cupboard carrying the name of the person in charge of the box must be provided. A trained first-aider is only required if there are at least 150 employees.

14 If an accident causes death, or absence from work for more than 3 days, the local authorities must be notified.

Failure to comply with any regulation under this Act renders you liable to a fine of up to £60, plus a further £15 for each day on which the offence continues, after conviction.

4 *Employers Liability (Defective Equipment) Act 1961.* Should any of your staff suffer injury from a defect in any equipment supplied by you as employer, you are deemed in law to have been 'negligent' and you can be sued for compensation. Having paid it, however, you can in turn sue the supplier or manufacturer of the defective equipment.

5 *Employers Liability (Compulsory Insurance) Act 1969.* All sensible employers have, of course, taken out insurance against liability in respect of personal injury, disease or death of staff sustained in the course of their work. However, since the implementation of this Act in 1972, you no longer have any choice about it. You must carry a minimum insurance cover of £2 million for any one accident, and to make sure you do so, you must also display your certificate on the premises. Any failure on your part to take out this insurance can bring a fine of up to £500, and up to £200 for failing to display the certificate.

6 *Occupiers Liability Act 1957.* This Act lays a responsibility on you to take care of all visitors to your establishment, from the postman to your guests, from your maiden aunt to the children of your staff. If you allow children entry, then you must take even more care for their safety than for adults'. Failure to take such care could result in your having to compensate any sufferer.

You have looked at but a skeleton of the legal side of your responsibilities for the health and safety of your staff. Look out for rapid changes—there will be many arising out of case law. Codes of practice are being produced, and the Secretary of State will make many regulations; the hotel and catering industry will be no exception.

The new laws and regulations are designed to cut down on accidents and deaths at work, but they also impose a heavy burden on all who employ staff in any capacity. You will not be liable now for damages only, but may also incur fines or even imprisonment. However, as a manager interested in retaining healthy staff in a safe environment, your concern will primarily be with constructive advice and help rather than a decalogue of forbidden actions.

12.2 A PRACTICAL APPROACH

No matter how small your establishment may be you cannot carry the burden for your staff health and safety singlehanded. Indeed, as you will have noticed earlier, in law everyone from the chief executive to the lowliest worker in any company or business has a personal responsibility in one form or another for safety. Surely this then points the way to a practical start to becoming the establishment with the best health and safety standards—get everyone interested.

Why not, as suggested by the H.S.A.W. Act (though not a legal requirement yet everywhere) begin by talking the whole thing over with your staff? Ideally you could aim to have a specific person assigned the role of safety representative for each department, and they could either be elected or appointed. Then you have the nucleus of a safety committee for the whole establishment. Clearly you must make sure that all grades of staff are represented and, above all, that there is the highest management commitment and interest shown. Without this the whole structure will be impotent.

Whatever safety organization is set up, allow it time to meet on a regular basis, perhaps under your chairmanship. You might consider it worth while to arrange that meetings of the committee are organized in such a way that one week, say, they meet to discuss specific safety measures, training and development ideas and to see a safety film, and the next they undertake a safety inspection of the whole establishment.

This last idea could be considered by some staff as unacceptable prying, if it is not carefully arranged and agreed by all. However, you could take all the steam out of any suspicion if you were to let everyone know that this inspection, apart from its obvious and declared purpose of improving the health and safety of all staff in the establishment, is being carried out as part of a competition to find the safest section or department. The safety committee should agree on a list of points to be checked in every department, from good housekeeping to safety-guards on slicing machines, from freedom of passages to unsafe actions on the part of staff, and so on. An agreed list of about twenty items could be drawn up to cover essentials; a system of handicapping could be instituted so that the inspection works out fairly wherever it is carried out. If this idea appeals to you and seems feasible in your business, then the following practical matters may help you set up this sort of competition:

1 Make sure all staff are fully briefed on the nature and purpose of the competition.
2 After the safety inspection has been completed in each

department, and the points allocated on the checklist, discuss it and argue about it there and then with the head of the department concerned.

3 Tally up the points scored quarterly and announce the winning department.

4 Award some sort of safety trophy to be held in the winning department for the next quarter.

5 At the end of the year make a final presentation to the department with the highest score for the four quarters, and perhaps reward them with, say, a special dinner.

Such a competition may not be possible or desirable in all hotels or catering outlets. Either in combination with such a competitive approach, or as a distinct activity, you may well consider it worth while to institute a system of hazard-spotting. This can take the form of a regular check by, say, the head of each department. If this approach is adopted, it should be made a separate duty of the person concerned to carry out this check at stated intervals, using an agreed checklist, and the results of the check to be given to you or the safety committee, if there is one, for consideration and any necessary management action. The following guidelines may be useful.

1 Discuss the idea of hazard-spotting with each head of department.

2 Conjointly, draw up an agreed checklist (see Appendix 20, p. 200).

3 Rectify any defects or omissions that may be reported upon as soon as practicable.

Accidents

Unfortunately in even the best regulated establishments, where safety-consciousness is of a high order, accidents will still occur. However, they can be turned to benefit if you have a system that allows for the recording and analysis of all accidents, however small, that take place in your establishment.

There is a legal obligation under the National Insurance (Industrial Injuries) (Claims and Payments) Regulations 1964 for every employer of ten or more staff to keep an accident book. Indeed this applies, however few your employees, in any premises subject to the Factories Act 1961.

In addition, common sense dictates that the first essential step in any programme to reduce accidents is to collect comprehensive information, based on accurate and detailed recording. This information is necessary if you are to take steps to avoid similar accidents in the future, as well as provide information for insurance companies (in the event of claims), the Health and Safety Inspectorate and the Ministry of Social Security. Some establishments will use the accident book (Form Bl 510) that is mandatory in any factory. On the other hand, since you will wish to use the information for accident prevention, you may feel that it will meet your stated obligations and provide you with the sort of information to allow proper analysis if you keep a simple accident book in each department, together with a supply of accident report forms to be completed for each entry in the book by the injured person's supervisor.

In the event of accident take the following action:

1. Attend to injured person.
2. Remove or isolate the danger: for example, switch off electricity, mop up spillage.
3. Inform appropriate authority.
4. Start an investigation of the cause.
5. If possible, take an account of the accident from the injured person.
6. Collect any evidence.
7. Interview witnesses.
8. Establish the nature and severity of the injury.
9. Make an entry in the accident book.
10. Complete an accident report form (by head of department).

An example of an entry in the accident book, and an associated accident report form, are shown in Appendix 21 (p. 202).

An accident is a historical event, rarely resulting from mere chance. Therefore your next step must be to carry out an analysis of the accident to prevent its future occurrence.

You are really concerned with two types of analysis: the first is an immediate analysis of any accident that takes place so as to quickly remedy the situation causing the accident; the second, which is equally important, is to review the accidents taking place in a period so as to spot trends or weaknesses that will aid you in taking appropriate preventive action. An example of collated information for analytical purposes is given at Appendix 22 (p. 203).

Training in Health and Safety

Last, but by no means least, comes the need for systematic training to be carried out in all aspects of health and safety. Indeed the H.S.A.W. Act lays an obligation on all employers to train staff at all levels in this important field.

By reviewing your induction training you can ensure that all new staff coming to work for you will be given a basic introduction to the health and safety requirements in your establishment. Briefly this should cover the following points:

1 Your company policy.
2 Health/safety rules.
3 Health and safety organization: for example, representatives, committee.
4 First-aid and medical facilities.
5 Accident procedures.
6 Protective clothing.
7 Fire procedures.
8 Hazard-reporting.

All craft/operative training on-job should incorporate the essential elements of training in health/safety matters. You may therefore include such things as the following:

1 How to spot potentially dangerous situations.
2 How to deal with these.
3 How to use safety equipment.
4 What company standards there are and how to maintain them.
5 What routine checks to make or expect.

You may well consider it advisable to have certain people trained over and above their job requirements in special aspects of health and safety care. These would include any safety representatives and a safety officer, as well as any department head or manager who might be called on in his normal duties to deal with crises. While no specific list of training requirements can be given here, because each type will require separate consideration, great emphasis should be placed on the reasons behind your safety procedures and systems. Preventing rather than handling crises should be the attitude.

A Last Word on Safety

Experience shows that it is very difficult, initially, to persuade managers and staff to take an active interest in matters of health and safety. It is too easy for them to take the line, 'We're busy enough!',

'Our record is good enough' or 'What a bore!' If you meet this sort of response, counter it with shock treatment. Point out how, under the new legislation, every single person has a legal responsibility for the health and safety of others at work; that every manager and supervisor can personally be prosecuted if it is proved that he has been negligent or consented or connived at breaches of health and safety regulations; that indeed it is much easier for a company to sustain a case of fair dismissal for breaches of safety rules than for almost any other offence.

On the positive side there are immense benefits to be obtained in a business where everyone is safety-conscious and concerned about the health of all who work there. Generally speaking, staff are happier to work where hygiene and safety standards are known to be high, and customers, too, soon learn to distinguish between places whose housekeeping and general standards of cleanliness and safety are of a high order from those where none of these things seem to matter.

Finally, because the whole subject of health and safety at work is so wide and in some respects so complex, you may feel that you need further advice and assistance. To help in this respect, you will find in Appendix 23 (p. 204) a list of sources of advice and assistance, and in Appendix 24 (p. 205) a list of training aids and courses in health and safety subjects.

CHECKLIST

1. Have you a written policy statement on health and safety, and is it available to all staff? Is it signed by the managing director or equivalent? Who is the senior executive responsible for health and safety matters? How often is the statement reviewed?
2. Does your statement allocate authority and responsibility at all levels of your management? Does it allocate sufficient resources to health and safety?
3. Have you a written list of safety rules?
4. What maintenance checks and reports are made, and when?
5. What arrangements are made for training all staff in health and safety measures?
6. What form of consultation takes place with staff on health and safety issues?
7. Do your disciplinary rules cover health and safety matters?
8. What steps are you taking to make sure you do not consent to, connive at, or neglect action to deal with health and safety measures?

9 Do staff have access to thermometers where they work?
10 Are staff provided with suitable toilet and washing facilities?
11 Do you supply staff with accommodation for outer clothing?
12 Have you checked to make sure staff below 18 years of age are not employed in cleaning dangerous machinery?
13 Have you taken out suitable insurance against liability for death, disease or injury to staff at work?
14 Is the insurance certificate properly exhibited?
15 What steps have you taken to see that all staff are concerned with implementing your policy on health and safety at work?
16 Would it help if you organized a regular competition to establish higher standards?
17 Does each departmental head or supervisor have a distinct responsibility for health and safety checks at regular intervals?
18 Have you an agreed safety checklist for each department?
19 Is there an accident book in each department?
20 What steps have you taken to collect accident statistics and to analyse them regularly?
21 Have you made accident report forms available?
22 What arrangements have you made for all staff to be given appropriate training in health and safety matters?

CHAPTER THIRTEEN

What is Welfare?

As we saw in Chapter 12, the H.S.A.W. Act imposes an obligation on all employers to take care of the health, safety and *welfare* of all staff. Unfortunately, not only is the term itself not given any definition, but it would be difficult to derive any sort of description of its significance from the Act. A late Lord Chief Justice once said, 'A sausage is a sausage', so we are almost forced to say 'Welfare is welfare'. If you turn to the dictionary for help, it will probably describe the word as meaning 'the state of doing well, freedom from calamity, prosperity'. Such descriptions, or lack of them, do not help the practising manager a great deal in his concern for the welfare of staff. A common-sense viewpoint must prevail.

A great deal of emphasis has been placed throughout this manual on the need for managers to look upon their staff as people, and the real asset of the business. Concern for their well-being at work is another facet of this management outlook, and it is this aspect in particular that this short chapter deals with. Welfare, in this chapter, means your concern, and its practical demonstration, for the particularly human needs of your staff while they are at work.

You need not delve very far back into industrial history to find examples of employers who took the line that workers themselves should be responsible for their own security against death, injury and old age: Henry Ford is a prime example. On the other hand, others, like Seebohm Rowntree, generated a live concern for their workers' welfare, which gave rise to what has been generally described as 'paternalism'. Such concern was not only expressed in improving the physical working conditions of staff but also in providing recreational facilities and giving opportunities for further education at the employer's expense.

All this has led to the present day, when it can be very difficult to distinguish between welfare benefits and fringe benefits. If you ask many managers in our industry what provisions they make for staff welfare, you are likely to be given a list that includes free uniform, discount-buying schemes, Christmas bonuses, living-in accommodation—to name but a few. Doubtless a number of such benefits started out under the banner of welfare, but nowadays they are more likely to be viewed by staff as part of their total remuneration, as fringe benefits. This chapter is not concerned with fringe benefits; welfare is to be understood here as concern for staff well-being.

13.1 PRACTICAL WELFARE

The way in which you may show this concern for staff will be dictated by a number of varying factors, such as the type of business you are in, its location and the age-groups of staff. In addition to any specific welfare requirements, there is a general welfare role in providing a counselling and advisory function to assist all staff experiencing difficulties or problems.

On a number of occasions in this manual you have been advised to be a good listener, to be ready to receive staff into your office and, indeed, to encourage staff to come forward with their views. With regard to welfare a good staff manager should be recognized as having an 'open-door' policy that encourages all staff to seek his counsel and advice with any problem that concerns them. Such problems may be connected with sickness, bereavement, domestic situations, financial difficulties and their work. If at first reading you think these sorts of problem have nothing to do with an employer, you must remember that they can and do affect staff at work. Apart from obvious humanitarian considerations, a staff manager who helps his staff with these problems will be able to show that it raises morale.

Practical Tips

1 Let all staff know by your attitude and expressed views that you really are concerned about their welfare.

2 When staff seek an opportunity to see you, give it a high priority. It may require a lot of courage on their part to come to you with a problem, so do not cause such courage to evaporate by your delay in seeing them.

3 Do not try solving problems by taking them upon yourself. Your aim should be to encourage staff to help themselves, with your advice. For instance, if John Smith comes to you because he is having difficulty with his landlord, advise him to whom he can go for legal advice, say, rather than taking it upon yourself to ring up the appropriate body. You may well consider it worth

while allowing John the time off to go and get such advice. Your role must be *to help staff help themselves*.

4 Provide whatever advice or assistance you can with the best interests of the individual in mind, which might be quite different to what he is asking. For example, if John comes to you and asks for financial help to meet an outstanding h.p. commitment, you may well be doing him a greater favour by not giving him the money but advising him how he can rearrange his payments, and in the meantime helping him to restructure his personal budgeting to avoid further difficulties of this sort.

5 Tell staff that anything you are told or asked about will be treated as private. This is essential if you are to encourage them to seek your counsel. On the other hand, what you are told cannot always qualify as confidential; there will be occasions when a third party has to be brought in to help. In these cases make sure staff are told of the third party.

6 Brush up your knowledge of likely sources of advice and help; this will establish greater confidence in your ability to help.

Applied Welfare

Apart from your general role as a welfare counsellor and helper, you might also take occasion to look for practical ways in which your concern for staff well-being can be expressed. Here are some examples:

1 *Staff Meals*. The provision of meals on duty is nowadays taken as part of an employee's remuneration, and can therefore be described loosely as a 'fringe benefit'. However, within this chapter your concern should rather be that of seeing to the quantity and quality of the meal. So frequently staff complain that what passes for a meal is nothing more than left-overs from the kitchen. Surely you will agree that, where staff meals are provided on this basis, there is no thought for the well-being of staff. It is here that you must consider costs, and this is no invitation to managers to provide staff with the choice that the paying customer can expect. On the other hand, if you are really concerned with your staff as people, you will be prepared to see that the food you provide is palatable, varied and well presented.

An additional demonstration of your thought for staff in a welfare sense will be found if you provide food to suit the special tastes of staff. For instance, where you have staff of varied nationalities, you should avoid giving pork to Muslims or beef to Hindus. It is equally thoughtful on your part to provide no meat at all for vegetarians. All this can be done without undue cost but with much to commend your concern for staff welfare and the benefits that can bring.

2 *Staff Canteen/Rest-room.* Again it is a frequently justifiable complaint among staff that they are provided with meals, and allocated so-called rest-rooms, in parts of the establishment that no manager would dare let the general public visit—let alone encourage the health inspector to go there. Surely, as a self-respecting manager concerned for welfare, you must see to it that such rooms are as comfortable and as well decorated as an average home. It is true that some staff behave at times like vandals, but your other staff systems should be used to remedy their behaviour and not allow them to prevent you from providing decent accommodation for them to rest or eat in.

3 *Living-in Quarters.* For many staff the accommodation you provide is their 'home'. You should therefore furnish it as best you can and see to it that the decoration is kept in good order. Again, do not be put off by the odd member of staff who, from his actions, shows no appreciation of your efforts; curb his activity through disciplinary channels and allow the majority to feel the benefit of your concern.

4 *Provision of Amenities.* Staff in our industry can often be asked to work odd hours. Many of our establishments are sited in places where it is difficult for staff to find a normal social environment. In circumstances like these you should, in consultation with staff, consider providing them as far as you can with some sort of facilities for recreation. This can take many forms, from allowing them the use of table-tennis tables to a television room, and from helping them to arrange competitive sports to encouraging them to hold events such as staff dances. The list of possibilities is endless, and whatever you agree to help them with in this respect can do nothing but good for you and your staff, showing them your worth as an employer.

5 *Care for the Young.* This industry employs a large number of young people, many of them straight from school. Here is where you can fill a dual role as a considerate staff manager in, firstly, thinking of their personal and social requirements as exuberant and energetic youngsters, and, secondly, in dealing with them *in loco parentis* without their being aware of it. It is a difficult role to

play, but you may be helped here by remembering your own welfare needs at that age.

13.2 A LAST WORD

Welfare is a difficult business, subject to a great deal of misunderstanding and, sometimes, denigration. However, properly understood by a staff manager, it will avoid the paternalistic on the one hand, and the failure to provide anything for staff on the other. Much that passes today for welfare is in reality an accumulation of fringe benefits—pension and sick pay schemes, for instance.

Your true concern for the welfare of staff will make its primary appearance in your attitude towards them. You will wish to be regarded by all staff as someone to whom they can come with their problems and worries, knowing that they will receive a sympathetic hearing and be provided with sound advice and help.

In addition, your staff will also find real evidence of your concern for their true welfare in the way you interest yourself in providing at work normal and acceptable amenities, as well as in being truly approachable with regard to allowing them opportunities to behave in a normal social manner, through dances and sporting activities, for example.

If you have sought in this chapter a list of 'welfare facilities', you must surely be disappointed. Such a list would not best serve the interests of your staff welfare; what really counts is your attitude to it and the way in which you are prepared to express your concern in practice.

CHECKLIST

1 Have you made it known to staff that you welcome their coming to seek your advice and assistance on problems affecting them?

2 Do you make it your business to grant such interview requests as soon as possible?

3 How well versed are you in sources of advice and aid in the community at large, and in your own particular locality?

4 When did you last check on the standard of meals offered to staff?

5 Do staff rest-rooms and personal accommodation feature regularly on maintenance schedules?

6 What welfare activities have you initiated to help living-in staff cope with loneliness?

7 What special welfare measures have you instituted for young members of staff?

CHAPTER FOURTEEN

Fire—Everyone's Enemy!

14.1 THE FIRE PRECAUTIONS ACT 1971

Few things are as comforting as being seated before an open fire, in a grate, and nothing is as terrifying as being engulfed by a fire in a building. No wonder the conventional Christian concept of hell is Fire!

Fire is indeed the enemy of any living being, and hence justifies this brief chapter in a manual dealing with staff management. The number of fires that break out in the United Kingdom increases annually, and the hotel and catering industry shares ignominiously in such increases, often with loss of life. The tragedy is that, in the majority of cases, such fires should never have happened.

Since the Fire Precautions Act 1971 became law a great deal has been written about its implications for our industry, especially in respect of the cost of complying with the new legal requirements to improve fire prevention standards in hotels, restaurants, guest-houses, pubs and all other sections of the industry. While none of these difficulties should be under-estimated, you may well agree that at least there has been the concomitant blessing of greater consciousness of the need for awareness of the dangers of fire.

The sole concern of the Act is the protection of life in the event of fire. The fact that by complying with the new legal requirements you also afford greater protection to your building against fire is quite incidental.

The Act applies to any hotel and boarding house except those that do not provide sleeping accommodation for more than six persons, guests or staff, not above the first floor or below the ground floor. It also covers any premises, whatever its use, to which the public have access.

The essential requirement, enforced by the Act, is that all such places be issued with a fire certificate. This is issued by the local fire authority when they are satisfied that the means of escape and other precautions appropriate in each case are such that loss of life in the event of fire would be minimized as far as is practicable.

The Fire Certificate

Your first step in meeting the legal requirements is to send off a form, supplied by the fire authority, registering your premises. Failure to do so in the required time may end in your having to close down. Nothing more is needed until your premises are inspected, when you will be issued with either the essential fire certificate or a set of recommendations for work to be done to meet the legal requirements before a fire certificate is issued. Each case is treated on its merits, and the requirements may vary considerably, according to the inspector's judgement of the fire risks in your establishment and what precautionary steps need to be taken.

An overview of these possible requirements can be seen by looking at what the fire certificate will cover. It will specify the following:

1 The particular use of the premises covered by the certificate.
2 The means of escape, probably by showing a plan.
3 The means for ensuring that the 'means of escape' can be safely and effectively used at all times. This may specify such precautions as lighted 'Exit' signs, smoke stop-doors and so on.
4 The fire-fighting equipment in the building.
5 The means of giving warning in the event of fire.

In addition to these items, your fire certificate may also cover the need for fire training of staff, the upkeep of records, a limit on the number of people who may be in the building at any one time, and so on.

If you fail to get a fire certificate until certain work has been undertaken, you will also be given a time limit in which to complete what is necessary for its issue. Once it has been issued, the inspectors retain a right under the Act to return periodically to ensure constant maintenance of all items.

Failure to obtain a fire certificate, or any breach in its requirements, can result in fines up to £400 and/or imprisonment for up to 2 years. You can also be fined up to £400 for giving false information to the inspectors or forging a certificate.

No more need be written here about the Act itself: there are many worth-while guides that can provide you with full details of what is legally required. What is of much greater importance is your commitment to implementing the total spirit of this Act.

14.2 YOUR RESPONSIBILITIES TO STAFF

As you have seen earlier in this Part, you do have responsibility for the safety of those you employ, so that you must make sure that the premises you occupy are as free of fire risks as possible, and that every means of saving life is available in the event of fire. You also have a moral obligation to help all staff become fire-conscious and learn how to deal with outbreaks of fire, and help in the safe evacuation of your buildings.

You may well agree that you cannot make a better start than by encouraging all members of your staff to become fire-conscious. This is no easy task, since most people find difficulty in disciplining their minds and their behaviour to adopt a preventive role, especially if they have no direct experience of the horrors of fire and its devastation. So the starting point is in fact one step back from this: the need for you yourself to become supremely fire-conscious and by your example to instil the same outlook in staff. Once you have gone some way along this path, you can then strike out more hopefully with positive steps to encourage staff to help themselves take fire-prevention measures.

If you have implemented any form of competitive hazard-spotting and checks, as suggested in Chapter 12, you should find it easy to add similar checks to cover specific fire hazards. But whether it is done in this way or not, what must be encouraged is a systematic approach to maintenance checks to be completed regularly by responsible staff.

It depends on the size of your establishment whether or not it is worth while appointing one member of staff with specific responsibility for fire prevention. If you do so, he/she could also be the one designated as responsible for fire training of all other members of staff. In any event, it seems sensible to make each departmental head personally responsible for the fire safety of his department. A fire checklist should be drawn up, preferably through co-operation with the department head concerned, and agreed intervals and reporting systems installed. This should combine easily with the safety checklists previously described, and the whole become part of a general system of health and safety measures.

Practical Tips

1 Agree with each departmental head a checklist covering:

(a) The main fire risk areas in the department, such as store-rooms and electrical and mechanical equipment.

(b) All fire-fighting equipment.
(c) Escape routes.

2 Agree the various intervals at which these checks will be carried out. Specifically these will vary from daily checks delegated especially to night staff to the six-monthly check of all extinguishers.
3 Arrange for reports to be made following any check—even negative reports—and specify that you should receive these reports as soon as possible after the check has been completed.
4 Commit yourself publicly to take action on any matter brought to your notice that could indicate a fire risk or any weakness in your fire-prevention measures.
5 Make it a clear part of your disciplinary rules that a breach of a safety measure designed to prevent fires, or any action that gives rise to a serious fire risk, will constitute a prima facie case for summary dismissal.

Staff Training

The second obvious responsibility to staff is to see that all of them have the appropriate training to help them spot fire hazards, take the necessary action in the event of fire to evacuate the premises safely, and deal with fires within their capability. None of this will come naturally to staff. Positive steps will need to be agreed for them to be given suitable training.

Where a senior member of staff has been designated fire prevention officer and is himself trained for the role, it would make sense to delegate the responsibility for all fire training to him. The details of this training will vary according to the size and nature of your business, but you may consider the following guidelines as the minimum required:

1 All new staff to be given specific fire-prevention training within the first month, in addition to anything included under this heading in the normal induction process.
2 All staff to be trained in procedures for evacuation and the use of basic fire-fighting equipment.
3 All staff to be acquainted with the warning system of your establishment.
4 All day staff to be practised in evacuation drills once every six months, and all night staff every three months.

Whether or not the fire authorities specify the need for staff training in issuing you with a fire certificate, you should need no convincing that any worth-while manager sees it as a major responsibility to make sure that staff are well trained in what to do in the event of fire breaking out. Only if this is done, can you be reasonably happy that, together with your normal fire-prevention measures, you have taken steps in the best interests of staff safety.

Finally make sure you keep suitable records of all the training carried out under the banner heading of fire prevention. Apart from other obvious uses for these records, it is one way in which you personally can make sure that the system you have devised is operating and that, if you are unfortunate enough to have a fire in your unit, all your staff have been equipped with the knowledge and skill needed to prevent loss of life and, hopefully, to reduce the damage to your premises.

It is so easy to shut your eyes to all that is required to comply with the Fire Precautions Act, but it is even easier to take the largely common-sense means necessary to reduce the risk of fire, and to implement fire-fighting measures. Unfortunately many adopt the attitude 'It can't happen here'. Remember one thing: fire need happen only once, and that can spell disaster for your business. Worse than that, if even one member of staff loses his life and you know that you could have reduced that risk in any way, how easily could you live with that thought? Fire is a risk in any establishment, no matter how carefully you plan to prevent it or to meet it if it arises. Make sure you have done all you can to protect the lives of your staff and, through this medium, the lives of others.

CHECKLIST

1 Have you registered your premises with the local fire authority?
2 Have you obtained a fire certificate to meet the requirements of the Fire Precautions Act 1971?
3 Has anyone been specifically delegated the responsibility for fire-prevention measures and fire training of all staff?
4 Has each departmental head a personal responsibility for regular checks covering fire risks and fire-prevention equipment?
5 Do all members of staff attend fire training?
6 Are fire drills practised on a regular basis?
7 Do you encourage all staff to be alert to fire hazards and report them?
8 Do you take action to remedy reported fire hazards immediately?
9 Are all staff given written instructions on how to deal with an outbreak of fire?

Part III Bibliography

Brewers' Society. *Safety in the Pub* (Brewers' Society, 1973).

British Institute of Management. *Health and Safety at Work*, Management Information Sheet No. 44 (B.I.M., 1974).

British Safety Council. *Safety Audit Checklist* (B.S.C.).

—— *Management Guide to Hazard Spotting* (B.S.C.).

—— *Hygiene At Work, Employees' Guide* (B.S.C.).

—— *First Aid and Hygiene* (B.S.C.).

—— *Who Does What In Health and Safety* (B.S.C.).

—— *Manager's Guide to Health and Safety at Work* (B.S.C.).

Christie, M. *Food Hygiene and Food Hazards* (Faber & Faber, 1969).

Confederation of British Industries. *Company Safety and Health Policies – C.B.I. Guide for Employers* (C.B.I., 1974).

Dept of Employment. *Protecting People at Work – An Introduction to H.S.A.W. Act* (H.M.S.O., 1974).

Food, Drink, Tobacco I.T.B. *Training for Health and Safety at Work* (F.D.I.T.B.).

Harvey, B. and Murray, R. *Industrial Health Technology* (Butterworth, 1958).

Health Education Council. *Your Guide to the Food Hygiene (General) Regulations 1970* (N.E.C., 1971).

Health and Safety Committee. *Health and Safety at Work etc. Act* (1975).

—— *Employers Policy Statements – a Guide* (1976).

Heinrich, H. W. *Industrial Accident Prevention* (New York: McGraw-Hill, 1959).

H.M.S.O. *Basic Rules for Health and Safety at Work* (H.M.S.O.).

—— *Clean Catering* (H.M.S.O.).

—— *H.S.A.W. etc. Act*, various leaflets (H.M.S.O.).

—— *Hygiene in Operation on Coin Operated, Food-Vending Machines* (H.M.S.O.).

—— *Office, Shops and Railway Premises Act 1963* (H.M.S.O.).

—— *The Safe Use of Slicing Machines* (H.M.S.O., 1970).

Hobbs, B. C. *Food Poisoning and Food Hygine* (Edward Arnold, 1968).

Hopkins, R. R. *A Handbook of Industrial Welfare* (Pitman, 1955).

Howells, R. and Barrett, B. *The Managers' Guide to the Health, Safety at Work etc. Act* (I.P.M., 1976).

Industrial Society. *Guide to H.S.A.W. etc. Act* (I.S., 1974).

Institute of Industrial Safety Officers. *The Training of Safety Officers* (I.I.S.O., 1970).

Jackson, J. *Health and Safety – the New Law* (1975).

Kinnersley, P. *The Hazards of Work – How to Fight them* (Pluto Press, 1973).

Mitchell, E. *The Employers' Guide to the Law of Health, Safety, and Welfare at Work* (Business Books, 1975).

Paper and Paper Products I.T.B. *Training In Accident Prevention* (P.P.I.T.B., 1976).

Powell-Smith, V. *Questions and Answers on H.S.A.W. etc Act* (Allan Osborne Association, 1975).

Rentokil. *Preventive Catering Hygiene* (Rentokil).
RoSPA Publications. *Occupational Safety Committees* (RoSPA).
T.U.C. *Health and Safety at Work – a T.U.C. Guide* (T.U.C., 1975).

JOURNALS

Industrial Relations Review and Report. Monthly. 286 Kilburn High Road, London NW6. (01-328 6633).
Industrial Safety. Monthly. United Trade Press Limited, 42/43 Gerrard Street, London W1V 7LP.
Occupational Safety and Health. Monthly. 6 Buckingham Palace Road, London SW1. Also a monthly supplement available to RoSPA Members only.
Protection Monthly. Official Journal of the Institution of Industrial Safety Officers. Alan Osborne & Associates, 11–13 Blackheath Park, London SE3.
Safety and Rescue. Monthly. British Safety Council, National Safety Centre, Chancellors Road, London W6 9RS.

Appendix 20 Checklist for Hazard-spotting

HEAD OF DEPARTMENT CHECKLIST
(to be completed every 6 months)

DEPARTMENT Kitchen

DATE: 1 March 1977
TIME: 10.30

ITEM	IN ORDER	COMMENTS
1 WORK AREA		
1.1 Floors	x	
1.2 Walls	x	
1.3 Stoves	x	
1.4 Stairs and steps		Linoleum torn
1.5 Electric leads		Frayed lead to potato-peeler
1.6 Machine guards in use	x	
1.7 Pipework		Clip insecure above basin
1.8 Gratings and covers	x	
1.9 Passages clear	x	
1.10 Fumes	x	
1.11 Thermostats		Large oven thermostat cracked
1.12		
1.13		
2 FIRE PRECAUTIONS		
2.1 Extinguishers	x	
2.2 Asbestos blanket	x	
2.3 Waste bins	x	
2.4 Loose rubbish		Polythene bags on floor
2.5 'No Smoking' notices	x	
2.6		
2.7		
2.8		
2.9		

ITEM	IN ORDER	COMMENTS
3 WASHING FACILITIES/TOILETS		
3.1 Towels	x	
3.2 Soap	x	
3.3 Hot and cold water	x	
3.4 Basins	x	
3.5 Urinal		Blocked
3.6 Floors	x	
3.7 Walls	x	
3.8		
3.9		
3.10		
4 OTHER ITEMS		
4.1		
4.2		
4.3		
4.4		

Signature: ....

Appendix 21 Accident Book/Report Form

ACCIDENT BOOK

DATE	TIME	PERSON INJURED	NATURE OF INJURY	SIGNATURE
1.4.97	10.00	A. Smith—chef	Left thumb cut with knife	J. Brown

ACCIDENT REPORT FORM

1 Department ....

2 Injured person: Surname .... Initials ....
Appointment ...... Age ....

3 Date and time of accident ....

4 How did accident happen? ....
....

5 If accident was caused by machinery:
(a) What kind of machine? ....
(b) Was it mechanically powered at the time? ....
(c) What was injured person doing at the time? ....
....

6 Nature and extent of injuries: ....
....

7 Has an entry been made in the accident book? ....
By whom is it signed? ....

8 Names of any witnesses: ....
....

9 If first aid was given: Name of attendant ....

10 If taken to hospital or sent home: ....
Address ....
....

Signed .... Department head ....
Date ....

Appendix 22 Accident Analysis Sheet

XYZ INDUSTRIAL CATERING COMPANY

ACCIDENTS RECORDED BY MEDICAL DEPARTMENT TO CATERING PERSONNEL 1.7.76–17.12.76

NUMBER OF PERSONNEL IN DEPARTMENT 88
NUMBER OF ACCIDENTS RECORDED 32

TYPES OF INJURY	CUTS	SCALDS	BURNS	ABRASIONS	BRUISES	PULLED MUSCLES	OTHERS
Head	—	—	—	—	—	—	—
Eyes	—	—	—	—	—	—	1
Arms	2	—	4	—	1	—	—
Shoulders	—	—	—	—	—	1	—
Hands	7	1	4	1	1	—	—
Legs	1	—	1	3	—	—	—
Feet	—	2	—	—	1	—	—
Back	—	—	—	—	—	1	—
Totals	10	3	9	4	3	2	1

Causes of reported accidents	*Number*
Careless use of hot equipment or utensils (hot plates, service counters)	7
Sharp edges on tins or small equipment (knives, urns, metal equipment)	5
Accidents with doors (fridge door handles, swing doors)	4
Broken crockery	3
Falls due to wet or hazardous floors (spillage, milk crates)	3
Careless handling or spillage of hot liquids (tea urn taps, pans of hot liquid)	3
Splash back of hot fat from fryers	2
Carelessness in handling small equipment (dropping tray and scissors on to self)	2
Improper bending and lifting	1
Misjudgement of distance between static and mobile equipment	1
Flying object causing eye injury (crumb from roll while cutting)	1

(*Note*: In addition, the company could ascertain from its accident book the number and types of accident by occupations or examine in particular the time of day/night of accidents.)

Appendix 23 Sources of Advice and Assistance

1 *Statutory Bodies*
HEALTH AND SAFETY COMMISSION and HEALTH AND SAFETY EXECUTIVE
Baynards House, Chepstow Place, London W2 (01-229-3456). Incorporating H.M. Factory Inspectorate and Employment Medical Advisory Service.

2 *Advisory Bodies*
ASSOCIATION OF ENVIRONMENTAL HEALTH OFFICERS
19 Grosvenor Place, London SW1 (01-235 5158)
BRITISH SAFETY COUNCIL
Chancellors Road, London, W6 9RS (01-741 1231)
BRITISH STANDARDS INSTITUTION
2 Park Street, London W1A 2BS (01-629 9000)
CONFEDERATION OF BRITISH INDUSTRY
21 Tothill Street, London SW1H 9LL (01-930 6711)
HEALTH EDUCATION COUNCIL
78 New Oxford Street, London WC1A 1AH (01-637 1881)
INSTITUTION OF INDUSTRIAL SAFETY OFFICERS
222 Uppingham Road, Leicester (Leicester [0533] 768424)
ROYAL SOCIETY FOR THE PREVENTION OF ACCIDENTS
Royal Oak Centre, Brighton Road, Purley, Surrey CR2 2UR (01-668 4272). Information on publications and membership. Extensive range of safety training courses for all levels of employee. In-company courses can be arranged.
TRADE UNION CONGRESS
Congress House, 23–8 Great Russell Street, London WC1B 3LS (01-636 4030)
TUC CENTENARY INSTITUTE OF TROPICAL MEDICINE, INFORMATION SERVICE
London School of Hygiene and Tropical Medicine, Keppel Street, London WC1E 7HT (01-636 8636)

3 *Organizations dealing with First Aid*
BRITISH RED CROSS SOCIETY
9 Grosvenor Crescent, London SW1X 7ES (01-235 5454)
ST JOHN AMBULANCE BRIGADE
St John's Gate, Clerkenwell, London EC1M 4DA (01-253 6644)

4 *Industrial Body*
INDUSTRIAL TRIBUNAL
Ebury Bridge Road, London SW1 (01-730 9161)

Note. Further information may be available from relevant trade associations and employers' organizations.

Appendix 24 Training Aids and Courses

FILMS

Hygiene in Catering. Summarizes ten key points of hygiene regulations in kitchen. 16 mm, colour, 10 minutes. *For hire from* Training Films International, St Mary's Street, Whitchurch, Shropshire (Whitchurch 2597)

It Shall be the Duty. Introduction to Health and Safety at Work, etc. Act. 16 mm. Produced by C.O.I. *For hire from* Central Film Library, Government Building, Bromyard Avenue, London W3 7JB (01-743 5555)

Make Light of Lifting. 16 mm, colour, 17 minutes. *For hire from* Millbank Films Ltd, Thames House North, Millbank, London SW1 (01-834 4444)

Key to Cleanliness. Emphasizes personal hygiene. 16 mm, colour, 21 minutes. Produced by J. Lyons & Co., Ltd. *For hire from* Guild, Sound & Vision Limited, 85–129 Oundle Road, Peterborough, Cambs PE2 9PY (Peterborough 63122)

The Uninvited Guest. Fire in hotel and how to overcome it. 16 mm, colour, 38 minutes. Produced by J. Lyons & Co., Ltd. *For hire from* Guild, Sound & Vision Limited (address above)

TAPE/SLIDE SETS

Health and Safety At Work. Produced by MKW Services. *For sale from* Sales and Supervision Analysis, Selsdon Park Hotel, Sanderstead, South Croydon, Surrey, CR2 8YA (01-657 8811)

Hygiene in the Job Situation. Series of kits for training food workers, e.g. hygiene for tea bars and trolleys, hygiene for people who serve food. Produced by J. Lyons & Co., Ltd. *For hire from* Guild, Sound & Vision Limited (address above)

Keep It Clean. Produced by K.L.P. Film Services in conjunction with Selfridge's Limited. *For hire from* Selfridge's Limited, Training Department, 400 Oxford Street, London, W1 (01-629 1234)

COURSES

Hotel and Catering Industry Training Board. Seminars are run regionally on Health and Safety at Work (1 day), and Fire Precautions (1 day).

Royal Institute of Public Health and Hygiene, 28 Portland Place, London W1 (01-580 2731). Certificate in Food Hygiene and the Handling of Food. Diploma in Food Hygiene.

Royal Society of Health, 13 Grosvenor Place, London SW1 (01-235 9961). Certificate in the Hygiene of Food Retail and Catering. Certificate in Nutrition in relation to Catering and Cooking.

Training Services Agency, Ebury Bridge House, Ebury Bridge Road, London SW1W 8PW (01–730 9661). Job Safety Courses for Trainers (1 week). Job Safety Courses for Supervisors (15 hours).

Appendix 25 Publications and Films Dealing With Fire

TITLE	TIME (mins)	DESCRIPTION	AVAILABLE FROM
Red Warning	12	This 16 mm film shows the ways fires are started, the damage they can cause and stresses the primary responsibility of top management for fire prevention	British Insurance Association or Central Fire Liaison Panel—free loan
What is Fire?		This is a 16-page booklet that covers in some depth the following four areas: 1 The three needs of fire. 2 Growth and spread of fire. 3 How fires can start. 4 What to do if fire breaks out.	Fire Protection Association
Planning Guide to Fire Dangers from Smoking.		Information Sheet. Reference No. J.82	Fire Protection Association
Study Report on Fire Dangers in Hotels.		12-page booklet containing several case studies of hotel fires and incorporating a manager's checklist. Reference No. J.83	Fire Protection Association
Fire Protection Association Catalogue		A 4-page folded sheet listing the above three publications as well as many other booklets, posters, leaflets and film-strips about fire.	Fire Protection Association
Visual Aids		A list of visual aids concerning fire and fire prevention	Fire Protection Association

TITLE	TIME (mins)	DESCRIPTION	AVAILABLE FROM
The Nature of Fire	19	This 16 mm film gives the basic facts about fire and how it can be prevented and controlled. If people know what fire is, they will more readily know how to avoid acts leading to fire. Dramatized situations and simple laboratory demonstrations are used to illustrate the point of this film. F.P.A. production.	Fire Protection Association. Central Film Library—free loan
The Control of Fire	19	Produced mainly with factory fires in mind, this 16 mm film shows how fire in a factory office rapidly gets out of control. The point of the film is to show that, with a knowledge of fire-fighting procedures, many fires can be controlled in the early stages. F.P.A. production.	Fire Protection Association. Central Film Library-free loan
The Prevention of Fire	15	Although set in a factory, this 16 mm film shows the simple precautions needed to prevent fires being started anywhere by the following: 1 Misuse of electrical equipment. 2 Smokers' carelessness. 3 Heat and sparks from machining and uncontrolled rubbish burning. 4 Intruders. F.P.A. production	Fire Protection Association. Central Film Library—free loan
Go to Blazes	15	This 16 mm film shows the work of a fire inspector and investigates fires that have happened, are happening or could happen, highlighting dangerous practices. Carelessness is shown to be a major cause.	National Film Board of Canada or Guild Sound & Vision—small hiring charge
Know your Fire Extinguishers		Small wall chart in two colours, showing the various types of fire extinguisher that should or should not be used when fighting fires.	British Safety Council
Fire Code		Small 12-page booklet outlining the following four aspects of fire: 1 Prevention. 2 Fire protection for buildings. 3 Fire extinguishing equipment. 4 What to do in the event of fire.	Royal Society for the Prevention of Accidents

TITLE	TIME (Mins)	DESCRIPTION	AVAILABLE FROM
Fire Protection		A monthly journal containing a lot of information about fire, fire prevention and fire-fighting. Each issue contains a number of recent case histories as well as special treatment of a particular area.	Fire Protection Association
'Fire Prevention', Hotels and Boarding Houses		Excellent Home Office official publication for management of hotels and boarding houses, showing pictorially main fire dangers.	Home Office
Fire Chemistry	30	Dealing with the triangle of combustion, this 16 mm film illustrates methods of fire extinction and demonstrates the use of various extinguishing agents in an aircraft fire. This film was primarily intended for the training of fire services. Central Office of Information production.	Central Film Library
The Uninvited Guest	25	Produced by Strand Hotels. Excellent film highlighting main fire dangers in hotels and steps needed to prevent and control fire. Useful general purpose staff-training film.	Guild Sound & Vision

Appendix 26 Organizations Concerned with Fire

NAME	ADDRESS	TELEPHONE
The British Fire Services Association Concerned mainly with the organization of fire brigades. This association often arranges courses for fire officers and provides advice on fire protection.	86 London Road, Leicester, LE2 5DJ	Leicester 24063
Royal Society for the Prevention of Accidents This society is concerned with the prevention of accidents of all types. On the subject of fire, advice is available regarding courses, seminars and literature.	Royal Oak Centre, Brighton Road, Purley, Surrey, CR2 2UR	01-668 4272
Fire Protection Association This is a central advisory organization, largely financed by insurance companies, providing technical and general advice on all aspects of fire protection.	Aldermary House, Queen Street, London, EC4N 1TJ	01-248 5222
Joint Fire Research Organization This body carries out research on fire, its causes, nature, extent and locations. Statistical analyses on hotel fires have been produced by this organization.	Melrose Avenue, Boreham Wood, Hertfordshire	01-953 6177
British Safety Council Concerned more with other elements of safety than with fire, this council does, however, produce occasional posters and leaflets on fire prevention and protection.	Chancellors Road, London, W6 9RS	01-741 1231

NAME	ADDRESS	TELEPHONE
Fire Service Technical College This college organizes courses and seminars designed mainly for the fire service but open to industrial fire officers and others.	Moreton-in-Marsh, Gloucestershire	
Fire Brigades These can provide valuable information on fire-fighting methods and are often willing to arrange speakers at courses and seminars.	Local	
Technical Colleges Most technical colleges have investigated fire as a course subject and are prepared to mount courses or seminars to meet a demand.	Local	

PART IV

STAFF DISCIPLINE

CHAPTER FIFTEEN

Interviewing—a Tool of Discipline

15.1 AN UNDERSTANDING OF DISCIPLINE

The inclusion of a separate Part in this manual on the subject of discipline is simply to recognize that, even if you succeed in acquiring all the skills and qualities of an ideal manager of staff, there will still be occasions when you will need to perform a disciplinary role. No self-respecting manager enjoys this part of his work, but he recognizes its necessity, and should be able to exercise discipline effectively without destroying his dignity or his subordinate's. This must be your objective.

Discipline means instruction, training in accordance with rules, and the maintenance of order. Unfortunately to many people it is equated with 'punishment' and harsh impositions, and therefore to be abhorred in our modern society; this is not the true concept of discipline at all. This chapter sets out to provide guidelines which ensure that any form of discipline is constructive, instructive and in no sense retributive.

Any organization, however small, has a need for order if it is to survive. Indeed you are likely to agree that if order is a necessity for survival, it is even more necessary if the organization is to grow. This order can only be achieved if there are recognized rules and procedures helping to govern how people act. This is the very basis of what is sometimes described as 'Works Rules' or, more commonly in our industry, 'Staff Rules'. Of course, not all such restrictions on what staff may or may not do necessarily appear in a rule book; this would be far from desirable even if it were possible. Perhaps you need a written record of only the most important rules. The remainder are known by everyone through tradition—the need to arrive on time for duty, say—or by the general requirements of the work being done, such as working tidily.

Not so long ago, when you started working for an employer, it was assumed that the boss was entitled to be autocratic in directing you in the way you would behave. This tacit agreement was virtually a condition of employment. It is not so today for two main reasons:

1 It is now recognized that it is often far from wise to exercise one's rights in a dictatorial fashion; it does not produce the best from people.
2 There is now a strong legislative concept of discipline that requires remedies to be available to people treated unjustly at work.

These two factors have changed the whole emphasis of industrial discipline; modern discipline aims to bring people into line with the needs of the whole organization, so that it can operate successfully and be seen to be fair to both employer and employee.

The following guidelines may be considered in establishing a fair attitude to discipline, which can be expressed in whatever code you design for the benefit of both company and staff:

1 Base your discipline on rules and not on your personal whims. This will make sure that the rules are made because the organization requires them rather than simply as an expression of your own likes and dislikes. Your test of a rule might be, Is this imposition required to further the proper progress of the business?
2 Your discipline should be corrective. Criticism that destroys staff initiative or implies that staff are 'useless' turns you into a management spectator rather than a leader. The effective manager uses discipline to correct mistakes constructively.
3 Let the situation support your need to discipline by suggesting another course of action when circumstances demand it rather than acting on status or rank. Discipline will not suffer then when occasionally your suggestion is rejected.
4 Aim to correct what is wrong rather than to attach the stigma of blame. In this way your staff will not be seen as insubordinate or impertinent, or even seen as a threat, when the natural reaction is to attack them from a position of authority, out of pique perhaps.
5 Treat all staff fairly in disciplinary matters; if they suspect any form of discrimination, it is bound to lead to resentment.
6 If staff work operates on the basis of procedures and established practices, rather than on the basis of following individual management orders and instructions, then discipline is easier to enforce. The likelihood of feeling a personal affront because your orders are flouted is removed, and staff will not experience

the normal resentment associated with having someone in power over them.

7 Discipline should never leave a person bereft of dignity. No matter how serious may be the act or omission that calls for discipline, the offender must be able to retain his self-respect. Your reprimand must therefore be given in private and directed at the offence and not the person of the offender.

Practical Tips

1 Make it known by your behaviour that you view discipline as a means of instruction, not punishment.
2 Draw up a list of the important rules of behaviour designed for the successful running of your business.
3 Do not make your rules on the assumption that staff are dishonest, irresponsible and lazy.
4 Phrase all your orders and control procedures in language staff readily understand. Avoid the tendency to use legalistic jargon.
5 Impose disciplinary measures in accordance with the spirit of your rules rather than with the letter.
6 Always act constructively in using discipline.

15.2 THE DISCIPLINE INTERVIEW

If you have established the discipline in your unit along the guidelines outlined earlier, most of your action in this area will be confined to day-to-day instructional correction. However, there will be times when a member of staff steps so far out of line that something more than informal corrective action is needed. For example, you may feel that the time has come to issue a formal warning about future behaviour; this could be part of your agreed disciplinary procedure, described in detail in Part V. You can best deliver the warning at a formal interview.

All the skills of interviewing described in Part I of this manual apply equally to interviews designed as a tool of discipline. Just as necessary is the need for you to be properly prepared, so that the offender leaves knowing full well that he has been disciplined but still ready to improve in the area that has formed the subject for his being disciplined.

1 First you must gather all the facts that might have a bearing on the interview. Do not accept hearsay evidence or call someone for interview on general impressions only. In most cases it

should be possible, in dealing with any disciplinary matter, to have facts related to the following:

(a) Name and background of offender.
(b) Date, time and place of offence(s).
(c) Names of witnesses.
(d) Nature of offence.
(e) Relevant records of employment.

With this information you will be able to carry out your role effectively.

2 Arrange for the interview to be held at a place and time that suit both parties best, and see to it that you are not interrupted.

3 Let the offender know not only that you wish to see him at a certain time but also that the purpose of the interview is disciplinary in nature. This is fair to the offender, who is then given a chance not only to recall his side of the story but also to gather any thoughts he might have in mitigation.

The basic reason for seeing the person in private is obvious, but that certainly does not mean that at the private interview anything can be said in a reprimand. It should be a dignified affair.

1 Start the interview by letting the person know the general charge and the specific details of the offence. Do not refer to general complaints or refuse to divulge details. All of this should be done in a factual fashion, without emotion and certainly without a trace of anger.

2 Stick completely to work behaviour and avoid all reference to personalities.

3 Having had your say, invite a response so that you can then listen to the other side of the story. It is very important to let the other person explain fully what happened and the reasons for it. There may be mitigating circumstances in some cases—conflicting orders or even orders you gave unclearly, which were at fault. Throughout this part of the interview listen carefully as much to what is not said as to what is said.

4 Keep control of the interview. Make sure both parties stick to the points at issue, and if you think it helpful, question the offender further. Use probing questions here to establish views and feelings, as well as facts.

5 Throughout the interview provide opportunities for the offender to admit his shortcomings. If he does so, the step to expressing your disapproval is an easy one, but couple this with

outlining the ways for him to remedy the situation and obviate similar shortcomings.

6 Compromise and understanding are virtues to be exercised throughout the interview, but once you have reached your decision and announced it, it is a grave mistake to relent. That would simply mean an admission that your first decision was wrong, and you will lose the effect of your reprimand.

7 Make sure the offender leaves you knowing that he has been reprimanded but not humiliated or short-changed. Rather, he should be quite clear about what is required of him and, if necessary, understand also that a failure to improve will inevitably lead to more severe discipline.

Post Interview

Once the discipline interview is over, the matter should be considered closed. Still, you will want to be realistic enough to know that not every member of staff who receives a discipline interview will live up to your company's expectations for ever and a day thereafter.

The next step to take then, after the interview, is to make a record of the disciplinary reprimand, preferably in the personal file or on the record card of the individual concerned. This then becomes a part of his employment record and can be used as evidence if he should need further discipline.

However, such an entry should not blot that man's record for ever. If you obtain evidence of correction, provided that the same person does not fail again in that same area for, say, a further 6 months, then justice would seem to demand that the record be wiped clean. Make sure your system is such that this is not overlooked, but if by chance it is, at least you should be prepared to ignore such a record as future evidence if he again requires further disciplining after 6 months.

Last, but by no means least, do not harbour a grudge against the person you have disciplined. The person required discipline, and he received it. Give him the benefit of real hope that it has achieved its true purpose, that of an instructional tool, and by both word and action let him know that you consider it a thing of the past.

Let This be a Lesson!

In moments of frustration managers will doubtless find themselves shouting orders to staff. However, you may hopefully now find not only that this so-called discipline has little lasting effect, but that a more considerate and civilized form of discipline, in getting people to work better and behave for the good of all, proves much more effective. The present climate, tending towards more participation and the breaking down of class and status barriers, makes temper tantrums less and less acceptable.

So far the bearing of legislation in the field of discipline has not been mentioned. It makes up the backdrop to the whole of the next chapter. All that need be noted here is that discipline at work, organized along the lines suggested here, can stand apart from all legal consideration and there will be no need for concern. On the other hand, the manager who uses rage and personal tyranny as a system of moving others to action not only must nowadays fear the effect of the law but should seriously look at himself and question his whole management approach. Let your disciplinary role be based on helping staff to learn from their mistakes. Do not allow the law to teach you an otherwise expensive lesson.

CHECKLIST

1 Does discipline in your establishment imply punishment, or does it lean rather towards civilized correction?

2 Are your house-rules based on the needs of the establishment for organized behaviour?

3 Are the most important rules made known to all staff in writing that is simple and clear?

4 Are your disciplinary actions carried out with dignity?

5 When staff attend for a discipline interview, have you made it clear in advance what sort of interview they are being called to?

6 Are you careful to avoid emotional outbursts during the interview?

7 Do you seek to provide opportunities for offenders to admit their faults, and then provide them with instructions for improvement?

8 Do you keep records of all formal disciplinary acts?

9 Once a disciplinary hearing is over, do you take care to avoid harbouring grudges by word or action against the offender?

10 Do you really try to impart discipline as a tool of constructive correction?

CHAPTER SIXTEEN

Dismissing Staff—Fairly

16.1 'YOU'RE FIRED!'—WHAT IT MAY MEAN TODAY

When all else fails, the ultimate disciplinary measure open to you as a manager is to dismiss a member of staff. It is a recognition of failure on someone's part, in that there no longer remains any confidence that a satisfactory contractual relation can continue. From your point of view you are having to administer the capital punishment of discipline: to take away a person's job, and therefore his livelihood. However it is looked at, firing a member of staff is a serious matter.

Unfortunately many managers do not realize the gravity of such decisions, nor consider too closely the justice of their action; staff are sometimes sacked on impulse—tempers have flared, patience has been exhausted or prejudices have held sway, and the dreaded words 'You're fired!' have followed. As in many other aspects of staff management, it is precisely because many managers have failed to behave with equity in dismissing staff that governments have intervened and imposed legislation. So, in 1971, the Industrial Relations Act introduced the statutory obligation on all employers to dismiss staff fairly, and spelt out the grounds for legally dismissing staff. In 1974 this Act was replaced by the Trade Union and Labour Relations Act, but the current legislation dealing with unfair dismissals is to be found in the Employment Protection (Consolidation) Act, 1978.

This chapter sets out to help you find your way through the minefield of legislation affecting the dismissal of staff, and offers a practical guide to help you reach this ultimate disciplinary decision on grounds of fairness to both the staff and the business. Mistakes, however well intentioned, can be costly, but remember this manual is a practical guide only; it is not a legal interpretation that can be quoted in defence.

Definition of Dismissal

Under the Employment Protection (Consolidation) Act a member of staff is treated as dismissed if the following conditions apply:

1 You bring the employment contract to an end, with or without notice.
2 A fixed-term contract expires and you do not renew it.
3 A member of staff terminates the contract, with or without notice, in circumstances such that he is entitled to do so, without notice, because of your conduct.

Once dismissal is established, you must distinguish between two main qualifications affecting it and the possible legal consequences:

1 *Wrongful Dismissal.* This is a term used to describe the situation when you fail to give staff any notice or insufficient notice. It is an offence under common law and you can be sued in the county court for damages equivalent to the actual loss suffered. Likewise, of course, you can sue for damages any member of your staff who leaves without giving you notice or agreed notice. Unfortunately the amount you receive may not meet the costs of bringing the case, but it might deter others.
2 *Unfair Dismissal.* This term is used to describe a dismissal that can be shown to have taken place for none of the reasons described in the Employment Protection (Consolidation) Act or was unreasonably decided upon or carried out. If an Industrial Tribunal finds staff to have been unfairly dismissed, it can order you to reinstate or re-engage them, or order you to compensate them financially.

This chapter concerns itself solely with the concept of fair/unfair dismissal.

Dismissal With Notice and Without

The usual means of dismissing staff is by giving them notice. How much notice you must give is contained in the statement you are required to give full-time staff under the Employment Protection (Consolidation) Act. Should a contract not specify a period of notice, the courts will decide what is reasonable. In any case you are bound to give minimum periods of notice depending upon length of service, as laid down in the Employment Protection (Consolidation) Act. The law does not clearly establish a right to give money in lieu of notice but in practice and by implication it is an acceptable alternative.

When staff conduct is such that you believe it challenges the very basis of the contract you can dismiss them on the spot, without financial compensation. You must, of course, be prepared to defend your action, if challenged, and this will necessitate your proving that you had fair grounds for summary dismissal and that you behaved reasonably in using them for sacking the man instantly. This subject will be examined in detail in Section 16.2; suffice it to say here that social attitudes and expectations are changing so much that what was once considered justified for instant dismissal may now no longer be thought so. For instance, if your chef, in a fit of temper, should swear at you, it may call for some form of discipline but not instant dismissal. Authority is not considered today to rest on the appearance of respect.

Staff Resignation

In the context of this chapter, staff resignation is not being used to describe the normal event when someone wants to leave you to take up another job, and they notify you to this effect. Instead, the sort of resignation now being described is that which takes place when a member of staff resigns or simply leaves the job because you make arbitrary changes to such items as his pay, benefits, status, place of work or working system so that they amount to a breach of contract on your part. If this should happen, then the law, as you have seen earlier, classes it as a dismissal, and you could be called upon to defend a claim against you for unfair dismissal.

When legal protection against unfair dismissal was first introduced by the Industrial Relations Act in 1971, some employers took the line that, since they had no legal grounds for getting rid of certain staff whom they would like to have dismissed, they would make life so difficult and unpleasant for those people that eventually they would leave of their own accord. In other words, they would resign. However, many such staff complained to Tribunals, and they were declared to have been 'constructively dismissed' and therefore entitled to compensation as if they had been unfairly dismissed. The definition of dismissal under the Employment Protection (Consolidation) Act, as you have seen, now specifically includes employee resignation in such circumstances.

You can make basic changes in staff terms and conditions of employment only if the contract itself allows for such changes, or staff accept the changes. What is important to understand here is that the changes referred to must be fundamental and serious ones. For instance, you would be quite entitled to ask waiting staff normally employed in a directors' dining room to work instead in the junior managers' restaurant. This is within the contract description of waiting staff. However, it could be a different matter if you were to insist on waiting staff working instead as still-room attendants or chambermaids, especially if it meant working on less favourable terms in any way. Staff would seem to be entitled to accept changes on a trial basis. The law allows no special limits on time other than in cases of redundancy where alternative employment is offered, but generally speaking it is likely to be a short period. If your staff make it plain that they are 'giving it a try', they almost certainly reserve their right to resign later and hold it as a dismissal.

Practical Tips

1 Look again at the terms and conditions you offer staff, especially those in the written statement you give them as required by law. Make sure they are not so tightly constructed as to allow no room for flexibility to meet future changes in your business needs.
2 If you do feel that it is necessary to change a fundamental term of someone's contract, do so only with their agreement.
3 Make sure any changes you suggest do not provide staff with less favourable terms, especially in relation to pay, status, hours and place of employment.
4 Avoid the temptation to invite someone to resign, especially if you offer a reference in return; it may well amount to a dismissal.
5 Never force resignation—'Resign or be instantly dismissed!' This will certainly be viewed by Tribunals as a dismissal.
6 If a resignation is offered, do not put it on ice for future use. If you refuse such a resignation or put it aside and then use it later, it will probably amount to a dismissal.
7 Do not be tempted to buy staff off. If you offer someone a sum of money 'in full and final satisfaction of all claims', it will not prevent you being sued for unfair dismissal; employees cannot contract out of their rights under the Employment Protection (Consolidation) Act.

As we have seen then, the legal understanding of the term 'dismissal' covers a much wider field than being given the sack. Most importantly it also covers the act of staff leaving of their own accord because they believe that you, as the employer, have acted in such a way as to breach a fundamental item in the employer-employee contract.

If you dismiss staff, with or without notice, or fail to renew a fixed term contract, then you must supply a written reason(s) for dismissal, upon request, within 14 days of the request. If you unreasonably refuse to do so or provide one with inadequate or false particulars, then an Industrial Tribunal can award two weeks' pay as compensation.

16.2 WHAT ARE FAIR GROUNDS FOR DISMISSAL?

Before you plunge into an examination of what both statutory and case law have to say about what makes for a fair dismissal, there are a few preliminary matters worth considering. One of the aims of the Employment Protection (Consolidation) Act is to give unfair dismissal rights to as many employees as possible. The position under this Act is as follows:

1 All staff employed for at least 16 hours a week can claim unfair dismissal rights.

2 Even if staff are employed for only 8 hours a week, they have these rights once they have been in your employment for 5 years.

3 All close relatives of an employer can claim, other than husbands and wives.

4 It no longer matters how many staff are employed; the rights are extended to all staff regardless of the size of the firm or unit.

5 To be eligible, all staff must normally have been employed for 52 weeks; however, if you sack someone who has served for only 51 weeks and give them no notice, or short notice in lieu, they will still be eligible to complain of unfair dismissal. Indeed it need be no more than 50 weeks and one day if you sack ordinary day workers on a Monday, or even 49 weeks and 2 days for those sacked on Monday whose starting date was on Friday. Only those below 65 (men) or 60 (women) at time of termination may complain of unfair dismissal.

6 If you dismiss staff for what the Employment Protection (Consolidation) Act describes as 'inadmissible reasons', then the requirement to have served a minimum of 52 weeks is waived.

Under the Employment Protection (Consolidation) Act staff are legally protected against dismissal for any of the following reasons:

1 Belonging to an independent trade union.
2 Taking part at an appropriate time in the activities of an independent trade union.
3 Refusing to join a non-independent trade union.

An independent trade union is one that is neither under the domination or control of an employer nor liable to any interference by him that could lead to such control. The Employment Protection (Consolidation) Act explains that the 'appropriate time' for trade union activities is either outside working hours or during working time agreed by the employer for that purpose. Remember then that to sack anyone for any of these reasons is automatically unfair, even if he has been in your employment for only one day. A guide to qualifying periods for various rights is given in Appendix 27 (p. 268).

The normal principle of English law about proof is that the burden of proof always lies with the complainant. So, if a customer complains to a county court that you have breached a commercial contract, the court will look to the customer to prove his case.

However, when the Redundancy Payments Act was passed in 1965, this principle took a knock; effectively the position was then stated that if a man lost his job, it was presumed to have been on account of redundancy, unless and until the employer proved otherwise. Again in 1971, when the concept of unfair dismissal was given legal definition for the first time, a man who was dismissed was presumed to have been unfairly dismissed unless the employer proved otherwise. To do so, you as an employer had to show that you had one of the reasons given in the Industrial Relations Act for sacking him. If you succeeded in doing this, the employee's last hope lay in challenging you with having acted unreasonably in using those fair grounds for dismissing him. If he did do so, the onus of proof reverted to the employee as complainant.

Now, however, under the Employment Protection (Consolidation) Act the position has changed once again: if you face a charge at a Tribunal that you dismissed a member of staff unfairly, the law requires that you prove, firstly, that you had fair grounds for dismissing him, and, secondly, that you acted reasonably in the circumstances in dismissing for the reason given. The only occasions in which the onus of proof rests with the complainants are in cases of constructive dismissal and being sacked for 'inadmissible reasons'.

To dismiss fairly therefore demands two separate requirements on your part:

1 To show what was the principal or only justification for the dismissal, and that it is a potentially valid one under the Act.
2 That you acted reasonably in all the circumstances in using that justification as grounds for dismissal, and in the way in which you carried out the dismissal.

To make for easier understanding it might help if you consider the two hurdles to be crossed to establish a fair dismissal in this way: (1) show the dismissal was potentially fair, and establish the grounds; and (2) show the dismissal was actually fair, and prove you acted reasonably.

To establish that the dismissal is potentially fair, you must show that the reason, or the main one, if there are several, was one of the following:

1 Incapability of doing the work for which engaged.
2 Lack of qualifications for the job.
3 Misconduct.
4 Redundancy.
5 A legal prohibition on you to continue employing him.
6 Taking part in a strike.
7 Other substantial reasons justifying dismissal.

This is a comprehensive list and your reason, to be fair, must fall under one or other of these headings. If, for instance, you claim that you dismissed Smith for redundancy but the Tribunal finds that you dismissed him so as to reduce costs by securing a lower paid person to do the work, this will be found to be a reason not covered by the above list. The same holds true if it is found that the real reason for dismissal is that you gave way to pressure from other staff who say they are no longer prepared to work with Smith. You must prove that the reason for dismissal is one of those given by the Act. Let us look at each in turn more closely.

Dismissal for Incapability

This heading is meant to cover any lack of skill, aptitude, health or any physical or mental quality required to do the job. In effect, then, you can still sack staff for incompetence, inadequacy or lack of skill, but it will of course be tested for fairness. Case law shows that it is very important to deal with incompetent staff fairly before deciding to sack them. This means you should have taken the following preliminary steps:

1 Given the person written warnings of possible dismissal within the last 6 months.
2 Given him a chance to improve with help and training.
3 Provided an opportunity for him to put his side of things.
4 If possible, offered him the chance to appeal to impartial management.

It should go without saying that all these steps should have been recorded.

Although this procedure is generally required, there can be exceptions. After all, senior management and responsible staff are supposed to know what is required of them and be able to check their own performance. Again you may feel that incompetence is so gross that giving warnings or a chance to improve may be of no benefit to the person concerned. You might win in such a case, but you are advised to go carefully; if you use extraordinary measures, you must show that the situation is extraordinary. Consider the following guidelines:

1 Think twice before you dismiss as incapable staff who have been recently promoted or whose job means big or rapid changes in their work. Instead you should train or retrain disappointing staff, and if that fails to work, give them a chance to revert to their old job or to a job that fits their real capabilities.
2 Provide documentary evidence of the man's ability, and do not contradict this by writing him a good reference or a letter of appreciation for this work just before you fire him.
3 Resist the temptation to soften the blow in dismissing a man whose best is not good enough by making him 'redundant'. Honesty must be your only policy.

Incapability also covers ill-health, which is looked at separately in Section 16.5.

Dismissal because of Lack of Qualifications

Qualifications is used by the Act to describe any degree, diploma or other technical or professional qualifications needed *on engagement* by a member of staff to do the job he is taken on to do. This heading is not designed to cover cases where staff fraudulently assert that they have qualifications. There are more serious penalties for this than dismissal.

There have been very few cases where staff have been sacked for lack of qualifications. What seems to be essential for success is to show that you behaved reasonably.

Dismissal for Misconduct

This term is not defined or described in any legal statute, so that misconduct is invariably a question of fact and not a question of law. Since this is the heading used by most employers under which to dismiss staff, it merits detailed consideration on its own. You will therefore find the whole of Section 16.4 devoted to this topic.

Redundancy

This is given by the Employment Protection (Consolidation) Act as a fair reason for dismissal, but it can be rendered unfair in three ways, as follows:

1 Making someone redundant for trade union activities.
2 Selecting him in contradiction to agreed procedure.
3 Selecting him 'unreasonably' in the circumstances.

Since redundancy is also a separate subject dealt with in Part VI of the Employment Protection (Consolidation) Act, the proof required under each part is different. If you wish to avoid incurring a redundancy payment you must prove that the reason for dismissal was for something other than redundancy; otherwise that is the assumed reason. But under Part V of the Employment Protection (Consolidation) Act, if you want to avoid paying unfair dismissal compensation, you must prove that the reason for dismissal was redundancy.

A further factor to keep in mind is that staff have to have two years' service before they can claim a redundancy payment but only need be employed for 1 year to qualify for unfair dismissal compensation.

Before looking at how selection for redundancy can render it unfair, here are some general points to note:

1 There is no fixed definition of 'unfair redundancy'—it is always a question of fact for Tribunals to decide.
2 It is rare for mass redundancies to be considered unreasonable; Tribunals generally accept company decisions to declare redundancies for economic or other business reasons.
3 Redundancy is judged as fair or not on the facts existing at time of the decision; subsequent factors have no bearing on this.

The first type of unfairness arises when you select staff for redundancy because of trade union activity. If therefore you select Smith because he proposes to become or stay a member of an independent trade union, because he is an active member in it, because he refuses to join a non-independent trade union or because he objects to being a union member on religious grounds when your business operates a closed shop, then the Act makes it clear that this is automatically unfair.

Another unfair selection for redundancy can arise if it goes against a customary arrangement or an agreed procedure; such a selection makes for automatically unfair dismissal. An agreed procedure is usually a written one, which covers what is to be done in a company if redundancy is necessary; it is usually agreed to by management and unions, or by the staff where unions are not represented. The terms of the procedure are usually incorporated into the terms and conditions of the individual contracts, either expressly or by implication. Tribunals will usually interpret any such agreement strictly. Customary arrangements are quite different: an expressed agreement is a unilateral declaration by the employer as to what he intends to do, whereas a customary arrangement is something that is so well known, so certain and so clear as to amount to an implied agreed procedure. In this case it is always a question of fact to be decided by the Tribunal.

Section 16.3 will look at what you might do to cope with redundancies, and particularly at the value of having an agreed procedure.

However, if an employee does not prove that his selection for redundancy was automatically unfair because it breached an agreed procedure or customary arrangement, he may still win a case of unfair dismissal if you fail to show that you acted 'reasonably in the circumstances'. This is the third type of unfairness for selection.

Case law has established the following examples of unreasonable redundancies:

1 Employer's failure to search for alternative employment.
2 Employer ignoring long service.
3 Employer using redundancy to see him through temporary difficulties.
4 Sex discrimination.

These are worth looking at more closely.

1 *Employer's Failure to Search for Suitable Alternative Employment*. The

I.R. Code of Practice (para. 46 [ii]) tells employers they have a duty to transfer staff to other jobs in the organization, if possible. Of course the Code is not legally enforceable, but Tribunals do take this proviso into account.

You need to look throughout the whole organization, not just your department or unit, to try to find a suitable alternative job. This means that you must make a genine effort to find another job; it will be no excuse to say that there is no administrative machinery available to scan the whole company. You are under no obligation to retain an employee in the hope that a vacancy will arise later, but clearly if one is foreseeable, you should offer the vacancy as soon as it arises.

2. *Employer Ignoring Long Service.* It stands to reason that if someone has given you long and loyal service and perhaps is now too old to find another job easily, this should not be ignored when selecting staff for redundancy. Certainly the Tribunals consider length of service. However, this does not mean the older men must always be kept. If a newer member of staff has great ability or shows more potential, then it is reasonable to suggest that he may be retained in preference to the older person. This is supported further if you can show that the younger person would suffer greater hardship than the older one, perhaps because of his family commitments and especially if he is in a depressed area. All in all, then, you must take into account a number of factors before deciding on who is to be selected for redundancy, such as length of service, initiative and drive, efficiency, future management potential and comparison of success rates.
3 *Employer using Redundancy in Temporary Difficulties.* It looks as if temporary difficulties besetting your business do not qualify as a sound defence against unfair selection for redundancy changes. Today you may qualify for subsidies for a fixed period to help you avoid making redundancies.
4 *Sex Discrimination.* The Sex Discrimination Act now bars all discrimination on grounds of sex or marriage in employment, and therefore you may not use such grounds to substantiate your selection for redundancy.

Finally the Employment Protection Act contains provisions which demand that in certain circumstances you must consult trade unions and notify the Department of Employment about redundancy proposals. This will be examined in detail in Section 16.3.

Practical Tips

1 Follow the I.R. Code of Practice, paras 45 and 46, whenever possible.
2 Consult, warn and listen to staff before making them redundant.
3 Do not put older staff automatically at the top of your list for selection.
4 Search for other suitable employment anywhere else in your company.
5 If you do have to make staff redundant, be generous with notice and payments. Do not forget that staff made redundant (after 2 or more year's service) are entitled to reasonable time off work, *with pay*, to look for a new job or to arrange for training for future employment; to refuse this right will result, at a Tribunal, in an award of compensation.

Dismissal because of Legal Prohibition

It is given as a fair reason for dismissal if to continue employing someone would render him or you as the employer liable to prosecution under another statute. This is best illustrated by the case of someone employed as a driver who subsequently loses his licence through, say, disqualification for drunken driving. Clearly if you were to continue employing him as a driver, there would be a breach of the Road Traffic Acts. It would therefore be fair to dismiss that employee.

Dismissal for Taking Part in a Strike

Under the Employment Protection (Consolidation) Act, you have an automatic right to sack staff who are on strike, provided you sack them all without exception. In addition, in order to use this reason to make the decision automatically fair, the strike must come within the definition of a strike, and those on strike must all be sacked during the strike because they are striking.

What then is a strike? The Industrial Relations Act gave a definition of this term but no such definition is given by either the Trade Union and Labour Relations Act or the Employment Protection Act; it would seem then that nowadays a strike can be any form of trade dispute, between employers and employees or between employees and employees. What does appear certain is that if the strikers are in breach of their contract, then this sort of strike allows for automatically fair dismissal. The second qualification mentioned above is that you must dismiss the strikers while they are on strike; if they tell you that the strike is off, it would rank as unfair to dismiss them during the rest of that calendar day. So much for strikes that qualify for being considered automatically fair grounds for dismissal.

You may still succeed in demonstrating fair dismissal if you select some staff for striking during the strike or when it is over, or if you sack all the strikers after they return to work. In these cases, however, you will be required to pass the test of reasonableness, presupposing you have put forward as the grounds for their dismissal industrial misconduct rather than going on strike.

Your alternatives are therefore quite clear: if your staff go on strike you can sack them all, during their strike, for going on strike; but if you select some for the sack or dismiss some or all afterwards, you may be called on to prove you acted reasonably in using the strike as industrial misconduct and therefore grounds for dismissal. However, good industrial relations suggests that to sack staff for going on strike should be seen as a last resort, and even then only after consulting the Advisory, Conciliation and Arbitration Service (A.C.A.S.).

What can you do if your staff take part in a go-slow or a sit-in or any other form of disruption? Are these fair grounds for dismissal? It would seem from the Employment Protection (Consolidation) Act that the same rules hold good here as for dismissing staff who take part in a strike; the same provisions apply to 'other industrial action'. Unfortunately this term is not defined in the law but it is usually considered to cover sit-ins, go-slows, work-to-rules and overtime bans. If you do decide to sack staff for any of these reasons, provided you sack them all while they are carrying out this disruptive action you may well be found to have acted on fair grounds for dismissal. However, if the Tribunal prefers to see their action as industrial misconduct or as 'some other substantial reason' for dismissal, you must be prepared to show that it was reasonable to sack them.

As a final note on this subject, you should remember that time spent on strike does not count as part of the period of employment. When you calculate someone's period of employment with you to assess whether they are qualified to claim protection against unfair dismissal (52 weeks) or to claim redundancy payments (104 weeks), any time spent on strike is deductable from this period.

Dismissal for Other Substantial Reasons

At first sight this appears to give you almost any other grounds for dismissing staff fairly. However, this is not the case; it simply recognizes that no Act can hope to list comprehensively all the circumstances in which an employer can justify dismissing his staff.

It must be a *substantial* reason; this means substantial in relation to the man being dismissed and in relation to the job he was doing. The more important the man and/or the job, the more substantial must be the reason. Here are some examples of reasons held to have been substantial in various cases:

1 Disrupting staff harmony, worsening staff relations.
2 Refusing to comply with reasonable changes made in the interest of greater efficiency.
3 A temporary post coming to an end. (Indeed the Employment Protection (Consolidation) Act specifies that an employer who dismisses the temporary replacement for a woman member of staff who returns to work after having her baby has to state 'some other substantial reason', and is subject to the normal test for reasonableness.)

If you do use this reason for dismissing staff, you do, of course, still require to show that you acted reasonably in all the circumstances. This constitutes the first stage in determining whether a dismissal is fair or not: to define the real reason why you dismissed a member of staff and to decide whether or not it fits into one of the statutory categories. Your evidence so far need only achieve that particular objective. The second stage to be considered is to determine whether you were justified in using this reason as the basis for dismissal.

16.3 WHAT MAKES A DISMISSAL REASONABLE?

Most cases of unfair dismissal have foundered for employers, not because they were unable to show they had one of the prescribed reasons, but at the second stage, when they failed to show they had been reasonable in sacking on those grounds. Nowhere is the term 'reasonable' given definition or description. It has been left to the courts to decide what it means, and they have tended to use the A.C.A.S. Code of Practice recommendations, as well as common sense and considerations of fair play, as the standards against which reasonableness is tested.

How then can you judge whether in sacking staff you are acting 'reasonably'? Make two tests:

1 Is your decision to dismiss fair?
   (a) Is dismissal the fitting punishment for the 'crime'?
   (b) Have you condoned earlier similar shortcomings?
   (c) Is any external factor influencing you, such as pressure from others?
   (d) Is it possible that somebody or something else is really to blame?
   (e) Is any weakness in management responsible?
2 Have you acted fairly before reaching your decision?
   (a) By making a thorough investigation?
   (b) By warning, in writing as well as orally?
   (c) By allowing him an opportunity to state his case?
   (d) By giving him time to improve?
   (e) By making it clear he could appeal to someone higher in the management ladder?
   (f) By complying with the A.C.A.S. Code No. 1. recommendations?

The division is only a convenient one under which to check reasonableness, for in practice the two aspects of reasonableness tend to run together.

Taking these and other checks into consideration, you will agree that it is usually impossible for you to decide if it is fair to dismiss someone until you have warned him, heard his story and given him a chance to improve. The Code of Practice provides the soundest guidelines to follow if you wish to be adjudged by a Tribunal as having acted reasonably in all the circumstances.

A breach of the Code is not a crime because it is not part of the statute. However, it does have a legal effect in that it may be admitted in evidence, and the Employment Protection (Consolidation) Act says that the courts must take it into account in their proceedings. The main sections of the Code, which you would be wise to study and consider, are these:

1 Disciplinary Procedures (A.C.A.S. Code No. 1).
2 Redundancy (paras. 44–6) – I.R. Code.
3 Managerial responsibilities (paras. 6, 31, 35, 41, and 51–9). I.R. Code.

Section 16.3 will incorporate a consideration of redundancies, and Chapter 19 will take account of the Code's guidelines on disciplinary procedures.

Tribunals may find that you have acted unreasonably in deciding to dismiss if part of the fault at least is due to your weakness as a manager. This can happen for instance if you fail in the following ways:

1 To provide proper training.
2 To give clear instructions.
3 To define lines of responsibility.
4 To take action to mend the situation before deciding to dismiss.
5 To consider mitigating circumstances.
6 To act in cases of serious misconduct on earlier occasions.

Finally, so as to keep the value of the Code in perspective, you should realize that there can be occasions when the Code need not be followed before you are considered to have acted reasonably. Some examples of this sort are those in which a shortcoming in competence or efficiency is such that warnings and a chance to improve not only will be of 'no benefit' to the staff concerned but also an 'unfair burden on the business'. Such cases are likely to be rare. Senior management and responsible staff are expected to know what is required of them and to monitor their own performance, so that warnings to them may not be quite so vital.

The most obvious example of where it may not be necessary to go through the whole Code procedure to establish 'reasonableness' is in a case of gross misconduct. Courts do recognize that such offenders may be summarily dismissed, although even then the right to a fair hearing would seem to be reasonable. In such cases you would be advised to suspend staff immediately, sending them off the premises and dismissing them only after hearing the other side of the story.

An employer's guide to dismissing staff fairly is given in Appendix 28 (p. 269).

16.4 WHAT IS MISCONDUCT?

Unfortunately, as we have seen earlier in this chapter, no legal definition exists for the term 'misconduct'. It follows then that every case of someone being sacked for misbehaviour of any sort is examined factually, to determine whether in the circumstances it justified the imposition of the ultimate disciplinary penalty—the sack. As we have noted earlier, the burden of proving that misconduct took place, and that it justified dismissal, lies on your shoulders.

You will not find here a list of the offences which justify you in dismissing staff on grounds of misconduct. That is not possible, since each offence has to be reviewed in all its circumstances before a decision can be reached as to whether or not it was so gross as to deserve dismissal. However, since industrial misconduct has featured so frequently as the reason for dismissal in cases brought before the court, it is possible to evolve some practical guidelines to help you reach a fair decision in any case.

Misconduct differs somewhat from the other statutory reasons given for dismissal in that it alone at times is used to sack staff on the spot—in other words, it is sometimes used to effect instant or summary dismissal. This is a breach of contract on your part, since it means no notice or pay in lieu, and carries with it strong evidence of unreasonableness; in such cases you must be able to convince Tribunals that your reasons for it justify your action. This can be done, of course, but you must be prepared to have your reasons tested fully. It follows then, as a first general guideline, that instant dismissal should be used sparingly. Instant suspension and a full investigation is the sensible and safest way to handle even the worst cases of misconduct.

What sort of things, in general, can you expect to be questioned on if a claim is made against you for unfair dismissal on grounds of misconduct? Basically there are two areas to be examined, as follows:

1 What were your reasons for dismissal?
   (a) What was the nature of the misconduct?
   (b) Where did it take place?
   (c) Had it anything to do with the job?
   (d) Did it affect discipline?
   (e) Did you ignore extenuating circumstances, like a good record?
   (f) Was the offender selected unfairly from others equally guilty?
   (g) Were you in any way to blame?
   (h) Is dismissal the justified punishment?
2 How did you reach and carry out your decision?
   (a) What sort of investigation did you carry out?
   (b) Was it a first offence?
   (c) Did you provide him with a chance to explain?
   (d) Had the offender been warned of the consequences?
   (e) How recent were these warnings?
   (f) Was an opportunity given to him to appeal?

While you can normally expect to be examined on any or all of these points, there are cases in which such a rigorous application of the A.C.A.S. Code No. 1 need not apply, such as explicitly deliberate misconduct, or where the discipline or safety of others, or where the firm's interests, are threatened. Even in these cases the person concerned should be given the opportunity to state his case, and your best plan, as noted earlier, would be to suspend before dismissing.

Here are some of the most common types of misconduct and tips as to how you might handle cases of the sort in your establishment.

Absenteeism/Lateness

Staff have an obligation to be at their place of work during the hours set, but minor breaches are unlikely to justify dismissal. Since lateness is a habit that can be cured, you would be well advised to ensure that staff guilty of turning up late are formally warned before you contemplate sacking them. This warning should preferably be in the form of an individual notice to the person(s) concerned, rather than a round robin on the subject, and it should spell out clearly your intention of dismissing if the offence continues.

Absence from work is rather more serious. Nonetheless before using it as grounds for dismissal, make sure your actions will pass the test of reasonableness. Consider the following factors:

1. Does your disciplinary procedure cover absenteeism?
2. Have you observed such a procedure carefully?
3. Does the nature of the job make absenteeism intolerable because of strict rotas or for safety reasons, for instance?
4. What about the offender's personal record of work attendance?
5. Was he given sufficient warning?
6. Was there any element of dishonesty in the absence—pretending sickness in order to do another job, say?

Dishonesty

This offence is generally considered by employers to be one of the more intolerable ones, which automically carry the penalty of dismissal. While the courts may generally agree with this view, they will still require you to pass the test of 'reasonableness'.

One point must be clearly understood: Tribunals are industrial courts of law and do not handle criminal proceedings; they see the crime only as potential grounds for dismissal and do not apply the Larceny Act. Because a person has been convicted in the ordinary courts does not necessarily mean that his dismissal will be seen to be automatically fair, nor an acquittal in these courts as grounds in themselves for rendering the dismissal unfair. Such a conviction or acquittal is clearly useful evidence in determining whether *at the time* your action was fair or unfair. What matters in such cases is whether you were right to dismiss the offender when you did, not whether you were right or wrong about his guilt.

The general guideline to follow, if you suspect dishonesty in a member of staff, is to suspend him, on full pay, until your investigations are complete. If the case is subject to criminal proceedings and the offender elects trial by jury, then of course suspension on pay may not be practicable. The solution to this problem, if you feel that you have insufficient grounds for dismissal until the case is resolved in the criminal court, is to suspend him, with pay suspended too. However, this can only be done if such a procedure is written into the man's contract or the company's staff rules, otherwise, like all suspension without pay, it becomes a breach of contract on your part and therefore dismissal, though the Tribunal may see it as justified in such cases.

Here are some examples of common forms of dishonesty, and how Tribunals might look on them as fair grounds for dismissal.

1 *Stealing*. Generally anyone who steals from the company or his colleagues at work may be summarily dismissed; this is especially true if it is covered in staff rules or where the sum stolen is not trivial. You are likely to be faulted only in the way you handle the case, and that means, especially, giving the man a chance to explain.

If the stealing takes place away from work it can still be grounds for summary dismissal if you can show that at the time you dismissed him you considered such convictions would harm your company's reputation with customers, say, or that it would harm trade or insurance terms. Play safe here by making sure there is a notice of warning covering such circumstances, and that this may lead to dismissal.

Finally cases of 'borrowing' from petty cash or from the till when the money is repaid may not at first sight appear to be gross dishonesty. Nevertheless such behaviour will usually be viewed by Tribunals as fair grounds for dismissal, provided your actions pass the normal test of reasonableness.

2 *Petty Theft*. This can amount to grounds for fair dismissal especially if done by responsible staff or staff in positions of trust regarding cash. Once again it will help your case if the matter is

covered in your staff rules, and you act reasonably in using this ground for dismissal.

3 *Fiddling*. Under this heading you may consider all such cases as clocking-in offences or falsifying time and expense sheets. Generally any offence of false clocking-in or clocking-in for others is serious, justifying summary dismissal, especially if it is covered by staff rules or by a warning of instant dismissal placed in the vicinity of the clock.

Fiddling time or expense sheets is equally serious misconduct, but in these cases you must make sure you have all the facts and do not spoil your case by acting inconsistently or condoning earlier offences, or by paying the fiddled accounts before dismissal; perhaps above all give the offender an opportunity to explain his actions.

Disobedience

Every member of staff has an obligation to co-operate, and this implies that he must obey all reasonable, lawful and non-dangerous orders within the terms of his employment. The crucial question to be answered in any case of disobedience is whether obedience to this order is an essential contractual condition. To warrant a summary dismissal, the disobedience must contain an element of 'wilfulness'. As in other cases of dismissal, what will be at stake is your reasonableness. Was it a breach of a vital term in the contract? Were you reasonable in using that disobediience as grounds for dismissal? If so, did you reach your decision and carry it out properly? Let us look at some examples:

1 *Disobeying Instructions at Work*. This is rarely seen by Tribunals as gross misconduct. If you want to use such disobedience as grounds for dismissal, be sure you can pass the test of reasonableness: (1) do not condone the offence by delaying your decision to dismiss; (2) do not overlook previous good records; (3) give due warning of the possibility of dismissal.

2 *Flouting Safety Rules*. You are almost certain to win any case against you for unfair dismissal if your reason for sacking a member of staff is a serious breach of a safety rule, such as refusing to use the guard on a slicing machine: that is gross misconduct. There is no real need for warnings here; the rules themselves incorporate such warnings, and the seriousness of the offence lies in the threat to company discipline and the safety of other staff. Even so, common sense demands that you

give a man the chance to put his case before dismissal, except where he blatantly refuses to follow a safety rule. Instant dismissal is a fair remedy.

3 *Refusing to Work Overtime.* The most important question to answer in this type of disobedience is, Is overtime provided for in the contract of employment? This may be expressly stated in a contract or be there by implication: staff in supervisory or management positions, for example, are usually expected to work overtime when necessary. Refusing optional overtime will rarely rank as a sound reason for dismissal; if your business relies on staff working voluntary overtime and if staff stop it suddenly when it is likely to hurt you most, you may be able to make out a case for fair dismissal. However, you would need to make out a good case because you are dismissing someone for not doing something his contract does not oblige him to do.

4 *Refusing Changes in Terms and Conditions of Employment.* Unless you are entitled, by virtue of the contract, to change essential items such as pay systems, shifts, hours and so on, then a refusal by staff to accept these changes is an expression of their right and not misconduct. If you dismiss anyone for such refusal, you are unlikely to be found to have dismissed fairly. As you have seen before, agreement by staff to the changes must be your objective.

Drinking

Most employers have strict rules about drinking by staff on duty, and if they carry the penalty of summary dismissal, Tribunals will usually recognize breaches of these rules as fair grounds for dismissal. They will still require you to pass the test of fairness and may ask the following questions:

1 Where did the drinking take place?
2 Was the person on duty at the time?
3 Was there a clear rule in the company about drinking on duty?
4 Was the offender in contact with customers?
5 Did you give a chance to tell his side of the story, when sober?

Violence/Swearing

Physical violence is another matter that is often incorporated in staff rules, and carries with it the penalty of dismissal. However, as you will expect by now, you must still be prepared to defend your actions as reasonable in dismissing. Points such as the following may be covered:

1 Was the violence serious enough to warrant dismissal?
2 Was either party a senior employee?
3 Have you enough corroboration to satisfy yourself as to the facts in the case?
4 Did you take into account mitigating circumstances, such as frustration or provocation?

Bad language used by staff against their superiors is likely to be seen as fair grounds for dismissal only if it is persistent or constitutes serious insolence. Are you prepared to face the test of reasonableness again? Consider the following points:

1 Can the act itself be considered so serious as to have fractured the employment relationship?
2 Was the language so wilfully offensive as to distress the ordinary person?
3 Was the status of the swearer or recipient a matter of importance?
4 Was a chance given to the offender to apologize?
5 Was he warned that refusing to apologize might lead to dismissal?
6 Did you take into account any extenuating circumstances, such as ill-health or an explosion of bad temper?

Misconduct Outside Work

If you read in your local paper that a member of your staff has been convicted of an offence outside work, does this justify your dismissing him? The short answer would seem to be, it may do so if such a conviction affects his work or the reputation of your business. What you must weigh carefully is whether the case justifies the further punishment of being sacked. The factors to take into account are these:

1 The facts you have at the time you think of dismissing him.
2 The nature of the offence and conviction.
3 The status and job of the offender.
4 The effect it might have on your business.
5 Whether your staff rules warn that convictions of this sort may lead to dismissal.

Where there is no conviction, your chances of succeeding in showing fair dismissal are much weaker. You need to show that the man's actions have affected his work or your reputation and interests. Offences committed off duty on your premises need careful consideration too. Could they affect working relations? Were outsiders implicated, and did they know that the offender was a member of the staff?

No doubt misconduct will continue to feature commonly as a reason for dismissing staff. No court will expect you to put up with gross misbehaviour by staff but, as you have seen, they will expect you to show evidence that the offence took place and that it was of a serious nature; and that, in fairness to both the business and the dismissed employee, you behaved in a reasonable manner in reaching the decision to sack and in the way you carried out your decision. The recommendations contained in the A.C.A.S. Code No. 1 will feature largely in determining this.

16.5 THE SICK EMPLOYEE

One of the biggest headaches for many managers is deciding when they can fairly sack one of their staff for sickness. At first sight it seems as if the Employment Protection (Consolidation) Act is on their side, since it specifically lists 'incapability' as the very first of the statutory grounds on which it is fair to dismiss staff. Surely, it is argued, if incapability means lacking in any physical or mental quality required to do the job, then illness is a classic example of incapability. Even if that is the case, the question remains, Would it be considered reasonable and fair to use these grounds for sacking?

What needs determining is, How do you balance fairness to the individual with fairness to the business and its efficiency? There have been a number of cases where staff have been dismissed on grounds of sickness, and certain helpful guidelines have emerged.

A contract can be automatically discharged whenever it is impossible for either side to fulfil the duties of the contract, through no fault of his own. This is the doctrine of frustration. A chef who loses his arms in an accident provides a simple example of this frustration: no dismissal takes place, notice is not required and there can be no presumption of redundancy or unfair dismissal. Few cases of illness can be so clear cut. Perhaps the first lesson then is that, if you think the point of frustration has been reached, you must take steps to terminate the contract, otherwise it will be adduced in evidence that the parties did not consider events amounted to frustration.

The real worry to managers are staff who have prolonged absences for sickness or other incapacity, or the chronically ill. Perhaps the best starting point is to remind you what the I.R. Code has to say on the subject: 'As far as is consistent with operational efficiency and the success of the undertaking, management should provide stable employment including reasonable job security for employees absent through sickness or other causes beyond their control' (para. 40 [i]). Every case needs to be considered on its merits, but the first guideline must be—move slowly, and act generously.

You may have a case in which someone has been off ill 'for a long time', or another where the person has relatively minor bouts of sickness throughout the year. You cannot safely apply the slide rule of time to each case so that after a certain period you can fairly dismiss. The nearest guide you can use in this respect is 26 weeks, a length of time arising from the Employment Protection (Consolidation) Act's limit to continuity of employment in sickness absence, and from many company sick-pay schemes operating for a period of six months. But use this figure only as a guide: it does not mean that if you wait that long before dismissing you will be guaranteed a finding of fair dismissal, nor does it necessarily mean that to sack someone in a lesser period of time makes for an unfair dismissal.

In cases of illness the Tribunals invariably expect employers to implement the same recommendations of the A.C.A.S. Code as applied to cases of misconduct. Therefore, pursue the following course:

1 Take stock of the case and get the facts.
2 Issue a warning that it may be necessary to replace the sick man, and therefore he will lose his job.
3 Listen to his side of the story.
4 Give him a chance to prove his future health and capability.
5 Give him the chance to appeal against your decision.

Practical Tips

1 Look at the terms of the contract, especially the provisions for sickness. Not every company operates a sick pay scheme, although para. 41 of the I.R. Code recommends one. However, most employers do make up wages for a time, perhaps to be followed later by half-pay and even unpaid leave. On the other hand, in some companies the only benefit staff can obtain during sickness is state security benefit. Whatever the case in your company, remember the requirements of the Code 'to keep employees on through reasonable bouts of temporary sickness'.

If you have a sick pay scheme, it is most unlikely to be a fair dismissal if you sack anyone while it is still operating. If you do not operate such a scheme, nor provide benefits to sick staff, then clearly you should be in even less of a hurry to dismiss them.

2 Consider the length of time the job is likely to last, and whether or not the person holds a key position in your establishment. This means in practical terms that you may be able to show reasonableness more easily if you dismiss someone who is close to retirement. The same will be true if the position held is an indispensable one, or one that greatly affects the work of other staff (so that when the job holder is off sick there is a big strain put on others). If you do use this approach, be sure you do not quote the needs of the job as the main reason for sacking; they should be used to support your reasonableness only.

3 Consider carefully the nature of the illness. What matters here is the information you have at the time of dismissal; subsequent events neither favour nor harm your case. Medical evidence is what counts in this context, and it has to be weighed in relation to the job he will do on his return.

4 Take into account length of service. This guideline speaks for itself: someone who has given you loyal and faithful service surely deserves special consideration.

Another way to tackle the problem in certain cases, which might well support your attempt to show how reasonable you have been, is to offer the person affected a lighter job or one with fewer hours. If you do this, and it is acceptable to staff, take care that, if later, because this new job comes to an end and you offer him another job that he refuses because it is beyond him, you do not sack him for misconduct (unreasonable refusal of an order within his contract). The Tribunal might well see this as a dismissal on the grounds of ill-health, because it arose out of the original incapacity, and probably unfair, especially if the original illness arose out of the employment with you.

Pregnancy and Maternity

Under the Employment Protection (Consolidation) Act it is no longer fair to dismiss a member of your staff who becomes pregnant unless at the time you dismiss her she cannot or will not be able to do her job, or unless to go on employing her would be against the law.

On the other hand, if you can prove that you offered her more suitable, not less favourable, work before her job ended, or that no such work was available, then this will act as a defence to any claim of unfair dismissal. So in practice you must allow a pregnant employee to work right up to the time the baby is due, either at her own or another suitable job; if you sack her on pregnancy grounds, this will rank as an unfair dismissal.

If you offer alternative employment, it must meet certain criteria:

1 It must follow on immediately upon her old job.
2 It must be suitable for women.
3 It must be suitable for a pregnant woman.
4 The place and terms and conditions of her employment must not be substantially less favourable to her than her old conditions.

It is worth noting in passing that the Act does not say this right is vested in married staff only.

You should be prepared then to accept that during her pregnancy a woman may require time off to attend clinics and may indeed have days at home 'on the sick'. This is unlikely to be accepted as grounds for showing she was incapable of doing her work.

Allied to the right not to be dismissed for pregnancy after 12 months' service, women have other new rights under the Employment Protection (Consolidation) Act. In brief, female members of staff now have a right to return to work after confinement, and since 6 April 1977 the right to a maternity payment. Basically this means that at any time up to 29 weeks from confinement, your female staff have the right to return to work with you, or your successor, in the same or a similar job on no less favourable terms than would exist had she not been absent. To obtain this right, women must have had 2 years' service with you, remain at work until at least 11 weeks before confinement, and let you know at least 3 weeks before their absence that they intend to return to work with you.

Staff must give you a week's notice before they intend to return. You can delay the return by a month from the day she notifies you, provided you give your reasons. Similarly, the employee can delay her return for 4 weeks—until the 33rd week after confinement—provided she lets you know by the 29th week that she is not fit and produces a medical certificate if you require it. The failure on your part to allow such a member of staff to return is treated as dismissal for both redundancy and unfair dismissal purposes.

Practical Tips

1 Encourage any member of staff likely to leave her job to have a baby to let you know as early as she can whether she intends to return to her job. You would be well advised to ask for this notice in writing.

2 If you recruit a temporary replacement, make sure you inform her in writing that she will be dismissed when the original member of staff returns.
3 While the dismissal of the 'temp' will be legally for 'some other substantial reason' (as given by E.P. [C] Act), you will still be required to act 'reasonably'; this means, for instance, that you should offer her any suitable alternative work that may be available.
4 Keep records of any changes in terms and conditions, such as pay and holidays, which the returning member of staff will be entitled to on her return. Remember also that her weeks of absence count towards her rights.
5 You do not have to pay pension contributions during the leave of absence period.
6 Remember that all 'maternity absences' are now given unbroken service and weeks that count, for 26 weeks, and that if the mothers conform with all the requirements of the Act in claiming reinstatement, then they are given this continuity for their total absence, up to their notified day of return—even if you refuse to have them back. In either case it means in practice that, if they do come back, they will be entitled to time off for another pregnancy immediately.

Any member of your staff who has been in your employment for 2 years has a right to 6 weeks' paid leave once she reaches the 11th week before her baby is due, provided she has stayed in employment till then (even if she happens to be away from work at the time, perhaps through sickness), and provided she lets you know (in writing if you wish) at least 3 weeks before taking her leave that she will be away from work because of her pregnancy. You will be entitled to ask for a medical certificate showing the week the baby is expected, if you ask for it.

You should note that a woman who has been dismissed but who would have been 2 years in the job by the '11th week before' retains her full rights. It is worth noting also that 'confinement' is defined so as to cover any live or dead birth after 28 weeks of pregnancy.

You can pay the maternity leave weekly, monthly or in a lump sum. It amounts to 6 × 9/10ths of a full week's pay, less £18.50 state maternity allowance, whether in fact she is entitled to this or not. If you operate a 'service charge', which is added to staff's basic wages as part of their total earnings, then this counts as part of the 'full week's pay'. If your tipping system is such that the money passes directly from customer to staff, then no account of this is taken in calculating the week's pay.

You are still required to pay a full 6 weeks' leave even if staff work beyond the '11th week before', although they will lose any state maternity allowance for any weeks beyond that 11th week. Nevertheless the state allowance is still deductable from your payments.

You will not be required to include in the 'week's pay' any sums normally included to cover such things as fares and travelling, free use of car or health assurance. Nor need you take into account overtime unless there is a contract to provide and work it, nor to include payments for food and free accommodation not being used.

A Maternity Pay Fund has been set up, into which all employers levied for secondary Class 1 contributions pay, even if they themselves do not employ women. It is similar to the present Redundancy Payments Fund. You will be entitled to reclaim in full from this fund any maternity payments made.

16.6 WHAT HAPPENS AT A TRIBUNAL?

Even the best employer can find that he is the subject of a claim against him by one of his staff, whether it be for unfair dismissal, sex discrimination or an equal pay dispute, and he may therefore be required to defend himself at an Industrial Tribunal. This section sets out to describe what happens at a Tribunal hearing and to give guidelines as to how to present your side of the case.

Industrial Tribunals were first set up in 1964 under the Industrial Training Act to handle disputes over the Industrial Training Levy. Since then this jurisdiction has been expanded so that today they are empowered to deal with most claims arising from the Equal Pay Act 1970, Trade Union and Labour Relations Act 1974, Sex Discrimination Act 1975 the Employment Protection Act 1975 and the Employment Protection (Consolidation) Act 1978.

Tribunals usually consist of three persons: the chairman, who must be legally qualified, and two lay members appointed by the Secretary of State for Employment. These Tribunals sit in locations all over the country. Any appeal from Industrial Tribunals, on points of law only, are taken to the newly appointed Employment Appeals Tribunal, the successor to the National Industrial Relations Court; its central office is in London but it can sit where it chooses. The chairman in this case is a judge of the High Court, Court of Appeal or Court of Session, and the other members lay persons with special experience or knowledge of industrial relations.

An Industrial Tribunal has the same status as a county court, and while any decisions they may make are 'for persuasive effect' only, and do not set precedents that become part of case law, the interpretations given in past cases before Industrial Tribunals generally are followed by other Industrial Tribunals. On the other hand, the Employment Appeals Tribunal has the same standing as the High Court and Court of Session, and being a superior court of record it can make orders for contempt of court and its decisions do set precedents that must be followed by Industrial Tribunals. It is possible to appeal from decisions given by the Employment Appeals Tribunal on points of law only, and those appeals will be heard in the Court of Appeal in England and Wales, and the Court of Sessions in Scotland.

The first difference you will note between Industrial Tribunals and other judicial courts is the informality with which they operate. The Tribunal members wear ordinary clothes rather than wig and gown, and are addressed either as 'Sir/Madam' or by name. While having the status of county courts, they operate as courts of industrial common sense. You may present your own case or be represented by anyone you wish—employers' association, solicitor or friend. The hearings themselves are conducted informally, without too much attention being paid to the strict rules of evidence and procedure. You may therefore ask your own witnesses leading questions, witnesses may read prepared statements and hearsay evidence may be admitted. All the parties may sit while speaking, and conduct their case in the way they think best.

Anyone who wishes to institute proceedings at an Industrial Tribunal is required to complete an application form (IT1) obtainable at any Department of Employment office. An example of such a form is shown in Appendix 29 (p. 270); it sets out the grounds on which a Tribunal decision is sought. As an employer, the first thing you may know about the claim against you is when you receive a copy of this completed form from the secretary of Tribunals, together with another form (IT3), which constitutes a notice of appearance. An example of this form is shown in Appendix 30 (p. 274).

Briefly this form will invite you to state whether you intend to resist the application and, if so, the grounds on which you propose to resist. To secure your right to take part in the proceedings you must deliver your completed Form IT3, personally or by post, to the secretary of the Tribunals at the address given in the notification to you, and within the required time limit of 14 days. A copy of your completed form is then sent to the applicant.

Practical Tips

1 If you feel you have been given insufficient information by the claimant to prepare your reply, seek the required information directly from him; if he refuses to help, apply to the Industrial Tribunal, which can order him to do so.
2 Always 'enter an appearance' by completing Form IT3.
3 If, by chance, you have not been able to complete and return the form within the 14 days allowed, return it nevertheless, explaining why you have been late. An extension of time can be allowed.
4 Even if you do not intend to resist the claim you should complete the defence form; this will retain your right to appear at the hearing if you change your mind.
5 If you do not think you are the employer who should be named, do not pass the IT3 on; enter an appearance in case you are concerned after all.

Once the secretary has copies of the Forms IT1 and IT3, he will pass copies of these and any other statements to the conciliation officer of the Advisory, Conciliation and Arbitration Service, who will then try to assist the parties concerned to reach a settlement without a Tribunal hearing. Industrial Tribunals place a great deal of emphasis on the settlement of disputes by conciliation; an agreed solution is always preferable to one imposed by judicial decisions.

This is the time when you should try to weigh up the whole case objectively. Has the claim got any merit? It might pay you to settle a good claim either by negotiating directly with the claimant, registering the settlement with the Industrial Tribunal, or negotiating through the conciliation officer.

The conciliation officer will usually see the employee first and then the employer. Remember that he is not an executive in any sense; his job is to help the parties reach an amicable settlement. He will therefore only come to see you if requested to do so, or if he thinks his advice and help will meet with reasonable success. If you refuse to see him, this is an exercise of your right and will not prejudice your case at the subsequent Tribunal hearing. You should remember, however, that these officers have a lot of experience of Tribunal cases and can be useful in advising you whether or not to settle out of court. Moreover anything you say or put in writing to a conciliation officer is private and cannot be used at any hearing without your permission.

If the conciliation officer considers that you are likely to lose the case against you, he can negotiate with you a return to work of the claimant for unfair dismissal, on a basis of reinstatement or re-engagement, or he can try to reach an agreement on compensation to be paid by you. In many cases you may find it impossible, for a number of reasons, to take back the person dismissed; in this case you are left with negotiating a sum of money to be paid out in compensation. A review of the many cases that have been resolved by out-of-court settlements would seem to indicate that by taking this approach your compensatory award may be less than if it goes through the Tribunal. This is where the conciliation officer can be very helpful with his advice in calculating appropriate compensation on principles used by the Tribunals themselves.

The Tribunal Hearing

If conciliation is not used or fails to bring about an amicable solution to the claim, you will then receive notification of the Tribunal hearing at least 14 days beforehand, probably with notes on the hearing, witnesses and what documents you should bring.

If you wish others to give evidence on your behalf, you must arrange this yourself. If such witnesses refuse to come, you can then apply to the Tribunal for an order requiring them to attend, which you must serve on them yourself. You may need to pay their fare to attend, but you can reclaim this money after the hearing.

A question that vexes many managers faced with a tribunal hearing is, Should I engage a lawyer or barrister to represent me/the company? There is no one answer to this question—it depends on how complex the case is and also to some extent on how well you know the basic law under which the claim against you is being brought. However, you should remember above all that a Tribunal hearing, while it is a judicial proceeding, is nonetheless an industrial court in which formalities are kept to a minimum and where cases are generally resolved in the best interests of sound common sense rather than on the niceties of the law. To support this view you must remember that, in most cases, a majority decision of the Tribunal is sufficient, and in practice this frequently means that the lay members are in agreement while the chairman, the legal member, may not be happy until every legal 'i' has been dotted or 't' crossed. Additionally, Tribunals place a lot of weight on people who can state facts from their own direct experience and knowledge, which can be subject to detailed cross-examination. In the end you must reach the decision to employ an agent to act on your behalf, be he a solicitor, a member of an employers' organization or simply a friend, in the light of both the case itself and your own confidence in presenting your own evidence.

Tribunals have the power to regulate their own proceedings, and can therefore deviate from what might be considered the norm. Usually the applicant, or his representative, will make an opening statement in which he will try to make three main points:

1 That he is qualified to bring the claim.
2 That he is not an excluded person.
3 That he was dismissed according to the legal definition of the term.

If you do not dispute these matters, you may be asked to open the proceedings instead of the applicant.

The applicant may give whatever evidence he feels necessary to establish these facts, and he may call witnesses to support him. You then have the right to question him or the witnesses, and the applicant can re-examine any witnesses you may have questioned.

It is then your turn, and you will be required to make three main points also:

1 That you had a reason for dismissing the applicant.
2 That the reason is one of those declared by the Act to be fair grounds for dismissal.
3 That you were reasonable in using it to dismiss the applicant in these circumstances.

Once you have completed your evidence and called witnesses (if you wish), you and the witnesses will be subject to questioning by the applicant, and when this is complete, you may re-examine those witnesses of yours that were subject to cross-examination by the applicant. The Tribunal members themselves may ask questions at any stage of the hearing.

You may ask for an adjournment of the hearing, for a short or long period, so as to consider matters put forward. You may refer to any documents that have been submitted to the Tribunal. You may seek the guidance of the Industrial Tribunal at any time on points of procedure.

Hearings are normally held in public but Tribunals have power to sit in private if, say, confidential information is to be given in evidence.

Before you attend the Tribunal, you must make sure that you have gathered together all the evidence you need to rebut the case against you. It is worth recalling that in almost all cases centering on unfair dismissal the burden of proof is on you as the employer.

Take into consideration first those people who can give direct evidence of facts that may be called in question—those who witnessed events in dispute, the ones who took part in the investigation, and those who administered your disciplinary code, especially whoever made and carried out the decision to dismiss. You may not consider it necessary to call all these witnesses, but their value to your case should be weighed up carefully. Next you must assemble any useful documentary evidence—statement of main terms and conditions of employment, staff handbooks, personal files or records, letters, reports and so on. Any time spent beforehand meticulously preparing your statement so that it is presented logically and backed by supporting evidence will weigh well with the members of the Tribunal.

Clearly the reason you are attending a Tribunal at all is because you dispute a claim that has been entered against you. One party is claiming that their legal right has been infringed. It is the job of the Tribunal to resolve this dispute, and to do so will usually necessitate their determining matters of fact and matters of law. You may disagree with the facts presented by your ex-staff member or about the interpretation of the law. Even if you are both in agreement about the facts of the case, you will have to inform the court of those facts and may be called upon to prove them. In this case it will be a matter of applying the law to these facts. On the other hand, if the facts are in dispute, the Tribunal's task will then be to decide, from all the evidence, which version of the facts to take as correct, and apply the law to them. Every case then consists of a body of fact and a body of law. To succeed you can adopt one of two approaches, as follows:

1 Rebut the case made out by the claimant and substitute the facts and law in support of your side.
2 Take a positive line from the start and concentrate on winning your own case.

This second approach has the merit of your going for the win rather than making sure that your opponent loses: a case won is won, but a case lost is not necessarily won by the other side.

Before you make out your case at all in the Tribunal setting, you will recall that the Tribunal and the claimant already have copies of the facts of your case. How much detail is included will vary from case to case, depending on its complexity, whether facts are disputed, or whether the law can be applied to a broad situation of facts or not.

Practical Tips

1 Try to obtain as much agreement as possible on facts before attending the Tribunal.
2 Give as much evidence as you can from your direct experience.
3 Obtain the help of witnesses whose evidence is based on what they saw and heard for themselves.
4 As far as possible give your evidence without sheaves of notes.
5 Be prepared to interpret official documents used by you in evidence.
6 Be ready to provide proof of authenticity for any documentary evidence submitted.
7 Do not worry if you are not fully conversant with the law's provisions—that is the prime responsibility of the Industrial Tribunal members.
8 Nevertheless try to grasp the more salient parts of the law and be ready to support your case by putting forward legal points.
9 Use the Codes of Practice openly to support your view.
10 Speak clearly so as to be easily heard, and address all your remarks to the Tribunal.
11 Do not speak too quickly: the Tribunal members take their notes in longhand.
12 Aim throughout your evidence to show that because the facts are these, and because the law says this, therefore, the claim against you must fail.

The Decision and the Appeal

Once the case is over, it is normal for the Tribunal to announce its decision and the reasons on which it is based. All decisions are written up with the reasons, and sent to the Secretary of State, from whom you will receive a copy, usually about three weeks later.

In all cases of unfair dismissal, if you should fail to rebut the claim against you, the Tribunal may decide to order you to reinstate or re-engage the claimant, or they may award a monetary compensation to be paid by you. The details of these penalties form the subject of Section 16.7.

The decision given by an Industrial Tribunal is not necessarily final. The Secretary of Industrial Tribunals can review or revoke the decision if, for instance, the following apply:

1 The decision was made while eligible parties were absent.
2 New evidence has come to light since the decision was reached.
3 Justice generally demands it.

To seek an appeal of this sort you can either ask for a reconsideration by the chairman of the Tribunal as soon as he has announced his decision, or you can write to the secretary of the Tribunals, stating your reasons, within 14 days of the date on which the Tribunal decision is registered. (This is shown on the copy which is sent to you.) Finally you do have a right of appeal to the Employment Appeals Tribunal, provided it is notified within 42 days of the registering of the Tribunal decision. Information about this right of appeal is sent to you when the copy of the Tribunal decision is dispatched. However, this appeal can only be made on a point of law, not on any point of fact.

Very broadly your appeal in this case must be on the grounds either that the Industrial Tribunal failed to apply the proper legal principles, or failed to apply the legal principles properly. This can apply to the principles of law themselves or to procedures. Some examples from cases taken on appeal to the National Industrial Relations Court help to illustrate points of law:

1 Stating the burden of proof wrongly.
2 Wrongly interpreting time limits or dismissal dates.
3 Considering the wrong circumstances.
4 Coming to their decision wrongly on the evidence.

It is possible to bring forward fresh evidence at the appeal stage but you cannot be guaranteed that it will be allowed in every case. You can, however, be hopeful if the fresh evidence is credible, likely to have been decisive if known at the time, or was not brought forward at the Tribunal hearing for a very good reason.

Costs

Although Industrial Tribunals do have the power to award costs, generally no costs are awarded unless either party is 'frivolous' or 'vexatious'. There are no court fees. On the other hand, allowances are payable to both parties to cover cost of travelling, subsistence and loss of earnings. These allowances are equally payable to witnesses and anyone who represents you (except barristers, solicitors and full-time officials of trade unions or employment associations). The only payment you may have to make will be to the claimant if the tribunal is postponed or adjourned at your request, or because of some action or failure to act on your part.

Remember that Industrial Tribunals place a great deal of emphasis on conciliation—they encourage settlements out of court before and even during the hearings. Weigh up carefully any claim against you, and, if you have been at fault, it will save a lot of time and money if you can reach an acceptable solution before it reaches the Tribunal stage. Apart from the obvious example of the time needed in preparing to answer a case and perhaps the cost of being represented, a case going against you can damage staff relations, your image in customers' eyes, or even your own career as a manager if you should have succeeded in preventing or successfully answering the complaint.

On the other hand, if you feel sure that you have complied with the law and the Codes of Practice, do not be afraid to defend your case fully at an Industrial Tribunal. Make sure you prepare for it fully and support your refutation of the claim with substantial evidence.

16.7 THE PENALTIES OF DISMISSING UNFAIRLY

The emphasis at the end of the last section was on the value of conciliation. The Employment Protection (Consolidation) Act places re-employment, either through reinstatement or re-engagement, rather than monetary compensation as its prime objective and the most important remedy for unfair dismissal. Whether or not this objective will be reached in most cases will remain a matter of conjecture until cases are decided by Tribunals under the newest legislation.

If you decide to settle any reasonably well based claim against you, and you find it impossible or impracticable to re-employ the member of staff bringing a claim against you for unfair dismissal, you will be faced with the problem of assessing what sum of money to offer as fair compensation. Of course the conciliation officer will advise you here, if you wish, but otherwise you should follow the Tribunal's own principles, which are described below. If you do make such a payment, do not be tempted to give it 'in full and final settlement of all claims' unless it is reached through the conciliation officer; otherwise staff will still have a right to take their case to a Tribunal. However, the Employment Protection (Consolidation) Act does allow for any ex-gratia payments to be deducted from any award that may subsequently be made against you.

Reinstatement and Re-engagement

It is important to distinguish between these awards: reinstatement means that staff are given back their old job on the same terms and conditions as before without loss of continuity in employment or loss of money and rights; and re-engagement means that staff are given a job with their previous employer, without loss of continuity. It is not as favourable as reinstatement.

Tribunals, having judged a dismissal unfair, now have the following obligations:

1 To explain the remedies to the employee.
2 To find out which one he would prefer.
3 Use their discretion on all the facts as to which remedy they offer.

If the Industrial Tribunal decides to order re-employment, it must first consider reinstatement. It will take into account the employee's wishes, the practicability of it for the employer, and the justice of it if the employee was in any way himself at fault. How practicable will it be for you? The Tribunals will decide but they will ignore the fact that you have taken on a permanent replacement unless you can show that (1) you had to do it to cover the work, or that (2) you took on a replacement only after a reasonable period of time during which your ex-staff gave no indication he wanted re-employment, and it was unreasonable for the work to be covered without having a replacement.

If you are given a reinstatement order, you will be told that you must treat the ex-employee as if he had never been sacked, including any improvements in terms and conditions since his dismissal. The order will also specify:

1 The arrears of pay from dismissal to reinstatement (less any money received during that time, such as wages in lieu, ex-gratia payments and unemployment benefit).
2 Rights and privileges to be restored, including seniority and pensions.
3 The date on which you must comply with the order.

You should note in passing that both you and the reinstated person must pay state contributions in respect of the pay arrears.

If the Tribunal decides against ordering reinstatement, it will then consider re-engagement, taking into account the same factors as for reinstatement. If an order is issued on this basis, you will be told to give the ex-employee a job comparable to the one he held, or another suitable job. The Tribunal must specify the other terms that are applicable to a reinstatement order, and also the identity of the employer, the nature of the job, and the pay for the job.

A re-engagement order is not usually as favourable to the employee as one ordering reinstatement. The Tribunals can 'punish' anyone who has contributed to his own dismissal by making the terms of re-engagement less favourable, perhaps by specifying a different, though suitable, job or work place.

If you re-employ someone, as ordered, but fail to comply fully with all the terms of the order, the Industrial Tribunal must award compensation to the member of staff, up to a maximum of £6,250. If you simply refuse to re-employ the sacked person, despite the order, you will have to pay a basic compensation of up to £3,600, plus a compensatory award of up to £6,250 and an award of anything from 13 to 52 weeks' pay. If the dismissal was in any way founded on your discrimination against the employee, on grounds of Trade Union membership perhaps, or on grounds of sex or race, then the award will range from 26–52 weeks' pay. For all other cases the award will fall between 13 and 26 weeks' pay. A week's pay is set at a maximum of £120.

Cash Compensation

Under the Employment Protection (Consolidation) Act, unfair dismissal can attract two potential awards, as follows:

1 A compensatory award of up to £6,250 (and no longer a lower maximum of 104 × week's pay, as under Trade Union and Labour Relations Act).
2 A basic award of a minimum of 2 weeks' pay and a maximum of £3,600.

Other awards can be made over and above these: for example, failing to give written reasons for dismissal to a sacked person within 14 days of his request brings an award of 2 weeks' pay.

The purpose of the basic award is to make sure no one is any worse off than he would have been had he been made redundant. If he has already received a redundancy payment, this will be deducted from his unfair dismissal compensation.

The following are the guidelines Tribunals follow so as to arrive at a final figure of cash compensation:

1 They assess actual loss as a result of dismissal.
2 They consider all losses attributable to employers' action.
3 They seek evidence of loss from the employee.
4 They consider all the circumstances.

5 Where the employee is in any way to blame, they reflect this in a reduction from award.
6 They weigh up how far the employee has tried to lessen his losses.
7 They provide a breakdown of figures to illustrate how the net figure has been reached.

The following losses are totted up for total compensation purposes:

1 Loss of earnings, immediate and future.
2 Loss of protection against unfair dismissal and redundancy.
3 Money loss flowing directly from the manner of dismissal.
4 Lost notice, holiday and sick pay.
5 Loss of entitlement to longer notice.
6 Lost benefits and expenses.

The total compensation for all these losses is then reduced by anything received or earned after dismissal—such as unemployment benefit, tax rebates, training grants, ex-gratia payments, pay in lieu of notice and any earnings in a new job. The maximum a tribunal is allowed to award is applied *after* all deductions have been made from the total.

Tribunals take into account any part the employee had in effecting his own dismissal when assessing the final figure for compensation. In some cases staff have won cases for unfair dismissal but had their compensation reduced by 100 per cent so that they received nothing. The following guidelines have evolved from cases heard by Industrial Tribunals: (1) contribution to own dismissal can result from misconduct, lack of ability and sickness; and (2) misconduct always reduces compensation, even if it is not the cause of the dismissal.

It should be clear by now that all employers, large or small, need to think carefully before deciding to dismiss staff. This is far from suggesting that you should never give staff the sack, but it does mean that, if you are to avoid the heavy penalties now imposed for dismissing staff unfairly, you must take the following precautions:

1 Review your whole disciplinary approach.
2 Draw up disciplinary procedures, preferably agreed with staff.
3 Train all those who are in any way responsible for administering discipline.

4 Maintain records and evidence to defend yourself against any claim you feel unjustified.

Failure in this area can amount to large sums in compensation, a weakening of staff-management relations and a poor image in customers' eyes.

CHECKLIST

1 Have you reviewed the terms and conditions of staff employment so as to render them flexible enough to allow for normal business changes?
2 If you find it necessary to change fundamental terms, have you obtained staff agreement to these before implementation?
3 What records do you keep of staff incompetence and of your efforts to assist them to improve?
4 What criteria will you use for selecting staff when redundancy arises?
5 What steps have you incorporated in your disciplinary code to make sure dismissals are carried out reasonably?
6 Do you generally apply suspension before dismissing staff summarily?
7 Does your disciplinary code incorporate provisions for dealing with absenteeism and lateness for duty?
8 Have you considered as part of your code a step allowing for suspension, with pay suspended, in cases of dishonesty?
9 Do your staff rules warn of dismissal for all forms of dishonesty?
10 What do the rules say about drinking on duty and its penalties?
11 What provision have you made for dealing with staff who are sick, especially to ensure any dismissals are reasonable?
12 In any claim against you for unfair dismissal do you make a genuine attempt at conciliation rather than pursue the proceedings in an Industrial Tribunal?
13 What provisions have you made to allow for re-employment if staff are found to have been unfairly dismissed?
14 What arrangements have you made to train staff who administer your disciplinary code so that they are fully acquainted with the concepts of fairness and reasonableness?
15 What arrangements have you made to cover the absence during pregnancy of staff who express the wish to return to their job?

CHAPTER SEVENTEEN

Coping with Redundancies

17.1 A POLICY FOR REDUNDANCY

Fortunately, unlike many other industries, the hotel and catering industry is not very often faced with having to make staff redundant. Precisely on this account it is important, therefore, to cover the main guidelines in a book like this, so that those who do reach a point where redundancy becomes a real possibility can make sure, not only that they remain within the existing legislation, but, more importantly, manage the situation in the best interests of both the staff and the business.

Redundancy takes place when staff are dismissed mainly because your need for them to work in a particular way in the place where previously they were employed either diminishes or ceases altogether. This does not necessarily mean that your total staff will have decreased. If, for instance, you decide to enter the conference trade and change a wing of bedrooms into small halls or syndicate rooms, some staff could become redundant, even if you have to recruit others for a different purpose. There is no need for staff to be formally declared redundant; if you simply cease trading altogether and your restaurant or hotel is closed down, all the staff may be deemed to have been dismissed on grounds of redundancy.

However remote may seem the likelihood of your having to make staff redundant, as a good manager you should incorporate your intentions in this area into your general employment policy. Briefly, this policy might cover what formulas will apply when redundancy arises, what safeguards and compensation will be given, and what consultation with staff will take place. Redundancy never happens overnight. Events leading to redundancy happen weeks or even months before the stage is reached when redundancy notices have to be sent out. Like every other aspect of good management-staff practice, you should have plans and procedures, agreed with staff, to cope with this situation, so as to minimize the effect on both the company and the staff.

In considering what might be included in such a policy you could start by looking at the I.R. Code of Practice for advice. There it is suggested that, in compliance with good company employment policies to provide as far as possible security of employment for all staff, you should take every reasonable step when redundancy threatens to avoid redundancies at all. Specifically the Code suggests that this can be done in a number of ways:

1 By restricting the number of new recruits.
2 By retiring staff who have already reached normal retirement age.
3 By reducing the amount of overtime worked.
4 By agreeing with staff to reduce normal hours of working to cover temporary fluctuations in your staffing needs.
5 By retraining staff or transferring them to other work.

The decision to prepare a statement covering redundancy as part of your general employment policy, or to take it a stage further and produce a redundancy procedure agreement, will depend on a number of factors: your own assessment of the needs of the business and the staff, the size of the establishment, and the organization of staff either in trade unions or in staff committees. At the minimum it is suggested that you cover redundancy as part of your general policy. If, on the other hand, you wish to consider drawing up a redundancy procedure agreement with staff, then you will find guidelines for this in Chapter 19.

First and foremost a policy statement should contain a general affirmation of the company's intention to maintain security of employment by all reasonable means. Following on this the statement might indicate that, when in a situation that looks as if it might result in staff being made redundant, every step will be taken to minimize or avoid redundancy. This could then spell out your willingness to explore such actions as cessation of recruitment, short-time working, the provision of alternative work, retraining, early retirement, and voluntary redundancy.

In order to reassure staff, if redundancies become inevitable, your policy should also specify your intention to consult with staff trade unions before selection is made, and perhaps outline the basis on which, generally, you would proceed to make selections. Finally the policy statement should indicate your intentions in respect of notice to be given to redundant staff, what basis of payment will be used and what provisions will be made for pensions that may be affected.

Your whole statement should indicate your consciousness of the provisions of the Employment Protection (Consolidation) Act, and your company's willingness to meet in all respects your minimum legal liabilities, and improve on them wherever possible. An example of a policy statement on redundancy is given in Appendix 31 (p. 275).

Once you have armed yourself with a statement of your intentions to cope with redundancy, you should then draw up a set of guidelines to help you implement both the letter and the spirit of your policy. Since the contents of policy statements may vary enormously from company to company, no specific guidelines are offered here other than to suggest again that it may best be accomplished by drawing up a redundancy procedure agreement, as outlined in Chapter 19.

17.2 LEGAL ASPECTS OF REDUNDANCY

Security of employment is seen increasingly as of paramount importance, and this has been reflected in the various pieces of legislation that have reached the statute book since World War II. However, it is also recognized that, as important as this may be, there are reasons and occasions when staff may lose employment, and one such obvious example is when the work for which they are employed no longer exists or changes in such a way that some staff are no longer necessary. Staff can then become redundant.

Some employers have always recognized this possibility, and have made provision to deal with such contingencies, thus ensuring that anyone affected by redundancy is compensated and helped in the very best way possible. Unfortunately not all employers have made such provisions, which is why it was seen as necessary to create in 1965 another piece of employment legislation—the Redundancy Payments Act. This made it compulsory for all employers to make lump sum payments to staff dismissed because of redundancy, or lay-off or short-time work for certain periods.

Redundancy Payments

The Redundancy Payments Act 1965 and 1969 were an amalgam of the original Redundancy Payments Act 1965 and the Redundancy Rebates Act 1969. Today their provisions are covered by Part VI of the Employment Protection (Consolidation) Act 1978. Basically it provides scales of monetary compensation to be paid to all redundant staff under the following conditions:

1 Staff must have been in your employment for 104 weeks.

2 Their normal working week must be of 16 hours or more.
3 If male, they must be aged 18–65, or female up to the age of 60.
4 They must neither be husband nor wife of the employer.
5 They must not have unreasonably refused your offer of alternative work.
6 They must have left your employment.

The following is the basis on which compensation is computed:

1 For each year's service at age 41 or over but under 65 (60 for women)—1½ weeks' pay.
2 For each year's service at age 22 or over but under 41—1 week's pay.
3 For each year's service at age 18 but under 22—½ week's pay.

The maximum sum payable is £3,600, based on the requirement that compensation is limited to the last 20 years before redundancy, and earnings above £120 a week are discounted.

No redundancy payments are made in the case of temporary lay-off or short-time working. If, however, the lay-off time or short-time working (where staff receive less than half their normal week's pay) has continued for 4 consecutive weeks (or a total of 6 weeks in any 13-week period), such staff may make a written request to you for a redundancy payment. They will be entitled to this unless you can show a good reason for the lay-off or short-time working to continue, and that there is a reasonable expectation that full-time working will be resumed within a further 4 weeks, and continue for at least a further 13 weeks. Industrial Tribunals will determine the adequacy of your reasons.

If you offer either a renewal of contract to take effect immediately or suitable alternative work, and this is refused, then staff immediately lose their right to a redundancy payment. Under the Employment Protection (Consolidation) Act you need no longer make this offer in writing. On the other hand, if the offer includes new terms, then staff now have the right automatically to a month's trial in this new job, although you can agree a longer period if you wish.

Staff can end the contract during this trial period or give notice ending it later, 'for whatever reason'. If this does happen, the date of dismissal is the date the previous contract ended and for the reason that it ended. If, however, staff bring the trial period to an end unreasonably when it contained new but suitable terms, then they lose their right to a redundancy payment. Only case law will help guide you as to when such circumstances might arise.

You also have a right to bring the contract to an end (or to give notice taking effect later) during the trial period for a reason 'connected with or arising out of the change'. If this happens, then, as before, the original date of dismissal counts and for the same reason that ended the contract.

If you have paid the statutory compensation to which redundant staff are entitled, you can reclaim 41 per cent of that sum from the Redundancy Fund. However, you must give prior notice in writing to the local Department of Employment office that such a claim may arise in consequence of your termination of staff contracts of employment. The amount of notice required depends on the number of redundancies:

1 If ten or more staff contracts are expected to terminate on the same day or within a period of no more than 6 days, then the Department of Employment must be given 21 days' notice.
2 In any other case the required notice to be given is 14 days.

The information required in this advance notice must be given on Form RP1, which can be obtained at your local employment office. Should you fail to give this notice in time without a good reason, you may find that your rebate is cut by 10 per cent. The reason for furnishing this information is to allow the Department to agree the claim for rebate if possible before the dismissals and the payments made by you take place.

Your claim for a rebate from the Redundancy Fund must be submitted on Form RP2, while your statement of calculation of the redundancy payment made, together with the employee's receipt, must be furnished on Form RP3. Once compensation has been paid, you are allowed up to 6 months from the date of paying staff in which to reclaim your rebate.

You should note that paying out a redundancy payment does not preclude a claim being made for unfair dismissal.

The Employment Protection Act

In this Act the main changes affecting redundancies concern the procedures for handling them. More specifically, these procedures apply only if you recognize an independent trade union for staff, whether or not they belong to the union. In these circumstances you then have two main obligations: (1) to consult the trade union representatives in advance, and (2) to notify the Department of Employment.

The consultation process must begin by your notifying the trade union representatives in writing of the following points:

1 The reasons why redundancy is necessary.
2 The numbers and which type of staff you propose making redundant.
3 The total numbers of those types you employ at the unit concerned.
4 How you propose to select the staff.
5 Your proposals in regard to the method of dismissal and the period over which the dismissals are to take effect.

You must consider any counter-proposals put forward by the trade union representatives and reply to them, giving your reasons if you reject any.

When this consultation must begin depends upon how many staff are likely to be made redundant:

1 If 100 or more are to be made redundant during a period of 90 days or less, consultation must take place at least 90 days before the first dismissal.
2 If 10 or more are being made redundant during a period of 30 days, the consultation must take place at least 30 days before dismissals.
3 If there are less than 10 to be made redundant, there is no legal obligation to consult within a predetermined period.

This duty to consult covers all staff in the class the union bargains for, even if they are not union members. The union representative means the official or other person the union authorizes to bargain with you.

Your second legal obligation is to notify the Department of Employment of your proposed redundancies not later than the minimum time set for consultations to begin. They have no power to delay the redundancies. You should note that this notification must be made whether there is a trade union concerned or not. If there are fewer than ten redundancies, there is no need to notify the Department of Employment, except, of course, in the process of claiming your rebate from the Redundancy Fund.

If you fail in your duty to consult, the trade union concerned may enter a complaint against you before an Industrial Tribunal. If it is well founded, the redundant staff may be given a 'protective award' of wages as if they were still at work, to be paid for a 'protected period'. This period begins with the date the first of the redundancy dismissals takes effect or with the date of the award, and lasts for as long as the Tribunal decides is just and equitable considering your default. The maximum awards are one week's pay for each week of the protected period up to a maximum 90 days' pay where the dismissals affect 100 or more redundancies within a 90-day period, or 30 days' pay where ten or more are made redundant within 30 days, and 28 days' pay minimum in all cases.

Since it is up to the union and not the individuals affected to make the complaint, this would seem to allow the unions to waive their rights when following the rules would simply increase your problems as the employer and perhaps lead to yet more redundancies. However, once a protective award has been made, it is the responsibility of the redundant staff to complain to a Tribunal if you fail to make the payments, and they have 3 months in which to make their complaint.

If you fail in your duty to notify the Department of Employment you may have your rebate reduced by up to one-tenth or you could be prosecuted in the Magistrates' Court, where a fine of up to £400 may be imposed. The one defence allowed you under this Act, if you fail in your duty to keep the new consultation rules, is for you to show that the circumstances were such as to make it not 'reasonably practical' to comply and that you really did all you could to do so. This defence is unlikely to be of much use to the hotel and catering industry, which would have difficulty in showing that redundancies were forced on companies at shorter notice than the Act demands for consultation. It is worth considering that the whole idea of this amendment to the redundancy legislation is to bring about planned redundancy through reorganization of companies.

Finally, although a comparatively small number of companies in our industry may as yet be affected by these new provisions of the Employment Protection Act because of a lack of recognition of trade unions, the new rules should help you in drawing up your own guidelines for handling redundancies, especially in relation to any procedural agreement you may draw up incorporating staff consultations.

CHECKLIST

1 Have you formulated a redundancy policy?
2 What provisions have you made to consult with staff?
3 What guidelines have you drawn up to help select the priorities

on which you will base a selection of staff for redundancy?

4 What plans have you made to minimize the numbers of actual redundancies?

5 Have you considered the advantages and disadvantages of seeking voluntary redundancies?

6 Have you a procedural agreement to implement your policy on redundancies?

Part IV Bibliography

A.C.A.S. *Code of Practice I – Disciplinary Practice and Procedures* (A.C.A.S., 1976).

Anderman, S. D. *Unfair Dismissals and the Law* (I.P.M., 1973).

Ashdown, R. T. and Baker, K. H. *In Working Order – a Study of Industrial Discipline*, D. of E. Manpower Paper No. 6 (H.M.S.O., 1973).

Cooper, W. M. and Wood, J. C. *Outlines of Industrial Law* (Butterworth, 1974).

Cuthbert, M. H. and Hawkins, K. *Company Industrial Relations Policies* (Longman, 1974).

Flanders, A. *Collective Bargaining* (Penguin, 1969).

Foulkes, D. *Law for Managers* (Butterworth, 1971).

Greenhalgh, R. M. *Industrial Tribunals – a Practical Guide* (I.P.M., 1973).

Hyman, R. *Disputes Procedure in Action* (Heinemann, 1972).

Incomes Data Services *Supplements* 1–11 and *Handbook* No. 1 (I.D.S. Ltd, 1973–76).

Kahm-Freund, O. *Labour and The Law* (Stevens, 1972).

Martin, R. and Fryer, R. H. *Redundancy and Paternalist Capitalism* (Allen & Unwin, 1973).

Mepham, G. I. *Equal Opportunity and Equal Pay* (I.P.M., 1974).

Nash, M. *The Sex Discrimination Act – a Guide for Managers* (I.P.M., 1976).

Odiorne, G. S. *How Managers Make Things Happen* (Heron Books, 1961).

Rubenstein, M. *A Practical Guide to the Employment Protection Act* (I.P.M., 1976).

Wedderburn, K. *The Worker and the Law* (Penguin, 1971).

Whincup, M. *Modern Employment Law* (Heinemann, London, 1980).

Appendix 27 Qualifying Periods of Employment

	Rights of full-time staff	*Qualifying time in your employment (weeks)*
1	Statement of terms/conditions of employment	13
2	Minimum period of 1 week's notice	4
3	Unfair dismissal rights	52
4	Redundancy payments	104
5	Guarantee pay	4
6	Medical suspension pay	4
7	Not to be dismissed on grounds of pregnancy	26
8	Maternity pay and reinstatement in job	104
9	Union membership and activities	None
10	Time off for union officials, with pay	None
11	Time off for union members	None
12	Time off for public duties	None
13	Time off to look for work or arrange training	104
14	All insolvency payments	None
15	Written statement of reasons for dismissal	26
16	Itemized pay statement	None
17	Redundancy consultation and protective award	None
18	Discrimination on grounds of sex or marriage	None
19	Equality of pay	None

	Rights of part-time staff	*Qualifying time in your employment (weeks)*
1	Not to be dismissed on grounds of pregnancy	26
2	Union membership and activities	None
3	Some pay arrears, protective awards, insolvency	None
4	Redundancy consultation and protective awards	None
5	Discrimination on grounds of sex or marriage	None
6	Equality of pay	None

Notes

1 'Full-time staff' means staff normally employed for at least 16 hours a week or for at least 8 hours a week after 5 years' continuous service. 'Part-time staff' means all other staff employed.

2 In cases of dismissal for inadmissible reasons there is no qualifying period required.

Appendix 28 *Employer's Guide to Dismissing Staff Fairly*

(References are to E.P. [C] Act)

STAGE 1 Has the employee been dismissed? (S.55)
Have you a reason for dismissal? (S.57)

STAGE 2 Was the reason for:

Incapability (competence or health) or Lack of qualification 57 (2) (a)	Misconduct 57 (2) (b)	Redundancy 57 (2) (c)	Statutory cause 57 (2) (d)	Some other substantial reason 57 (1) (b)	Lockout 62 (1) (a)	Strike 62 (1) (b)	Exercising trade union rights 58 (1)
		but was he selected fairly?			but was he offered re-engagement at the conclusion?	but was he selected fairly?	then automatically unfair as an inadmissible reason

STAGE 3 Did you act reasonably in treating these grounds as a sufficient reason for dismissing staff? (57[3]).
Did you give him, on request, written reasons for dismissal? (S.53).

STAGE 4 If you fail to show that the dismissal was fair, what steps have you taken to allow for his re-employment?
Failing re-employment, the minimum compensation will consist of a basic award (maximum £3,600) and a compensatory award (maximum £6,250).

Appendix 29 Originating Application to an Industrial Tribunal

NOTES FOR GUIDANCE

Before completing the application form please read –
These notes for guidance
Leaflet ITL 1 which you were given along with this form
The appropriate booklet referred to under the relevant Act of Parliament – see paragraph 2 below.

1 QUALIFYING PERIODS AND TIME LIMITS

IN ORDER TO MAKE A VALID APPLICATION YOU MUST SATISFY ANY APPROPRIATE QUALIFYING PERIOD OF CONTINUOUS EMPLOYMENT AND YOUR APPLICATION MUST BE RECEIVED WITHIN THE APPROPRIATE TIME LIMIT. Information on both of these requirements is given in the booklets mentioned in paragraph 2 below. For example, to be able to complain of unfair dismissal you must normally have been employed by the same employer for the appropriate minimum period and the time limit for the receipt of such an application is normally 3 months from and including the effective date of dismissal. There is no qualifying period of employment for certain jurisdictions e.g. Equal Pay, Sex Discrimination or Race Relations complaints or where dismissal is for trade union activities, but time limits for making an application apply.

2 RELEVANT ACTS OF PARLIAMENT

You can ask the Tribunal to decide various questions as provided for in relevant Acts of Parliament. Details of these questions, the relevant Acts of Parliament and the titles of booklets explaining in simple terms the provision of these Acts and what the Tribunal can decide are given in Leaflet ITL 1 which should be issued to you with this form. These booklets are obtainable FREE from any employment office, jobcentre or unemployment benefit office. This form may be used for any of the matters referred to in leaflet ITL 1.

3 PREPARATION OF APPLICATION FORM

When completing the application form you should fill in items 1, 2, 4 and 12 and any other items which are relevant to your case. You should keep a copy of entries on the form. If in doubt about the respondent to name in item 4 you may seek advice from any employment office, jobcentre or unemployment benefit office. A Citizens' Advice Bureau or Trade Union may be able to help you complete the form or advise you as to whether you have a complaint which an Industrial Tribunal could consider.

4 PREPARATION OF YOUR CASE AND REPRESENTATION AT THE HEARING

At the hearing you may state your own case or be represented by anyone who has agreed to act for you. If you intend to have a representative it is advisable that he or she should be consulted at the earliest possible stage – preferably before the application form is completed (but see note above regarding time limits). In cases under the Equal Pay and Sex Discrimination Acts the Equal Opportunities Commission, and in cases under the Race Relations Act the Commission for Racial Equality, may provide assistance or representation – see appropriate booklet. IF YOU NAME A REPRESENTATIVE ALL FURTHER COMMUNICATIONS WILL BE SENT TO HIM OR HER AND NOT TO YOU; YOU SHOULD ARRANGE WITH YOUR REPRESENTATIVE TO BE KEPT INFORMED OF THE PROGRESS OF YOUR CASE AND OF THE HEARING DATE

Do not forget to sign the form.

PLEASE DETACH THESE NOTES before sending the application form to the Central Office of the Industrial Tribunals. KEEP THE NOTES FOR FUTURE REFERENCE.

Originating Application to an Industrial Tribunal

IMPORTANT: DO NOT FILL IN THIS FORM UNTIL YOU HAVE READ THE NOTES FOR GUIDANCE.
THEN COMPLETE ITEMS 1, 2, 4 AND 12
AND ALL OTHER ITEMS RELEVANT TO YOUR CASE,
AND SEND THE FORM TO THE FOLLOWING ADDRESS

For Official Use Only	
Case Number	

To: THE SECRETARY OF THE TRIBUNALS
CENTRAL OFFICE OF THE INDUSTRIAL TRIBUNALS (ENGLAND AND WALES)
93 EBURY BRIDGE ROAD, LONDON SW1W 8RE Telephone: 01 730 9161

1 I hereby apply for a decision of a Tribunal on the following question. *(State here the question to be decided by a Tribunal. Explain the grounds overleaf)*.

....

2 My name is (Mr/Mrs/Miss Surname in block capitals first):–

....

My address is:– ....

....

.... Telephone No. ....

My date of birth is ....

3 If a representative has agreed to act for you in this case please give his or her name and address below and note that further communications will be sent to your representative and not to you *(See Note 4)*

Name of Representative:– ....

Address:– ....

.... Telephone No. ....

4 **(a)** Name of respondent(s) (in block capitals) i.e. the employer, person or body against whom a decision is sought *(See Note 3)*

....

Address(es) ....

employer recognizing the union making application, etc.) ....

....

5 Place of employment to which this application relates, or place where act complained about took place.

....

6 My occupation or position held/applied for, or other relationship to the respondent named above (e.g. user of a service supplied in relation to employment).

....

7 Dates employment began .... and (*if appropriate*) ended ....

8 (**a**) Basic wages/salary ....

(**b**) Average take home pay ....

9 Other remuneration or benefits ....

10 Normal basic weekly hours of work ....

11 (In an application under the Sex Discrimination Act or the Race Relations Act)
Date on which action complained of took place or first came to my knowledge ....

12 You are required to set out the grounds for your application below, giving full particulars of them.

13 If you wish to state what in your opinion was the reason for your dismissal, please do so here.

14 If the Tribunal decides that you were unfairly dismissed, please state which of the following you would prefer: reinstatement, re-engagement or compensation. (Before answering this question please consult the leaflet 'Dismissal – Employees Rights', or, 'Unfairly Dismissed?'

....

Signature .... Date ....

FOR OFFICIAL USE ONLY

Received at COIT	Code	ROIT	Inits

Appendix 30 Employer's Reply to Complaint Form

Industrial Tribunals
NOTICE OF APPEARANCE BY RESPONDENT
To the Secretary of the Tribunals

Address

Case Number ....

For official use	
Date of receipt	initials

1 I *do/do not intend to resist the claim made by ....

2 *My/Our name is *Mr/Mrs /Miss/title (if company or organization) ....
address

telephone number ....

3 If you have arranged to have a representative to act for you, please give his name and address below and note that further communications will be sent to him and not to you.
name ....
address ....

telephone number ....

4 (a) Was the applicant dismissed? *YES/NO
(b) If YES, what was the reason for the dismissal?

(c) Are the dates given by the applicant as to his period of employment correct? *YES/NO
(d) If NO, give dates of commencement............and termination ....

5 If the claim is resisted, please state the grounds on which you intend to resist:

Signature.. Date ....

**Delete inappropriate items*

Appendix 31 Example of Policy Statement on Redundancy

It is in keeping with the employment policy of the XYZ Catering Company that we seek to provide security of employment for all our staff. However, in order to cover the eventuality of redundancy becoming unavoidable due to any situation in the catering industry or company changes in its methods of operation, this statement of policy is brought to the attention of all staff.

AIMS

The aims of our policy are as follows:

1 To take every reasonable step to avoid redundancy.
2 To consult with staff before redundancies take place.
3 To minimize the effect of redundancy.
4 To cushion the effect of redundancy on staff affected.

MINIMIZING REDUNDANCY

Whenever it becomes apparent that redundancy may have to be effected, the company will issue instructions to all management to take steps to avoid the need for staff reduction or to curtail the numbers likely to be affected. They will be encouraged to undertake the cessation/reduction of recruitment, to explore the possibilities of short-time working to cover temporary difficulties and to offer staff the opportunity to retire early or to volunteer for redundancy.

STAFF CONSULTATION

Whether staff belong to a trade union or not, no redundancy will take place without full consultation with representatives of all staff.

SELECTION

In the absence of any specific procedural agreement it is the policy of this company to operate the principle of 'last in, first out'. However, this principle will not operate with rigidity and the company reserves the right to apply this principle to the common-sense needs of both staff and the company.

REDUNDANT STAFF

If staff are made redundant, every effort will be made to find them alternative suitable employment in the company, and any necessary retraining to fit them for their new work will be undertaken. When this is either impracticable or unacceptable, the company will offer all staff notified of their impending redundancy the opportunity to seek other employment or to make arrangements for training, and to receive their normal salary during this time. Precise arrangements will be made by each manager.

All staff who are made redundant, provided they have a minimum of 6 months' service, will be eligible to receive compensation, paid as a lump sum on termination of employment. This sum will be made up of all monies due to them on any account, and an amount which in no circumstances will be less than the minimum sum due under the Employment Protection (Consolidation) Act, 1978. The company reserves the right to increase this sum, at its discretion, in recognition of long and faithful service.

RECALL

If circumstances change so that the company can offer re-employment, all staff so recalled within six months of their redundancy termination date will be allowed to count the time out of the company's employment for continuity of service purposes.

THE LAW

Nothing in this statement should be construed as in any way detracting from the company's legal obligations to comply with the Employment Protection (Consolidation) Act or the Employment Protection Act, where applicable.

PART V

STAFF RELATIONS

CHAPTER EIGHTEEN

Consulting and Negotiating with Staff

18.1 WHO HAS A MONOPOLY OF IDEAS?

What a pity that as soon as most people hear the terms 'consultation', 'negotiation', 'arbitration' or almost any other industrial '-ation', they immediately associate them with yet another '-ation': 'confrontation'! Perhaps it is understandable in that we live in an age where freedom is regarded more and more as the only real virtue, and because of that any interaction between management and staff is seen as necessarily antagonistic, especially if authority is thought to be the very antithesis of freedom. What does not help is the fact that the news media tend to highlight only the '-ations' that do show an 'us v. them' approach. Nor is this confined by any means to situations where the employees are represented by trade unions. Perhaps in the catering industry, where we do not have a long tradition of formal face-to-face relations between management and staff, we have an opportunity of putting these terms into proper perspective, and making the reality of the situation meet the true intent behind the words themselves.

You will be familiar with such people as medical consultants, management consultants and even trade consultants; what is common to each is that they are people to whom you turn to discuss difficulties and problems, and to listen to their advice and suggestions. Moreover they are people whom you respect because of their knowledge and experience, although they are not oracles. You may not necessarily agree with everything they say nor accept all their views. This consideration helps us to arrive at a working definition of consultation: it is the seeking of views, ideas and feelings of people whose experience and knowledge you value, *before* you reach a decision.

This section looks solely at consultation at work and Section 18.2 will examine the process of negotiation.

Your responsibility as a manager is to control and co-ordinate all the business functions, and to do this successfully you must rely on having accurate information and a supply of ideas, as well as the backing and support of your most important asset, your staff. As has been seen earlier in the manual, success can only come from team effort where you, by virtue of your position, are the leader. It is your role to take the initiative.

Communication has already been looked at in Chapter 8, and consultation is a special form of communication: it is not a briefing of staff, a talking to them, but rather a seeking of their views and ideas. Consulting staff has a number of obvious advantages:

1 Your decisions must be the better for using the knowledge and experience of the staff who have to implement them.
2 You are likely to obtain a higher degree of co-operation and commitment from staff whose views have been taken into account before decisions are made.
3 It is a sensible and vital form of management-staff participation.

You clearly cannot commit yourself to consultation with every member of staff, and so it must devolve upon representatives of all of them. If your members are already in trade unions that you recognize, it makes good sense to hold consultative meetings with already elected staff representatives. Indeed, if this is the case in your establishment, you probably already meet these representatives in negotiations; but if that is the only sort of meeting at which you both get together—to sort out conflicts—then you cannot be surprised if management-staff relations are somewhat brittle. However, while the basic guidelines offered here will hopefully be helpful in organizations where consultative and negotiating machinery already exists with trade union representatives, the following points may help managers in concerns which so far do not have any formal contacts with staff on a consultative basis.

If you already hold meetings of heads of departments, then this may seem the best form in which to express your view that consultative meetings with staff should be initiated. Get them to test out the staff in their departments and their general feelings about such a committee, making sure that at this stage the departmental heads have a clear idea as to what is envisaged in consultation and the part that representatives of all staff might be expected to play if such a committee is formed. It should surprise, even disturb you, if there is anything other than a favourable reply to the idea. Now you must get it off the ground.

Practical Tips

1 Draw up a list of 'constituencies' approximating as near as you can to the already existing organizational structure.
2 Make sure in this that you take into account any shift system that operates, so that all your staff are represented.
3 Suggest that each constituency elects or nominates its own representatives on the basis that he/she can truly speak on behalf of all the staff there.
4 Give your staff guidance on how to select their representative.
5 Try to keep the total number of representatives to a maximum of around ten people.
6 Nominate managers on the basis of their being a cross-section of all levels in the proportion of 1:2 to staff representatives.
7 If you are the senior manager, you should act as chairman.

Your First Meeting

If the whole idea of consultation with staff is novel in your establishment, then the first meeting with representatives will need to be handled with great care. You must expect staff to arrive in a somewhat suspicious frame of mind, especially if there has been any previous history of authoritarianism. As the chairman, it will pay you to spend some time on the following:

1 Describing in detail what consultation means and the purpose of this committee.
2 Persuading staff that you really do believe in consultation, by showing respect for every individual and a willingness to learn and to accept criticism.
3 Making it clear that any tangible benefits resulting from consultation will be shared by all staff.

You may also wish at this first meeting to find out how the committee views the idea of having a formal constitution and rules. How necessary this may be depends a great deal on the size and nature of your organization, but on the whole you may feel that some sort of framework committed to paper will be of benefit to everyone. An example of a constitution is given at Appendix 32 (p. 315).

Once you have set up the machinery, commit yourself wholeheartedly to making it a success. This is not an easy task. You can help enormously as the chairman if you behave as follows:

1 View consultative meetings as having value in their own right and not as simply another staff amenity.
2 Recognize that all staff have a contribution to make in helping the business.
3 Handle the meetings with enthusiasm.
4 Stimulate discussion to produce new ideas.

Like most meetings, it helps everyone attending if there is an agenda to work from. Immediately this prompts the idea that to illustrate your understanding of consultation you can invite any representative to submit a topic for discussion so long as you reserve the right to decide whether it is a proper matter for their consideration. The main responsibility for the agenda must be yours—certainly until these meetings are firmly established you and the management team should contribute at least 70% of the items to the agenda. After all, most of what comes up for discussion should be matters of policy, proposals and briefings, which you invite staff to comment on, so that when, later, you make decisions, it is with the benefit of their consideration. On the other hand, you must leave room for staff to make proposals and to express ideas of their own—but still the responsibility for successful consultation lies with you.

If you yourself have no firm idea of what represents good material for consultation of this sort, there is a great danger that such meetings will degenerate into a discussion of trivialities and to the airing of individual grievances. This should not be the forum for such things. Some examples of possible topics for a consultative committee are given in Appendix 33 (p. 317).

Meetings should be held regularly, about every two months, and the agenda should be sent out to all representatives about a week in advance; this serves the twin purpose of reminding representatives of the meeting date and time but more importantly, to give them an opportunity to canvass the views of staff on agenda items. The appointed secretary should be responsible for taking minutes of every meeting, so that a record is available of what items come up for discussion, what viewpoints are expressed and what action is recommended.

There is no scope in this manual for notes on how best to conduct meetings, but a number of special points might help in getting the best out of consultative meetings.

Practical Tips

1 Use the meeting to *inform* representatives of your business

activities and decisions that have been taken following earlier consultation.

2 Do not make other than administrative decisions at this meeting.
3 Pose actual problems for the committee to work on and supply them with enough information for them to express considered views as to possible solutions.
4 Do not hog the meeting yourself. Encourage everyone to take part and bring in the shy members.
5 Encourage your management colleagues on the committee to speak their own minds freely and not become mere mirrors of your thoughts.
6 Give reasons for every view you express, and to support any proposal you wish to be discussed.
7 Do not use the meeting to sidestep your responsibilities for other meetings with, say, heads of departments.
8 Encourage your heads of departments to maintain informal contact with their staff lest the consultative meetings be seen as a substitute for everyday sound management.
9 If some of your staff do belong to trade unions, make sure their officials are kept informed of what happens at the consultative committees and invite them to attend occasionally.
10 Avoid putting the conventional 'any other business' on the agenda, so as to encourage serious thought about agenda items in advance and to discourage a 'free-for-all' at the end of meetings.

Perhaps the most important action you take once consultative meetings are over is to reach a decision on matters discussed while everyone's view is fresh in your mind. Since this will not be practical in every case, the minutes of meetings then take on their real importance and value as a record of the feelings and views expressed. Consult these minutes when decisions pertaining to agenda items must be made.

Another important post-meeting responsibility, usually delegated to the Secretary, is to make sure that the minutes are prepared as soon as possible and circulated, not only to the staff representatives, but also to all managers and supervisors who do not attend the meetings themselves. You should also make sure copies are placed on staff notice boards. Finally, if in the course of the meeting you make a promise to seek further information or to investigate matters discussed, keep that promise promptly.

Summary

This section has looked at the process of staff consultation, and you would do well yet again to remind yourself of the descriptive meaning of 'consultation'. If you set up a formal consultative structure, make sure that it adheres strictly to its consultative role: subjects will inevitably come up that will form matters for later negotiation; by all means discuss these topics, but do not fall into the trap of negotiating about them in this meeting.

If you are really in earnest about improving the efficiency and profitability of your unit, there can be no doubt but that there is a place for a genuine consultation of staff views. Neither you, nor the management team as a whole, hold a monopoly of good ideas. Tap the minds of all who work in the enterprise; give them genuine grounds for believing that you view them as an integral and valuable part of the whole business, recognizing the simple fact of business life that the success or failure of any business depends entirely upon *all* the people who work in it.

18.2 NEGOTIATION—AN ART OR A SKILL?

As we have just seen in the previous section, many matters that come up for discussion at a consultative meeting can also be matters that form a basis for negotiation. It is not necessarily that the subjects are so different but the way they are tackled that clearly distinguishes them. One easy way to see the difference is to look at the end results to be achieved: consultation leads to subsequent management decisions, whereas negotiation finishes with an agreement that both management and representatives have a responsibility to keep. Negotiations also concern themselves with points of conflict, or at least with divergent views, which the process of negotiation seeks to resolve by the saving grace of all collective bargaining—the compromise. In many cases the atmosphere between the two processes can be different.

However different the two processes, some of the people who attend the consultative meetings are also bound to be the ones conducting negotiations. If your staff are represented by trade unions, elected staff representatives no doubt already take part in both processes. But if the trade unions are not represented among staff, you may question whether it is wise to give consultative representatives the authority to negotiate. Whatever your arrangements, the crucially important point to remember is that when you consult, you consult; when you are negotiating, you are negotiating; the lines should never be crossed.

Finally, before you look at negotiation and the guidelines offered to help you, you need to determine what your attitude and policy are towards negotiation. If you operate in a company in which your staff belong to independent trade unions, the sensible attitude must be to recognize that they have a right to belong to unions and that trade unions represent a legitimate power base, external to the company, from which the staff can negotiate on anything that affects them. On the other hand, while still recognizing staff rights to join unions if they wish, you may be in a company in which staff so far have not chosen to join a union. Should this be any reason for denying them the opportunity to negotiate? It would not appear so. Negotiation between management and staff is a matter that is quite independent of unionized staff organization. The major difference likely to arise between companies that recognize trade unions and those in which staff have so far shown little interest is that the negotiation procedure will be different. In the former company it will be a demand of right by staff representatives, whereas in the non-unionized concern it will either not take place at all, or will do so as a result of a management policy to foster negotiating practices. This section holds out no view about the merits or demerits of either case, but is solely concerned with giving those who have to negotiate an insight into the skills and the art required.

No specific guidelines are offered here as to how the negotiating machinery should be set up, since each company's requirements will vary with its size and whether or not it is unionized. However, two general matters need to be mentioned:

1 The 'bargaining unit' needs to be agreed: there should be a reasonable degree of common interest represented, and it should exclude mixing of staff with supervisory/management personnel.
2 Some procedures need to be agreed to cover the representatives of each side and the frequency of meetings. Much help can be obtained from the I.R. Code of Practice, paras 71–95, which make a number of basic recommendations about collective bargaining and negotiation.

Just as it is impossible to learn to drive by reading about it, so you must recognize that you cannot become a good negotiator merely by following a set of rules. Your personality determines the way you negotiate to some extent, especially in the way you use it. Moreover each time you sit down to negotiate, it will be different, because the issues and people's reactions will differ. It is in this sense that negotiation can be termed an art to be studied and not a routine to be learned, though at the same time it can be described as a skill to be practised and perfected face to face with other negotiators.

Having said that, let us look at some basic guidelines. An effective negotiator can be distinguished by three special characteristics: (1) he plans tactics as well as strategy; (2) he is an effective communicator; and (3) he is in control of his own behaviour. That is the ideal to be aimed at; it provides a neat framework within which to highlight some of the skills and some of the rules of the game if you are to be an effective negotiator.

The first constraint you must recognize is that bargaining in industrial relations means a *continuous* relationship, so that, when you prepare for a round of negotiations, your objective should never be total victory or total defeat. The art is to effect an acceptable compromise.

Your approach should be based on something positive; avoid at all costs the starting point, 'We will concede nothing that can be avoided, but give in if really pushed'. Your preparation must include collecting as much information as you can, not only to support your case but, very importantly, about the interests of the staff side. Are the aims of each side reconcilable? What really is behind their differences with you? What deterrent sanctions are at their disposal?

You must decide how far you are prepared to go to achieve a satisfactory settlement. Put at its simplest, this means that you must identify three positions beforehand:

1 The 'ideal settlement', which represents your starting point.
2 The 'realistic settlement'—the position you believe you have both the power and the ability to achieve, and which you will aim for, and
3 The 'fall-back position'—the very worst settlement you are prepared to accept.

This gives you a certain freedom of movement in the 'give and take' nature of all negotiations.

Practical Tips

1 Put yourself in the position of the other side—try to understand their feelings and motives.
2 Consider the consequences of different types of approach, and decide how far you are prepared to go on the issue.
3 Prepare yourself to meet the likely arguments put forward

by the staff, arming yourself with any relevant information about earlier agreements, and about the history, precedents, custom and practice behind their case.

4 Decide who will form your negotiating team and the role of each person—and who alone will make any decisions and what action you will take if you find signs of disagreement within your own team.

5 Make sure you have the authority to take any decision likely or to agree a final solution; reference back to higher authority other than by exception serves only to undermine your position.

6 Consider what will happen if agreement is not reached.

Once you have completed your preparation you are then ready to meet the staff across the negotiating table. There are two major matters now to consider—your tactics and your behaviour.

Negotiating Tactics

There cannot be any hard and fast rules about tactics, since so much of what takes place is not under your control. However, some guidelines can be considered:

1 *The Opening*. Whichever side opens determines to a large extent what sort of bargaining game is to be played. For instance, if the staff opens with a demand set at a deliberately high level, there is the possibility of an eventual settlement higher than your fall-back position or a greater likelihood of open confrontation. If you are faced with this situation, you would be well advised to avoid what might be considered the natural reaction—to make a counter-offer immediately. If this should be low, then it raises the possibility of confrontation and at the same time makes it seem more legitimate. On the other hand, if your counter-offer is high, it immediately places you in the arena of high demand/high settlement claims, which is unlikely to be within your predetermined position. The tactic to be used in this situation is to make no counter-offer at all but rather to attempt to moderate the demand, bringing it within the limits of your planned positions.

If the opening demand is a very general one, couched in terms like 'a substantial increase', then you should spend whatever time and effort is needed to have this translated into specific terms before you consider making an offer. The golden rule must be, 'Never make an offer without hearing the size of the demand'.

2 *The Agenda.* It is unlikely that you will be engaged in negotiations on a single specific issue, even if occasionally negotiations are established apparently on that basis, Other items will enter into your discussions. You may find it helpful and useful in reaching an ultimately successful agreement if you set out to discover the major items put forward by staff but withhold agreement of any kind until your major item is discussed. Then the two can be brought together and a better trading arrangement reached. You should therefore try to get the staff to agree to look at the negotiating agenda as a whole, with a view to achieving a general agreement rather than agreements on each item separately.

If, so far, the conduct of negotiations is seen to have been rather vague and indeterminate, this is quite deliberate. Strategy and tactics cannot be learned by reading about them or by following set rules. If you wish to improve in this area, the answer is to undertake specific training. However, of equal importance to the successful negotiator is the way in which he conducts himself during negotiations—the manner he adopts, the form of communication he follows and the personal behaviour he exercises. Here more specific guidelines are possible.

Practical Tips

1 Because negotiations always bring about some sort of conflict, keep your emotions firmly in control. A cool reasoning approach, even in the face of the utmost provocation, pays handsome dividends.

2 Stick to the subject matter rigidly, and avoid personalities at all costs.

3 Be careful not to use emotive words or phrases, which serve only as irritants. Thus to qualify your offer with a description that it is 'generous' may serve only to draw cynicism or even anger, which could destroy any hope of acceptance.

4 Exercise patience, especially when negotiations seem to be protracted needlessly or when a deliberate attempt is being made to provoke you.

5 Avoid extreme positions that leave the staff no alternative way out. Adopting the attitude 'only over my dead body' might have disastrous consequences for your company.

6 On the other hand, take care you do not find yourself being

totally negative until sanctions are being threatened. If at that stage you find yourself saying 'Yes', you will have displayed a fundamental weakness as a negotiator.

7 If you do make a mistake, admit it openly. Take responsibility for any problem that is your fault or which might be seen as a fault by the staff. They know that managers are as fallible as anyone else, but it helps your case a lot if you are prepared to admit your own knowledge of your fallibility.

8 Spend a good deal of time asking questions of the staff and seeking information that helps you to understand their feelings and motives better.

9 When you have heard the other side, check it out with them to make sure your understanding of what has been said accords with what has really been stated.

10 When you are making out your case, especially when it is lengthy or complex, take occasion to flag up in advance what you are about to say. For instance, 'Well, now I'd like to ask you a question', 'Here is my proposal', or 'Can I summarize where I think we have got to then'. This helps everyone to a better understanding of what you are saying, and avoids the danger of inattention.

11 Once proposals have been made, steer the discussion along the lines of your strong points and the weak points in the other side.

12 Keep strictly to the point.

13 When the staff side is being put, listen carefully to everything that is being said, making notes of the main points covered, and checking out your understanding. If this means them advancing a number of reasons in support of their case, pay especial attention to these. They cannot all be as strong as each other, and it therefore gives you the opportunity to come back at them and dilute their case by attacking the weakest links in the chain of their argument.

14 On the other hand, do not interrupt. Hear the other case out.

15 Finally, do not crow over any apparent 'victory' you may win; humility may help you the next time, when your case may be a weaker one.

The Agreement

The ultimate aim of any negotiation must be to reach an agreement. It is worth noting here that that does not necessarily mean the same thing as saying it must be just in every sense. There is no value in arguing that what you propose would be declared by any objective judge as fair. The outcome of any negotiation is what both parties are prepared to live with—hopefully a just solution but not necessarily.

Once agreement is reached, make sure it is written down, including the date, time and responsibility for its execution. Check it out there and then, so that there is no misunderstanding about its interpretation.

Whatever the subject of the negotiation, the outcome will clearly affect far more than those who take part in its attainment. Do not leave it to the staff representatives to tell all those concerned. Make sure that you let everyone know what agreement is reached and how it is being implemented.

Should you fail to reach agreement, make sure that a 'failure to agree' is recorded. The next step to resolve this situation depends upon any procedural agreement you may have, since it will cover such an eventuality. If you do not yet have such a procedural document, then, in the absence of, or after exhaustion of, any internal arbitration system, you may agree to ask A.C.A.S. to conciliate or arbitrate.

The criteria by which you can judge the effectiveness of negotiations are these:

1 They are judged to be effective by both sides.
2 They conclude satisfactory agreements.
3 The agreements are lasting ones.

One of the characteristics of industries with wages councils, and indeed one of the reasons for such industries being subject to wages councils, is that collective bargaining (management-staff negotiation) either does not exist at all or the machinery for it is inadequate. At present the hotel and catering industry is in this position, but with the increasing influence of the trade union movement this may not remain so for ever. These questions may, therefore, prompt themselves:

1 In the more participative climate of present-day industrial relations, should you not institute a system of management-staff negotiations?
2 Why should you wait until collective bargaining is forced upon you?
3 What training and preparation are you undertaking to prepare yourself to take part in negotiations effectively?

It is a management role to take the lead, and therefore good management to take a consistently positive and constructive approach and institute sound industrial relations practices.

CHECKLIST

1 Are you clear what consultation means?
2 If you have a consultative committee, are all staff represented?
3 Do you have an agreed Constitution? If not, should you have?
4 Do you encourage staff to submit topics for the Agenda and *vet them* as suitable for a consultative meeting?
5 Do you rate your attendance at these meetings as of a high priority?
6 Do you attend these meetings with the full intention of listening to the views of others rather than to air your own in detail?
7 Do you encourage everyone to participate in the consultative process?
8 Are minutes circulated quickly?
9 How quickly do you take any action you promise at the meeting?
10 Have you a policy in respect of management-staff negotiations?
11 Have you determined at least two bargaining units—one for staff and the other for junior management/supervisors?
12 What procedure exists for initiating negotiations and regulating its conduct?
13 Does your preparation give a lot of consideration to the question, How do the staff view this matter, and what are their feelings and their motives?
14 Have you checked on the extent of your authority to make decisions and agreements?
15 Do you seek to achieve a general agreement rather than to bargain piecemeal?
16 Do you resolve before any negotiating takes place to 'keep your cool', whatever turn the exercise may take?
17 Are you ready to admit your own fallibility?
18 Do you regularly check out your understanding of the other side?
19 Do you make sure that all staff are notified officially of any agreement reached?

CHAPTER NINETEEN

The Use of Procedures

19.1 FORMAL AND INFORMAL PROCEDURES

Are you tempted to by-pass this chapter dealing with procedures as not having any application in the industry or your business? Perhaps it is understandable if you do feel that way—after all, in many cases managers in the industry equate the idea of procedural arrangements with industrial relations conflicts in other industries. But have you ever stopped to examine what is really meant by a 'procedure', and to find out if in fact it could be a help to you if you had some?

No organization, however small, operates without procedural arrangements of some sort; to do so would deny its entitlement to the very term 'an organization'. A procedure is basically an established way of carrying out a part of your business, such as how you order your wet and dry stocks. All those working together in a business need to have a common understanding about how things are normally done, so that efforts are co-ordinated. Procedures are really concerned, therefore, with how things are done, and that they are done sensibly, humanely and acceptably.

If you are in agreement so far, then it must be asked why procedures should not also have a place in regulating the working relations of people. If you check the dictionary definition of the word, you will find that particular mention is made of parliamentary and legal business, both of which are concerned with solving differences of opinion and interests. In the business world it is primarily because of the need to provide orderly, consistent and known methods for dealing with working relations between everyone in employment that procedures have such importance in what can be described generally as industrial relations.

Of course procedures dealing with things which affect staff interests, such as where, when and how they get their wages, exist wherever people are employed. They are a necessary part of normal business operations. Such procedures are based on customary practice rather than on formal arrangements. Are such customary practices suitable for all occasions, especially those that may lead to conflict?

The argument for keeping all arrangements as informal as possible usually rests on the contention that formal written procedural arrangements are seen to be restrictive and prejudicial to relations based on mutual trust. It could be countered by arguing that a preference for informality stems from a reluctance to accept commitments. What has become firmly established informally is not necessarily capable of being readily changed. Effective constraint on freedom of action arises from the strength of the parties to the agreement. Where there is no established mode of doing business, the opportunities for exploiting weaknesses by constant pressure are greatest. Formal, and written, procedures limit the area of uncertainty—they are a stronghold against arbitrary and unpredictable action.

The Case for Formality

It makes no sense to try and constitutionalize everything, so that the case for drawing up formal procedures does not rest on trying to achieve a comprehensive and essentially static means of dealing with what will always be an evolving situation. Procedures should be planned to deal with known problems, and this implies that you review the industrial relations problems you might have. Apart from any particular problems you now have in your business, procedures for dealing with matters such as grievances, discipline and redundancy seem of most obvious importance. If factors such as technical innovation, expansion or decline, mergers, and changes in organization, products or pay systems throw up unforeseen pressures, you may also find there is a case for other procedures.

To an employer the following points show the advantages of drawing up formal procedures:

1 The process of drawing them up provides an opportunity for discussion of the points likely to arise.
2 A document, especially if agreed, helps to reduce later misunderstandings.
3 A written text helps in disseminating the knowledge of the procedure among all who may be affected by it.
4 A procedure demonstrates your commitment to fairness.
5 Some basic rules help you to avoid acting inconsistently.

6 When changes of staff take place, continuity is more easily maintained.
7 The absence of procedures could prejudice your case at an Industrial Tribunal.

Procedural arrangements, however, must be seen in perspective: they are valuable in regulating management-staff relations but even more valuable if you are conscious of their limitations. Good procedures cannot ensure that all disputed issues will be settled peacefully. Human behaviour cannot be made to conform to prescribed rules just because there are prescribed rules. Your procedures can only be effective if they reflect a generally good relation between management and staff and a determination by both sides to use them.

Mutual goodwill may be an essential ingredient but it is not the whole recipe. The procedure must be well designed, and in practice this means that it is sufficiently flexible to suit all circumstances and able to be applied with common sense rather than with rigidity. After a time it should be reviewed in the light of experience and suitably amended, if need be. A procedure is only useful if it corresponds with reality and fulfils its ends.

A last but very important point to help you keep procedures in perspective is to remember that a procedure is not a substitute for a policy. You must have worth-while employment policies first, and then procedures can be very valuable in helping their implementation.

If you see it as exclusively your right, in the capacity of employer, to prescribe the objectives of your business and the procedures for attaining them, you must still, of course, recognize that you need to pay some attention to the views of staff if procedures are to have the acceptability needed to ensure they operate. If procedures are jointly agreed, the backing of them ceases to be solely your responsibility. The procedures become far more than an arid formalism, a codification of agreed rules: they incorporate a common understanding about how best to deal with certain matters in which both parties have a mutual interest.

Agreement of procedures is not impossible where no trade unions are recognized, although, where this is the case, the organization for discussion and agreement is likely to be at hand through staff representatives. Staff consultative committees offer a forum if the staff are not organized under a trade union banner.

Apart from acceptability, there are stronger arguments in

support of procedures being agreed. For you as a manager there will be a loss of sole discretion and authority in some aspects of running your business, but there can be a return in goodwill and more effective operation. From the staff side, whether unionized or not, there is a renunciation of their complete freedom and discretion to use their strength to press a case. So on both sides there is a dilution of unilateral power.

Agreed procedures constitute the practical expression and tangible evidence of both sides' understanding of their mutual interest and relations. Using the procedures becomes a concern transcending their interest in a transient case.

What really generates the need for agreement is the potential for conflict. Agreement needs at least two parties, and on the staff side this means they must be organized so that representatives can speak on behalf of all. The organization must have strength not only to advance their views to good effect but to see that agreements, once reached, are kept. This is clearly where the trade union role works best.

Formal and informal procedures can and should co-exist on a complementary basis. Ones that have been formally drawn up should be backed with the authority of mutual agreements, with both sides committed to upholding them. However, do not look on any procedure as the complete solution to any conflict of interest: the value of a procedure is that it can help to reduce misunderstanding and ensure that all possibilities of reaching agreement are fully explored and reasonably considered. Above all, procedures are only as good as the policies they express.

19.2 DISCIPLINARY PROCEDURE

In the light of all that has been said in Chapter 16 about the administration of discipline it is unlikely that much more emphasis needs to be given here to the need to have some sort of arrangement for its just and equitable application—in even the smallest of companies. Indeed, in light of Part I of the Employment Protection (Consolidation) Act the need to have a disciplinary procedure is implicitly required now in law.

Any procedure here normally centres around a staff code of conduct, perhaps formalized into a set of staff rules. Here is a basic outline of what a disciplinary procedure might be expected to cover:

1 A description of the most important rules, with examples of

circumstances in which breaches may justify instant dismissal.
2 Standards of behaviour in general that are necessary for the running of your particular business.
3 An indication of the progressive steps in disciplining staff for breaches of company rules and regulations.
4 A definition of who is authorized to take disciplinary action of various kinds.
5 A statement of an individual's right to be accompanied at various stages of the procedure.
6 An appeals procedure.

There can be no disciplinary procedure to suit all firms. You must set about tailoring a procedure to fit the nature of your business and the number of staff you employ, and especially to fit the organizational structure that exists.

Start by taking a look at the present rules governing staff and their behaviour. It is quite useless to attempt to draw up a list of rules covering every aspect of staff employment, so concentrate on the most important behaviour necessary for the smooth running of your organization, and take into account any particular aspect of the work that needs carefully regulating. In addition to this, review the subject matter of past discipline application to determine if there are any particular weaknesses needing to be specifically covered. For instance, if absenteeism is a particular problem, make sure your disciplinary code covers this, and that this is included in your procedure for handling breaches of duty to attend work faithfully and regularly.

Here are some examples of specific subjects companies have incorporated in their rules:

1 Smoking in prohibited areas.
2 Drinking on duty.
3 Quarrelling and fighting.
4 Absenteeism and lateness.
5 Theft.
6 Breaches of safety, especially fire, regulations.

Be selective in determining actual examples of what you consider serious misconduct and at the same time make sure you indicate clearly that the list is not intended to be comprehensive. Rather, make it clear that any form of misconduct is liable to be punished.

Penalties

Apart from any specific examples of gross misconduct, which will carry a possible penalty of summary dismissal, a sound disciplinary procedure should specify a graded series of penalties. Today it is normal for such a list to start with an oral formal warning and progress to suspension from duty and ultimately to dismissal. More particular types of penalty may be cited, but they need careful consideration. Such penalties may be suspension without pay and fining staff in breach of regulations, but since these could well be illegal in practice, they are best avoided altogether.

Most disciplinary procedures nowadays incorporate a series of oral and written warnings. A formal oral warning is exemplified in Appendix 34 (p. 318), written warnings in Appendix 35 (p. 319), and letters of dismissal in Appendix 36 (p. 321).

Perhaps because of the dangers of having to defend your disciplinary actions in Tribunals, most procedures today require that any penalty beyond a first warning be administered by a progressively more senior person, and that the decision to dismiss someone is vested in only those with senior status in the organization. This is probably a good thing in itself, since the offender may well begin to see the errors of his ways by virtue of the seniority of the managers who impose the severer penalties. It also relieves more junior management of the increasing responsibility of making decisions to discipline staff. A disciplinary procedure should therefore specify *who* has authority to do *what* at each step of the procedure.

Incorporate in your provisions the right of an individual to be accompanied, if he wishes, at each stage of the procedure. It is usual for the first step, when a formal verbal warning is administered, to be confined to the individual and his immediate superior, but thereafter for staff to be accompanied by a friend or trade union representative (if any). Certainly at the later, more serious, stages the level of representative may change, as does the level of manager, and thus you may allow in the procedure for the alleged offender to be accompanied at times by his shop steward, his branch or district officer or even a national officer.

An essential part of any disciplinary procedure must be the built-in right of staff to appeal against disciplinary decisions or penalties. This right usually implies a series of steps and may terminate at various points. It is also normally tied to a time-scale, which should not be protracted.

Practical Tips

1 Look on your disciplinary procedure as a code of fair practice rather than as a punishment charter.
2 Make sure you cover an appeals system in the procedure that is now required, by implication, under the Employment Protection (Consolidation) Act.
3 Use straightforward English, comprehensible to all staff, and avoid the temptation to use legalistic jargon.
4 If the procedure contains anything that fundamentally changes any term or condition of employment, make sure it is incorporated only with staff agreement.
5 When the procedure has been agreed, let all staff either have personal copies of it or bring it to their attention.
6 See that all those administering the procedure are properly trained and briefed in its application.

An example of a basic discipline procedure is given in Appendix 37 (p. 323).

19.3 GRIEVANCE PROCEDURE

The grievance procedure is in many ways the converse of the disciplinary procedure: the latter is concerned with handling dissatisfaction in the employer about a member of staff's behaviour and performance, whereas the former deals with dissatisfaction of staff with an employer's performance, or at least behaviour within the employer's power to alter. Action in a grievance procedure is initiated by staff.

A grievance is essentially a complaint by an individual member of staff. This section deals with the kind of procedure that aims to allow a grievance to be aired and settled satisfactorily and quickly.

Grievances can arise over almost any issue at work—the make-up of a person's pay, his holiday arrangements, shift working, job methods and working conditions. No organization is so perfect that staff need never complain. Even if it did exist, staff may still *feel* justified in raising a grievance. The whole purpose of encouraging you to draw up a grievance procedure, as with all procedures, is to provide staff with a course to follow in order to resolve their conflict as quickly as possible.

The Employment Protection (Consolidation) Act places a legal obligation on all employers to include in their written statements of terms and conditions of employment to staff details of how they can take up a grievance in the company. This is not the same thing as saying there is a legal requirement to draw up a formal full-blown grievance procedure—but it points strongly in that direction.

If that is not sufficient motivation, allied to common sense, there is another reason to have a procedure that can be followed in order to air a grievance. This can be derived from the findings of the Commission on Industrial Relations Report on the Hotels and Restaurants sector. In para. No. 189 it is recorded that: 'We found few written grievance procedures, and frequently discovered that staff either did not know how they would proceed or said they would proceed in a variety of ways varying from "speaking to the chef" to "going up to the manager when he came round". Some said the only way in which they would deal with a grievance would be to get a job in another hotel. We heard arguments that where there was no formal grievance procedure a worker might give up his job without taking up his grievance with management, thus leaving the cause of it behind him unremedied and perpetuated. This happening on any scale could be a factor in high labour turnover figures.'

The usual feature of the procedure is that the aggrieved person can have recourse to one or more levels of management. Invariably he airs his grievance first of all with his immediate boss, and if it is not settled there, he may take it to the next level, and so on, until it is resolved. What needs to be stressed here is that every effort should be made to have grievances resolved as near the point of origin as possible. If a commis chef feels that he is not being treated fairly in the hours he is expected to work, he should see the head chef first of all. Only if he gets no satisfaction there should the procedure allow him to take it to, say, the staff manager, and so on.

Of course the response he is likely to get from the head chef is conditioned by both the ability of his supervisor to settle it himself and by his readiness to do so. Basically, whether he is able to settle the grievance or not depends on both the nature of the grievance and the authority given to the head chef. It is unlikely that he will be able to give much satisfaction to his commis chef if the complaint is over basic wages—unless he fixes the rates of pay. On the other hand the head chef may have the authority and the ability to help, but be unready to do so. That would then look like a case for you to handle under the banner of training or perhaps discipline.

As with a disciplinary procedure, it is usual to allow the aggrieved person an opportunity to be accompanied at any stage of the procedure. Certainly if your staff are unionized, it would be sensible to build into the procedure a staff option to be accompanied by a staff representative.

Another feature of any procedure is that it embodies time limits for each stage. This makes sense if you consider that a person with a grievance is like a time bomb—the longer the grievance is allowed to burn the more likely it is to become enlarged and eventually to explode. On the other hand, if you are next in line to hear a staff complaint, you will need time to collect the facts and fit the hearing into other duties. Hence, on balance, you would be wise to build into the procedure some time limits to provide you with the chance to consider the problem and to provide an answer within a fixed period of time.

Finally you might consider it useful to require in the procedure that a written record of each step taken in resolving the grievance is maintained. Such a record helps to clarify the facts and contentions of the parties, and must be helpful to the person in line in the procedural routine.

Practical Tips

1 Keep your formal grievance procedure as simple and as straightforward as you can.

2 Whatever form it takes, make sure it contains the following essential features as a minimum: (1) progressive levels of appeal; (2) staff's right to be accompanied, if wished; and (3) time-scales to encourage an early settlement.

3 Train all who may have to handle grievances.

4 Build in a proviso that any time limits set may be extended by mutual agreement.

5 Make sure all managers encourage staff to use the grievance procedure without fear of retribution.

6 When a grievance has been settled, prepare a written and agreed statement to ensure that there are no misunderstandings.

An example of a grievance procedure is shown in Appendix 38 (p. 326).

19.4 REDUNDANCY PROCEDURE

All staff are concerned with job security, and this concern reaches major proportions when there is a threat of redundancy. Chapter 17 has indicated the legal requirements to be complied with should redundancies become likely in your company, and it has also highlighted the pitfalls awaiting any manager who tackles the problem without due thought and planning.

On this account, as well as acting as a general indication to all your staff of your concern to act fairly in all conceivable employment situations, you may well consider it worth while to produce a redundancy procedure. This will consist of contingency arrangements made in anticipation of any future reduction in your staffing needs. Because they are merely contingency plans, the procedures will be concerned with principles of conduct rather than with details. The latter can be attended to when arrangements must be made to meet a specific problem likely to give rise to redundancies.

You may find that if your staff are organized as trade unionists, they may not wish to take part in producing a redundancy procedure, preferring to reserve their position completely. On the other hand, if you can obtain agreement to the procedure, which, after all, deals with principles of conduct only, operating within the agreed procedure, when the need arises, should protect both you as the employer and the staff from any claim of unfairness.

Your procedure may take into account compensation payments and other monetary terms. The amount of compensation can have a significant effect on the smooth handling of redundancies, if they arise: for instance, they may help in encouraging voluntary redundancy.

Finally your redundancy procedure may not need to incorporate a separate appeals provision, since any grievance arising out of redeployment or redundancy can be handled through the normal grievance procedure.

Practical Tips

1 Keep your redundancy procedure on general lines. Stress the principles to be followed, but avoid specific details, which can hardly be anticipated.

2 Make sure the procedure leaves you free to take essential manning decisions, and therefore provides some degree of flexibility.

3 Include a clause giving you the right to vary the general rule, following consultation with staff.

An example of a redundancy procedure is given in Appendix 39 (p. 327).

CHECKLIST

1 Have you incorporated in your discipline procedure a list of the most important rules required to operate your business efficiently?

2 Does your requirement for issuing written warnings say that they should specify the reason or reasons behind them and highlight what further disciplinary action may be taken if the warning is ignored?
3 Does your disciplinary procedure incorporate clear steps of progressively severe penalties?
4 Is there a right for an alleged offender to be accompanied when subject to discipline?
5 Does your procedure cover an adequate appeal system?
6 Do all staff have copies of the procedure?
7 Have all supervisory or management staff administering discipline been fully briefed and, if necessary, trained in how to operate the procedure?
8 Does your grievance procedure establish that any grievance is normally discussed initially between the member of staff and his immediate superior?
9 Are there established further stages of discussion of unresolved issues?
10 Do staff have the right to be accompanied, if they wish, at least from the second level of the procedure?
11 Have all staff been given a copy of the procedure?
12 Have you complied with the A.C.A.S. Code of Practice recommendations?

CHAPTER TWENTY

Working with Trade Unions

20.1 THE ROLE OF A TRADE UNION

Why are there so few trade unionists among employees of this industry? Why have the trade unions not made more impact? Why are so many managers, if not actually opposed to, at least uninterested in their staff joining trade unions? Why are so many staff apparently apathetic about belonging to trade unions?

A whole book could be written in an attempt to answer questions like these, and it is no part of this manual's purpose to attempt to do so. However, you might well agree that possibly a part of the answer lies in a basic ignorance of what is the function of the trade union movement; and ignorance is often a cause of fear, which in turn can lead to antagonism. Whatever the other reasons may be—fragmentation, small units with close working relations between proprietor and staff, lack of a tradition of staff organization, or any one of a number of other reasons—you should recognize that a basic lack of knowledge of the aims and structure of trade unions is not excusable. Indeed, despite the spectacular stories of strikes and friction carried by the media, which tend to show the whole of the trade union movement in a poor light, an understanding of trade unionism can lead to an understanding of what it can offer as a help towards achieving better business results through a more effective working relation between management and staff.

The term 'trade union' is used to describe an association of employees with common interests based particularly on their occupation or their employment. This association gains its legal standing from being registered as a trade union with the Registrar of Friendly Societies, although the Certification Officer set up under the Employment Protection Act has taken over the duties of the Registrar of Friendly Societies.

There are approximately 11,000,000 members in the trade union movement, organized into nearly 500 separate trade unions, which can differ markedly in size, type, political orientation, openness to new members and form of administration. While the total number of unions has been dropping in recent years, the total membership has been increasing. In terms of size about 253 unions have fewer than 1,000 members, while around 24 each have a membership of over 100,000.

In the catering industry, most union membership is concentrated in the industrial catering section, which is represented by the General & Municipal Workers' Union, Transport & General Workers' Union and the Union of Shop, Distributive & Allied Workers. On the hotels and restaurants side these three unions also have a number of members, with the balance probably favouring the General & Municipal Workers' Union. If you are therefore called upon to establish a working relation with a trade union, it will probably be with either the General & Municipal Workers' Union or the Transport & General Workers' Union.

A trade union is a body that sees itself as an association of individual members without full corporate status—that is, it has not got the standing of a fictional 'person' for legal purposes. This allows it certain immunities in law.

The primary purpose of any trade union is to defend and advance the interests of its members, specifically by regulating the terms and conditions of their employment. Of course, as a responsible organization, the union takes into account such considerations as the interests of other trade unions, employers and the country as a whole.

Naturally, in seeking to satisfy its members' interests, the action of the trade union is conditioned by circumstances and can vary from place to place and from time to time. It is very important, however, to keep in mind the prime role and function of the trade union: to defend and advance the interests of its members.

On the other hand, the prime responsibility of management is to the proprietor or shareholders, to operate the business as efficiently as possible. It is here that conflict can be born; but good industrial relations are concerned with identifying and recognizing the distinct interests of each party, accentuating those that are held in common and reconciling those that are not.

Trade Union Structure

If your company is unionized, most of your industrial relations activities will be with *shop stewards* or staff representatives, whose function has grown in importance in proportion to the increase in local activities nowadays. In many unions shop stewards are not recognized as part of the official union structure. They have two particular functions—to further the interests of those who elect them and to represent union policy and interests in your company. Section 20.3 will look in more detail at the role of the shop steward.

Your union staff will be members of a specific *branch* of the union, usually based on a geographical division, and organized by a branch secretary. This is where meetings will be held regularly, but attendance normally represents but a small percentage of total membership.

A collection of local branches in most unions are gathered together into a *division*, *district* or *area*. This is controlled by a district committee elected by members from the branches, and the district secretary or organizer is usually a full-time official. He spends a lot of his time visiting companies in the district to help shop stewards with disputes and negotiations. There may be a divisional committee elected by members of the division, which exists to strengthen union organization and to provide services and officials dealing with branch problems throughout the division.

Finally, at *national level*, there will be a national executive council of the trade union responsible for carrying out the policy of the union agreed at the national conference. This committee consists of the main full-time national officials of the union and some elected 'lay members'. The general secretary of the union who is a full-time official, is the chief executive.

The Trade Union Congress lays down broad policy for the trade union movement, and can be asked to carry out actions on behalf of trade unions if they find them individually impossible or difficult to accomplish. The power of the T.U.C. derives solely from the consent of the trade unions themselves.

So much then for a brief outline of the function and structure of trade unions. It seems certain that the hotel and catering industry will become increasingly unionized, and it makes sense to consider what this implies.

The Commission on Industrial Relations was asked 'To report on the functioning and development of voluntary collective bargaining in the hotel and catering industry, with particular reference to the recommending of any improvements in industrial relations that appear necessary and desirable'. The report was published in October 1971 and one of the conclusions and recommendations reached was this: 'Companies and managements should make known their readiness to cooperate with trade unions and grant facilities for union recruitment within their establishments, as unions are hampered in their orderly development if there is employer opposition. They should pursue the possibility of developing joint agreements with the union which would not only demonstrate the effectiveness of voluntary collective bargaining to other companies and managements, but would also show the effective role of the union in joint regulation.'

Today, as you have seen earlier in this manual, the prime function of the Advisory, Conciliation and Arbitration Service is to further collective bargaining, and this is seen inevitably as bargaining with the trade union representing your staff interests. You are perfectly within your rights to decide whether or not to encourage your staff to join a trade union, while recognizing their rights to join an independent trade union and take part in all its activities., Whatever your approach may be, at least you should follow the Boy Scouts' motto and 'Be prepared', even if you are not yet ready to give a trade union *carte blanche* to come in and organize your staff if they wish.

20.2 A QUESTION OF RECOGNITION

Trade unions have had a legally defined freedom to organize since as long ago as 1824, but to date have had no similar right to recognition by employers. It is true that our present-day legislation leans considerably in the direction of recognition, as part and parcel of the emphasis on the value of collective bargaining.

The legal position is this: all your staff have a legal right to belong to an independent trade union and to take part in its activities, but if they, under the banner of their union, seek recognition by you that may allow them to negotiate terms and conditions of employment, you retain the right to say 'yes' or 'no'. Under the Employment Protection Act the union, if refused recognition, can then ask the Advisory Conciliation and Arbitration Service to help. This will mean that the A.C.A.S. will consult all the parties it considers may be affected, in an effort to act as a conciliator. Should the matter not be settled at this stage, the A.C.A.S. will prepare a report recommending recognition of some kind or giving reasons why no such recommendation is made. This report may follow a secret ballot of staff, although the result of this is not binding on the A.C.A.S.

If you receive a recommendation to recognize a union or unions from the A.C.A.S. but do not comply with it, the union can complain to the Central Arbitration Committee (C.A.C.) and claim that certain staff should receive some specified improvement in their terms of employment. If these are awarded, they become enforceable terms of the staff contracts. The law goes no further than that.

One of the first instructions given to the now defunct Commission on Industrial Relations (C.I.R.) was, 'The Government will expect the C.I.R. normally to favour recognition if the union is appropriate and can establish that it has reasonable support'. The very first annual report of the C.I.R. said that it had hoped to formulate the principles that should govern recognition policy but had decided that to do so would simply resolve itself into 'heavily qualified generalities'. As you have seen, the successor to the C.I.R., the A.C.A.S., has generally continued the same approach.

Guidance of the Code

If you are faced with a request for recognition, the first place to look for guidance is probably the I.R. Code of Practice (paras 82–9). Unions won't usually seek recognition unless they have members on your staff. If they do, these are the questions to consider:

1 *What is the support for the union?* You are not entitled to know the identity of those staff who belong to the union, but you are entitled to know the number of members. However, in trying to answer this question you will also want to know what support is likely to be given to the claim by staff who would join the union *if* it were recognized. If there is any dispute about the size of the support, it can be resolved either by holding a secret ballot of all staff, or by asking the A.C.A.S. to send an adviser to make an independent assessment.

   Of course, if you operate a 'check-off' system, this will enable you to estimate actual union support more accurately; for this is the means by which you deduct union dues at source from staff wages, and pay them to the union on behalf of staff. It is normal in these circumstances to negotiate with the union a commission of, say, 5 per cent to cover your administrative costs. It should go without saying that in your early discussions with the union you should agree what level of support is necessary before you grant recognition.

2 *Does the union seek to represent all grades of staff or not?* You might well consider that recognition of one union to deal with all staff has the greatest advantage all round. But how practical is this?

Are the interests of supervisory/junior management staff the same as staff at other levels?

3 *What sort of recognition is sought?* You may agree with the union in the first place that you will recognize a representational right only: this would give the union a right to represent any of their members who wish to use a grievance procedure or who are subject to action under your disciplinary procedure. On the other hand, what may be at stake is full negotiating rights, in which the union will have the sole right to bargain with you, as the employer, over the pay and other conditions of employment of staff. This is what will be at issue, at least eventually, on the argument that staff have a socially accepted interest in helping to determine their wages and conditions.

4 *Will you consult the staff about a recognition policy?* If the staff know that there is talk of recognizing a trade union in the air, do not be tempted to leave the communication side to the union or staff actively engaged with you in discussion. Not only would this be an abdication of your responsibility for keeping staff informed about things that may affect them but it would probably also be missing a good opportunity to show that you are concerned about recognition in the best interests of staff and the business. Consequently you should keep them officially informed of such points as the following:

(a) Your general attitude to staff joining trade unions.
(b) Whether you are ready to give the union facilities to recruit.
(c) What factors will determine whether you grant recognition.
(d) What sort of recognition you are considering.
(e) How staff who are not yet trade unionists might be affected by whatever recognition you may grant.

5 *What sort of things would be bargained about?* You may be able to agree with a recognized union a list of exceptions to negotiable items. However, unions would generally expect to be free to bargain with you over such things as wages, holidays, holiday pay, overtime and overtime pay, service charge distribution, shift systems, job evaluation, work study, redundancy, grievance and disciplinary matters, pensions and sick pay schemes.

6 *If recognition of any sort is granted, should you have a recognition policy?* If it becomes part of your employment policy to recognize a trade union then it might be sensible to draw up a policy

document giving the principles of recognition. An example of such a document is given in Appendix 40 (p. 328).

You alone can decide to grant or withhold recognition if this is requested by a trade union. You must weigh carefully what will be best in the interests of both staff and business. Ask other managers in the industry who have experience to tell you what they have found to be the advantages or disadvantages. Take advantage of the free advice available to you from the A.C.A.S. Remember that you can start by according a limited form of recognition until you have had a bit more experience of your own to judge from, and at all times consult the staff; after all it is going to affect them most of all.

If you do accord recognition of any sort, then staff will seek a representative system; this may well be formalizing, on a union basis, what consultative rights already exist. However, these representatives will then become officially shop stewards, a subject covered in Section 20.3.

If any form of recognition is accorded, you should draw up substantive and procedural agreements with the union. The points that may be covered in such agreements are suggested in Appendix 41 (p. 329).

20.3 THE FUNCTION OF THE SHOP STEWARD

The term 'shop steward' is not used universally for the person who, with trade union support, acts as a representative of a group of staff. More frequently in the hotel and catering industry he/she is known as the 'staff representative' or 'union representative'. Whatever the title may be, most people are familiar with the term 'shop steward', and it will be used throughout this section.

Once staff are officially unionized in your establishment, your dealings with union matters and interests are likely to be with your shop steward rather than outside officials of the union. Cordial relations right from the start are most important, and can be enormously helpful in setting up a sound system of industrial relations in your company.

One of the first points to agree upon with the union is the number of shop stewards to be appointed. This will depend to a large extent upon the size of your company or establishment, and the division you agree on in terms of areas and types of staff to be represented. In a typical hotel you might well have a shop steward in each of the following areas: kitchen, front of house, restaurant and housekeeping. However, weigh carefully with the union the clear advantages of having only one shop steward per unit. Another determining factor will be the number of union members among staff. This is also the time to consider whether it is necessary to have a senior shop steward, or convener, and deputies.

Your initial consultation with the union might also decide on any conditions to be imposed in terms of eligibility, such as minimum age qualification and length of service with the company. You should be able to agree with the union your right to veto any selection on the grounds of it not being in the best interests of the company or staff.

The election of stewards may be in the hands of the union, but ideally it should be organized jointly between management and union. You should be prepared to give appropriate facilities, such as helping them to publicize election details. Once elections are over, the union should be charged with the responsibility of letting you know the names of those elected and any subsequent changes.

A shop steward has two main responsibilities—to represent the interests of those who elect him/her, and to act as the linkman and spokesman for his union. However, the practical implication of these duties is that the shop steward may be expected to carry out very diverse duties, from recruitment of new members to acting as a local negotiator. What his precise functions are will depend on a number of different factors, as follows:

1 The formal responsibilities of being a shop steward.
2 The attitude towards him of various groups, including management and the union itself.
3 The system of industrial relations existing in your company.

Unfortunately the formal duties of a shop steward are not laid down as neatly and clearly as they might be. Most industries rely on custom and practice. Fortunately in the hotel and catering industry, where custom and practice are likely to be limited, you have an opportunity from the start to agree with the union a list of the steward's formal duties. These could include any or all of the following items:

1 To take up grievances of individual members.
2 To take up group issues.
3 To act as a negotiator.
4 To take part in a consultative committee.
5 To collect union dues.
6 To recruit new members.

Certainly in a newly unionized establishment one of the most important ways of starting on a sound footing is the establishment of the correct relationship between the steward and his local union official. This will give the former access to a wide field of industrial relations and enable him to draw upon experience he would take time to gain alone. You can help by encouraging this contact, and making his access to outside officials as easy as you can.

Contact between stewards is also an important formative element. Whether you allow them time during normal working hours to hold a joint shop stewards' meeting will depend on numbers and the particular circumstances of your company, but in principle it should be a good thing in that it will encourage a unified approach on the part of stewards throughout the company.

Your own attitude and that of fellow-managers is also very telling. If your approach is positive, it can help effective industrial relations.

However, the most important influence on the work of the shop steward is the staff he represents—his constituents. They appointed him and they sack him. He will normally be 'one of them' in almost every respect, and will be in close contact with them in his normal everyday life. In some cases the steward will be looked upon purely as a spokesman to management; in others he will be expected to undertake a leadership role. The important thing for him is that any agreement he reaches with you must be acceptable to the group he represents. You can help him by making sure he has the facilities to maintain contact with his members and to pass adequate information to them.

In the end the function of the shop steward will be determined by your own employment policies and by the existence or not in the establishment of procedural agreements. Once these are established, it will be part of the steward's job to see that you and management remain within the agreements, and to operate within procedures.

Once elected, a shop steward should be issued with written credentials. Ideally these should be jointly agreed and issued, and should spell out the period of office and the group he represents, his powers and duties within the union and his rights and responsibilities. An example of a statement of joint credentials is given at Appendix 42 (p. 330).

Facilities

If the shop steward is to carry out his functions effectively, he needs to be given the appropriate facilities. These may well vary from establishment to establishment, largely depending on his agreed functions, but some of the basic facilities required will include the following:

1 Time off from his normal work to carry out his industrial relations functions, with permission from his supervisor, which should not be withheld normally.
2 Maintenance of earnings while engaged on authorized union activities.
3 Notification of all new staff employed.
4 Accommodation for meetings with his members, inside or outside normal hours of work.
5 Access to a telephone.
6 Provision for displaying notices on union matters.

Training

If a shop steward is to be effective, he certainly will require specific training for his new role. Again this should be agreed jointly between yourself and the union, not only in terms of allowing the steward time off for, and payment for the time spent in, this training, but also in the subject matter of the training. Trade unions provide their own training courses for stewards, as do many colleges of further education up and down the country. When you are considering what contribution you can make toward this training, you might consider such factors as the following:

1 Company objectives and organization.
2 The financial structure of the company.
3 Employment policies and conditions of employment.
4 Wage structure.
5 Sickness benefit scheme.
6 Pension and life assurance scheme.
7 Safety and hygiene.
8 Company agreements and procedures.

Conclusion

As you would expect, the I.R. Code of Practice contains quite a lot of guidance on shop stewards. Paras 99–119 might well be a good starting point for your consideration of the whole question.

The whole of Part V has considered the subject matter of industrial relations and the role of trade unions in helping to build up and maintain them in good order. You will realize that the whole of the United Kingdom is undergoing quite significant changes in this area, with ever-increasing emphasis on the rights of individual members of staff and on their right as a body to participate in decisions that have traditionally been looked upon as an exclusive management prerogative. It is unlikely that the hotel and catering industry will remain unaffected by these events; and because it has been traditionally an industry that has relied on personal relations between management and staff rather than on more formalized relations through the medium of trade unions, the changes required of it may be more significant than in other industries.

The facts cannot be denied: trade unions of both manual and white-collar workers are becoming more organized and are receiving the general support of all political parties; terms and conditions of employment are becoming more regularized by collective bargaining; and the process of shared decision-making is evolving at an increasingly fast pace. You cannot act as the ostrich and ignore these facts which need not be a cause for concern. Here is a golden opportunity to develop positive employment policies, to put into effect sound practices and procedures to further the combined interests of both the business and staff. The whole purpose of this manual has been to help you do all this in a practical and realistic manner.

CHECKLIST

1 How many of your staff belong to an independent trade union?
2 What would the attitude of non-union staff be to any form of recognition granted by you to a trade union?
3 What effect would recognition have on existing bargaining arrangements?
4 Would you grant recognition to the same union to represent both staff and supervisory staff?
5 What sort of recognition would you be prepared to grant—full negotiating rights, representation only or consultation only?
6 If recognition is granted, do all staff have a document clearly setting out the recognition principles?
7 If recognition is on a full negotiating rights basis, do you have an agreed procedure for initiating and conducting negotiations, and for resolving any issues in dispute?
8 What help have you given unions to enable them to represent their members' interests effectively?
9 Have you offered to operate a 'check-off' system on an agreed commission basis?

Part V Bibliography

A.C.A.S. *Disclosure of Information to T.U.'s Code No. 2* (A.C.A.S.).

Allen, V. L. *Power in Trade Unions* (Longman, 1958).

Anthony, P. and Crichton, A. *Industrial Relations and the Personnel Specialist* (Batsford, 1969).

Armstrong, E. *Industrial Relations – an Introduction* (Harrap, 1969).

Balfour, C. *Participation in Industry* (Croom Helm, 1973).

——*Unions and the Law* (Saxon House, 1973).

Burns, T. *Industrial Man* (Penguin, 1969).

Clegg, M. A. *The System of Industrial Relations in Great Britain* (Blackwell, 1973).

C.I.R. *Hotels and Restaurants,* Report No. 23 (H.M.S.O., 1972).

—— *Employee Relations in the Smaller Firm* (H.M.S.O., 1972).

Dept. of Environment. *Code of Industrial Relations Practice* (H.M.S.O., 1971).

Donovan, Lord *Royal Commission on Trade Unions and Employers' Associations* (H.M.S.O., 1968).

Flanders, A. *Trade Unions* (Hutchinson, 1952).

—— *Collective Bargaining* (Penguin, 1969).

—— *Management and Unions* (Faber & Faber, 1970).

Goodman, J. F. B. and Whittingham, T. G. *Shop Stewards in British Industry* (McGraw-Hill, 1969).

Hughes, J. and Pollins, J. H. *Trade Unions in Great Britain* (David & Charles, 1973).

Hyman, R. *Disputes Procedures in Action* (Heinemann, 1972).

—— *Strikes* (Fontana, 1972).

Industrial Society. *A Practical Guide to Joint Consultation* (I.S., 1974).

McCarthy, W. E. J. *Trade Unions* (Penguin, 1972).

Ramsay, J. C. and Hill, J. M. *Collective Agreements – a guide to their Content and Drafting* (I.P.M., 1974).

Rhenham, E. *Industrial Democracy and Industrial Management* (Tavistock, 1968).

Singleton, N. *Industrial Relations Procedures,* D.E. Manpower Paper No. 14 (H.M.S.O., 1975).

Thomas, J. L. and Roberts, N. *Trade Unions and Industrial Relations* (Business Books, 1967).

Thomason, G. *A Textbook of Personnel Management* (I.P.M., 1975).

T.U.C. *A Guide for Negotiators* (T.U.C., 1972).

Whincup, M. *Modern Employment Law* (Heinemann, London, 1980).

Appendix 32 Constitution for a Consultative Committee

CONSTITUTION AND RULES OF THE XYZ CONSULTATIVE COMMITTEE

(non-unionized catering outlet)

CONSTITUTION

1 AIMS The purpose of the consultative committee is to provide a means of exchanging views between management and staff on all matters of mutual concern.

2 STRUCTURE

2.1 The committee will consist of both management and staff representatives, in a ratio of 1:2, under the chairmanship of a senior management representative appointed by the company. A secretary is elected from members of the committee.

2.2 Staff representatives are elected by any grade below managerial level from every department who may send two representatives if that department is subject to shift working.

2.3 Management representatives are to be nominated by the managing director.

2.4 The function of the committee is to discuss any matter as it affects constituency interests and those of the business as a whole, with the exception that they will not be competent to discuss individuals or matters that more correctly are the subject of a negotiating committee.

2.5 The committee will not replace the ordinary staff meetings of the company.

2.6 The committee year of office will be 1 January–31 December.

RULES

1 *Elections*

All elections will be by ballot, and the member of staff with the highest number of votes will become the representative. In the event of a tie a second ballot will be held between the tying candidates.

2 *Term of Office*

All representatives will hold office for a period of two years and will not be eligible for re-election after two consecutive 2-year periods without a break of at least 1 year.

3 *Vacant Offices*

If a constituency loses its representative for any reason, a new election must take place within a month of departure of the original representative.

4 *Co-option*

The chairman may invite members from management or staff to attend on occasion to provide information that might not otherwise be available to the meeting.

5 *Meetings*

Meetings will take place every two months, to be called by the secretary, who will be required to give all representatives a week's notice. An extraordinary meeting may be called by the chairman at any time, without notice, if circumstances demand an urgent and special meeting of the committee.

6 *Agenda*

All committee members will be invited by the secretary to submit items for the agenda, which will be distributed to all members a week before a meeting is held. The chairman shall have the right to exclude any item submitted only on the grounds that it is not a subject for consultative purposes.

7 *Minutes*

The secretary will prepare minutes for every meeting, and, once approved by the chairman, copies will be sent out to all committee members, other management and supervisors, and a copy posted on the main staff notice board.

8 *Other Matters*

Any other matter not covered by the rules or any interpretation of them will be considered by the committee chairman, and his decision will be binding.

Appendix 33 Possible Topics for Consultative Committee Discussion

Company annual report
Decoration schedules
Customer complaints procedure
Distribution of duties
Disciplinary rules
Induction of new staff
Uniform
Training facilities
Shift systems
Fire drills
Safety matters
Heating and ventilation
Staff rest-rooms
Attracting new business
Duty rosters
Trade union representatives
New equipment
Structural alterations
Improvement of service
Function trade

Appendix 34 Example of Letter Confirming Formal Oral Warning

Date ....

Dear ....

This letter is to confirm that on 17 December 19..... you were given a formal oral warning by me about your poor timekeeping.

You provided no reasonable excuse for turning up late for work on a number of occasions, and I therefore formally warned you that you would need to take every step possible to improve in this matter.

I hope you took this verbal warning seriously and will show an immediate improvement in your timekeeping, otherwise, as I told you, you will be given an official written warning as laid down in the company discipline procedure.

Yours sincerely,

Appendix 35 First and Final Warning Letters

FIRST WRITTEN WARNING

Date ....

Dear ....

OFFICIAL WARNING

You will remember that on 17 December I spoke to you about your bad timekeeping and formally warned you that things would need to improve.

There has been no real improvement in this matter since then, and so this letter is meant to record an official warning on the subject.

I have noted your lateness on the following occasions:

29 January—10 minutes late
4 February—25 minutes late
16 February—15 minutes late

If you should continue to arrive late for duty, a final warning may be given to you and any lateness after that may result in your dismissal.

Yours sincerely,

....

I acknowledge receipt of my first official warning.

Signature ....
Name .... Date ....

Final written warning

Date ....

Dear ....

FINAL OFFICIAL WARNING

You received a first warning letter from me on .... about your lateness of arrival on duty. Unfortunately you seem to have ignored this warning and I now am issuing you with a final official warning.

I again have noted your late arrival for duty on several occasions, and you have been unable to give me a satisfactory explanation for this. To be precise, you were late on the 27 February and again on the 4 March—on this occasion by 35 minutes.

I know of no reason for this failure on your part to be punctual in reporting for duty; if there is such a reason, please make sure you see me immediately.

If you should be late again on duty in the next 6 months, you will be liable to be dismissed from the company.

Yours sincerely,

....

Area Manager

I acknowledge receipt of this final official warning

Signature ....

Name .... Date ....

Note: A copy of this warning is lodged on your file.

Appendix 36 Letters Terminating Employment

WITH NOTICE

Date ....

Dear ....

NOTICE OF DISMISSAL

Following your suspension on ...., the company has examined the case against you, which is that you continue to fail in your duty to report for work on time.

You were given a verbal warning about this on ...., and two official letters, dated .... and ...., but despite these you continue to report for work late on occasions.

Your service with the company is therefore terminated with effect from ...., which takes account of the .... weeks' notice that is due to you, on the grounds of industrial misconduct.

This letter is given to you at your request in accordance with your rights under the Employment Protection Act.

Yours sincerely,

....

Area Controller

WITHOUT NOTICE

Date ....

Dear ....

NOTICE OF DISMISSAL

Following your suspension on ...., the company has considered fully the case against you, which is .... (a brief statement of the offence).

You were issued with a written official warning on ...., and a final written warning on ...., stating that if you made a further unsatisfactory return of cash in respect of sales of liquor stocks, you would be liable for dismissal.

Your service with the company is therefore terminated with effect from ...., without notice, on the grounds that you have shown yourself incapable of holding the appointment of a managed house manager.

This letter is given to you at your request in accordance with your rights under the Employment Protection (Consolidation) Act.

Yours sincerely,

....

Director of Managed Houses

Appendix 37 Example of a Disciplinary Procedure

INTRODUCTION

It is the policy of the XYZ Hotel to maintain a friendly, personal relationship among all staff in the hotel, and to provide security of employment. However, when a number of people work together, there have to be certain rules and regulations designed to maintain an organized working atmosphere. When such regulations are broken, some form of discipline must be exercised. This procedure document outlines the form discipline will take in this hotel. Every member of staff is to be issued with a copy of this document.

RESPONSIBILITY

All members of management are responsible for explaining company rules and standards of conduct to their staff, and for ensuring that they are followed. All staff are expected to familiarize themselves with their conditions of employment and the *Staff Handbook*, which give accepted standards of behaviour in the hotel.

OFFENCES OTHER THAN SERIOUS MISCONDUCT

If a member of staff's conduct is in question, the head of department or manager will investigate the facts. If he considers them established, he will endeavour to find the reason for the offence.

If the reason is outside the man's control, appropriate action to resolve the problem will be taken, or due allowance made. If domestic trouble is the cause, the staff manager will be advised and will take appropriate welfare action.

If the reason is within the employee's control, the head of department will decide whether an informal talk with the employee is wanted or whether Stage 1 of the Procedure should be invoked.

STAGE I—VERBAL ADVICE AND WARNING

If the failure is thought to be within his own control, the employee will be interviewed by his head of department in the presence of a friend or his staff representative (if he wishes), and given an opportunity to explain his alleged shortcomings and offered whatever advice, help or reprimand is felt to be necessary. He will be given an agreed specific time in which to improve, and will be informed that if this is not forthcoming, a written warning, which may be the final one, will be given. This verbal warning will be recorded on his personal file, and confirmed by personal letter.

STAGE II—WRITTEN WARNING

If the employee's conduct does not improve within the stated time, the head of department will arrange a meeting at which he will interview the man in the presence of a friend or his staff representative (if he wishes). A written warning will be given to the employee and all the circumstances recorded, with a copy placed in his personal file and a copy sent to the hotel manager. In the event of satisfactory conduct the record will be cleared within 6 months.

STAGE III—FINAL WRITTEN WARNING

Should there be no or inadequate improvement within the 6 months, a final written warning may be given, following again the procedure in Stage II.

STAGE IV—TERMINATION OR DISMISSAL

In the event of no further improvement in conduct, or the offence being committed again, the head of department, after consultation with the hotel manager, will indicate to the member of staff concerned, accompanied by a friend or staff representative (if he wishes), what penalty he proposes to recommend.

He may recommend termination of contract, with notice, or dismissal without notice.

Having given the member of staff an opportunity to reply to the penalty to be recommended, the head of department will then report to the hotel manager with his recommendation. Meanwhile, if the employee belongs to a trade union, he will be given the opportunity to inform his full-time official at this stage. If the recommendation is endorsed, the employee will be informed of the penalty to be imposed by the hotel manager himself, who will support his decision in the form of a letter of termination or dismissal, provided the employee requests the reasons for termination/dismissal, in writing within 14 days of dismissal. A copy of this letter will be placed on the personal file of the employee concerned.

SUMMARY DISMISSAL

The following offences are examples of the sorts of misconduct that may result in summary dismissal:

1 Being drunk on duty.
2 Any physical violence.
3 Any serious breach of a fire, safety or hygiene regulation.
4 Dishonesty.

In some circumstances it may be necessary to use immediate suspension as a precautionary measure so that a member of staff may be removed from duty during the investigation, without prejudice to the result or his future employment. If this takes place, he will receive average earnings for the period of the precautionary suspension.

In cases of dishonesty when a prosecution is pending, a member of staff may be suspended, with pay suspended too, until the outcome is decided in court. Should there be no conviction and he is reinstated, then payment will be made for the period of suspension. Should dismissal follow suspension with pay, then the procedure in Stage IV will be followed; otherwise the hotel manager will send the final notice of dismissal to the employee's home address.

ABSENTEEISM

Because this hotel is operated on a tight staff schedule, it is important that there is no unnecessary absence of staff from duty. The following provisions therefore apply to all cases of uncertified absence:

1 day's absence	—Formal verbal warning
Second day's absence within 3 months of first warning	—First written warning
Third day's absence within 3 months of written warning	—Final written warning
Fourth day's absence within 3 months of final written warning	—Termination, with notice

APPEALS PROCEDURE

1 If a member of staff indicates that he wishes to appeal against any penalty imposed at Stages I–III of this procedure, the matter should be placed within 48 hours in the hands of the staff manager, who will arrange for the hotel manager to hear the appeal within a further 48 hours.

2 There is no appeal against termination or dismissal, but staff retain their rights under the Employment Protection (Consolidation) Act to appeal to an Industrial Tribunal.

MISCELLANEOUS

1 It is not necessary in every case to progress through each stage of this procedure.

2 If warnings are issued, then subsequent warnings in the procedure will be issued only if they relate to the same or similar offences. If other offences are registered in the meantime, then another set of warnings may be necessary.

Appendix 38 Example of a Grievance Procedure

In accordance with our employment policy in the ABC Catering Company to provide a congenial working atmosphere and to maintain satisfactory relations among all employees, the following procedure is designed to allow any grievances among staff to be resolved satisfactorily and as speedily as possible. Therefore, if any member of the staff should feel dissatisfaction with his terms and conditions of employment, his working conditions, work methods or any other aspect of his employment, he should take the following steps to resolve the problem:

Stage 1 Discuss your complaint with your immediate superior as soon as you can. If you are not satisfied as a result of this discussion, proceed to Stage 2.

Stage 2 Tell your superiors that you would like the matter discussed with the catering manager. If you wish, you may be accompanied by a friend or staff representative at this hearing, which will take place within 24 hours of your request. Should your complaint remain unresolved after this stage, then you should ask the catering manager for an interview with one of the company's directors.

Stage 3 At this stage you are entitled to be heard by a director of the company, again accompanied as before, if you so wish. This interview will normally be granted within 48 hours of your request. The decision given by the director will be final.

Notes

1 The time-scales may be extended by mutual agreement.
2 A written record will be made at Stage 2, agreed by the aggrieved person, before Stage 3 is reached.
3 Whatever the result, a written statement will be given at Stage 3 setting out the official answer to the grievance.

Appendix 39 Example of a Redundancy Procedure

CONSULTATION

When redundancy is anticipated, consultation will take place with staff/the XYZ trade union on a time-scale at least as long as that required under the Employment Protection Act, and this consultation will include the following points:

1 Cessation of recruitment.
2 Cessation of contracting-out work.
3 Short-time working.
4 Work sharing.
5 Redeployment within the company.
6 Retraining arrangements.
7 Voluntary redundancies.

Redundancy procedures will be followed after the agreed measures have been taken.

WARNING

At least one week's warning will be given to all staff affected by redundancy.

SELECTION

The general principle of selection of staff to be made redundant will be 'last in, first out', but the company may depart from this practice where necessary in order to maintain efficient operation and to avoid exceptional hardship.

UNIT OF REDUNDANCY

The practice of 'last in, first out' will be applied to each grade of staff and to each trade.

COMPENSATION

Rates of compensation will not be less than those laid down in the Employment Protection (Consolidation) Act. All redundant staff who have completed at least 6 months' service will receive compensation at the following rates:

1 Service of 6 months to 1 year: $1\frac{1}{2}$ weeks' pay.
2 For each year of service below the age of 41: 2 weeks' pay.
3 For each year of service between 41 and 60 (female) and up to 65 (male): $2\frac{1}{2}$ weeks' pay.

Where less than complete years have been served, part years will be calculated on the following basis: 1 day's pay for every 2 completed months of service.

The compensation so calculated will be paid as a lump sum on termination of employment, tax-free.

VARIATION IN PROCEDURE

Any item in this procedure may be varied, if necessary, after consultation with the staff/the XYZ trade union.

Appendix 40 Company Policy Statement on Trade Unions

1 It is the policy of the XYZ Hotel Group to recognize the G.M.W.U. within the hotels, and the company and the union jointly agree to the following:

(a) It is in both our interests that staff should be encouraged to join the G.M.W.U. in order that negotiations between the union and the company be conducted on an authoritative basis.

(b) Procedures be available for settling any question affecting an individual or all staff, so as to arrive at a satisfactory conclusion.

2 Membership of the G.M.W.U. or any union is not a condition of employment.

3 In addition to encouraging staff to join the G.M.W.U., the company will provide the union with facilities to assist recruitment of members by notifying shop stewards of all new staff in their area.

4 The company and the union have a common objective in using the process of negotiation to achieve results beneficial to both the company and the staff.

5 The union recognizes the company's responsibility to plan, organize and manage each hotel. The company recognizes the union's responsibility to represent the interests of their members and to work for improved conditions of employment.

6 Any changes in terms and conditions of employment agreed between the company and the union will be implemented to benefit union and non-union staff alike.

7 The company and the union agree to refrain from lock-outs, strikes or other industrial action until appropriate procedures have been exhausted.

Appendix 41 Suggested Subjects for Inclusion in Substantive and Procedural Agreements

The I.R. Code of Practice recommends that collective agreements should cover both substantive and procedural matters, either in one document or separate documents. As implied in the term itself, *substantive* provisions cover terms and conditions of employment whereas *procedural* provisions describe the steps to be followed in such matters as consultation, negotiation and disputes, and the handling of grievances and disciplinary questions.

Here are typical subjects covered by such procedures:

Substantive agreements

Job grading scales
Probationary periods
Working hours
Meal breaks
Overtime payment
Public holiday working
Shift systems
Incentives/merit increases
Annual holidays
Public holidays
Periods of notice
Wages/salaries
Guaranteed pay
Sick pay

Procedural agreements

Parties concerned
Resolving grievances
Handling disciplinary cases
Matters to be negotiated
Levels of negotiation
Facilities for T.U. activity
Number, appointment, status and facilities of shop stewards
Settling collective disputes
Constitution and scope of consultative committees

Appendix 42 Example of Joint Credentials for Shop Stewards

The ABC Restaurants and the G.M.W.U. jointly agree on the following points for .... (name of shop steward), who has been elected as the staff representative for .... (name of constituency/area concerned).

1 You will be the recognized staff representative for a period of ...., commencing on .... Should you leave the company's employment during this period, your office as staff representative will cease immediately on termination.
2 In your capacity as a union representative you will comply with the rules of the G.M.W.U.
3 You will be subject to the normal terms and conditions of employment of all staff appropriate to your job.
4 In your capacity as a staff representative you will be specifically responsible for the following:

   (a) Collecting union dues.
   (b) Recruiting new union members.
   (c) Representing your members individually and collectively.
   (d) Communicating with your members on all union matters.

   You will be permitted to carry out those duties in normal working hours with the agreement of .... (name of immediate superior).
5 You will receive your normal wages while employed on any of the above functions.
6 Apart from the specific items covered in this agreement you will not be given any special privileges or immunities.
7 You will encourage your members to abide by any agreements made between management and the unions.

Signed .... Date ....
(for the company)

Signed .... Date ....
(for the union)

Note. Copies of these credentials should be given to the shop steward and to his immediate superior.

Appendix 43 The Employment Act

The Bill was published on 7 December 1979, had its second reading on 17 December and is now awaiting Royal Assent.

It will be published as an Act with effect from October 1980.

MAIN PROVISIONS

1 Closed Shops

All staff in or seeking employment in a business operating a closed shop will have the right not to be unreasonably refused membership of the Trade Union concerned nor to be unreasonably expelled from membership.

Complaints will be heard by Industrial Tribunals and E.A.T. who will judge cases on equity and merit of each case. If a Union complies with a Declaration by an I.T., the person can be awarded compensation for any loss sustained to a maximum of £9,850. If the Union fails to obey the Declaration then the E.A.T. can award up to £16,090 against the Union.

Dismissal. It will be unfair, in a closed shop, to dismiss anyone:

1 Where he objects on grounds of conscience or deep personal conviction to belonging to the Union;
2 Where he was employed *before* the closed shop agreement and has not been a member *since.*
3 Where the closed shop is not 'approved' (i.e. not approved in a secret ballot where at least 80% of those entitled to vote did vote for it).

Union Pressure. If an employer claims in an U.D. case that he was subject to pressure (threat of industrial action) to dismiss someone for his failing to join a Union, he has the right to join the pressuriser (T.U.) in proceedings. Any compensation awarded may then be payable, in part or whole, by the T.U.

2 Picketing

Lawful picketing will be confined to a. Staff picketing at their own place of work and b. Officials of their own Union accompanying them, provided it is in 'contemplation of furtherance of a Trade Dispute' (not necessarily with their own employer!)

Any breach of the new definition will render staff liable to legal action.

3 Coercive Recruitment

If staff at Hotel Company A take industrial action to compel staff at Hotel Company B to join a Union, they will be liable in tort for their actions. If the industrial action leads to interference with a commercial contract, liability for that interference will also arise.

4 Codes of Practice

The Employment Secretary may issue codes to improve industrial relations.

5 Small Businesses

(a) In all cases of U.D., the I.T.s will take into account the size and administrative resources of the business.

(b) Staff in *some* businesses will not have U.D. rights where:

1 They are dismissed within 2 years of the business recruiting the first employee.
2 At no time were more than 19 staff employed.
3 They were told in writing of these lack of rights and also told date of rights becoming effective.

6 Maternity

To exercise her job-back rights, a woman must notify her emplcyer in writing, at least 21 days before leaving, of her intention to return and the expected date/week of confinement.

Seven weeks after confinement the employer may write for confirmation of her expected return, and the woman then has 14 days in which to reply or lose her right. The woman must give at least 3 weeks' written notice of the day she wants to return.

There is no claim for U.D. when a woman is not allowed to return to her old job if:

(a) at the start of her absence there were fewer than 6 staff employed, and
(b) it is not reasonably practicable to offer her the old job or alternative work.

There is no right to return if, in any size of firm, it is not reasonably practical to give her the original job she had and she unreasonably refuses alternative work.

7 Burden of Proof

In all U.D. cases the employer will no longer have to show it was 'reasonable in the circumstances' to dismiss; this burden will now be 'neutral'.

8 Compensation

The following changes to Basic Awards will be made:

(a) minimum of two weeks' pay will be abolished;
(b) award may be reduced to nil if staff unreasonably refuse reinstatement or if their conduct (before or after dismissal) warrants it;
(c) years of work between ages 16–18 will count in calculating basic award.

9 Union Ballots

Unions may be re-imbursed for holding secret ballots:

(a) to call or end a strike
(b) to elect Union Officials
(c) to amend Union Rules
(d) to decide on amalgamation or transfer

10 Miscellaneous

(a) A.C.A.S. will lose power to enquire and recommend in recognition disputes: they will conciliate only.
(b) C.A.C. will lose power to award pay increases in 'general level' or 'recognized terms' disputes (Schedule 11 repealed)
(c) The 5 days entitlement for guaranteed pay will arise in respect of 'rolling' 3 month periods instead of the present beginning on 'Quarter days'.

INDEX

Index